Roots and
Branches

Roots and Branches

A Resource of Native American Literature—
Themes, Lessons, and Bibliographies

Dorothea M. Susag
Simms High School
Simms, Montana

National Council of Teachers of English
1111 W. Kenyon Road, Urbana, Illinois 61801-1096

Prepress Services: Precision Graphics
Staff Editor: Zarina M. Hock
Interior Design: Doug Burnett
Cover Design: Precision Graphics
Cover Art: Jack Real Bird

NCTE Stock Number: 41951-3050

It is the policy of NCTE in its journals and other publications to provide a forum for the open discussion of ideas concerning the content and the teaching of English and the language arts. Publicity accorded to any particular point of view does not imply endorsement by the Executive Committee, the Board of Directors, or the membership at large, except in announcements of policy, where such endorsement is clearly specified.

A portion of the royalties from sale of this book will be given to Montana tribal libraries.

Library of Congress Cataloging-in-Publication Data

Susag, Dorothea M.
    Roots and branches : a resource of Native American literature themes, lessons, and bibliographies / Dorothea M. Susag.
        p.   cm.
    "NCTE stock number: 41986"--T.p. verso.
    Includes bibliographical references and index.
    ISBN 0-8141-4195-1
    1. American literature--Indian authors--Study and teaching--Outlines, syllabi, etc.   2. Indian literature--Study and teaching--Outlines, syllabi, etc.   3. American literature--Indian authors--Themes, motives, etc.   4. American literature--Indian authors--Bibliography.   5. Indian literature--Themes, motives, etc.
6. Indians in literature--Bibliography.   7. Indian literature--Bibliography.   I. National Council of Teachers of English.
II. Title.
    PS153.I52S87   1998
    810.9'897--dc21   98-45105
                                                                CIP

CURR

This book was typeset in Palatino and Avant Garde by Precision Graphics of Champaign, Illinois. Typefaces on the cover and spine were Industria and Syntax. The book was printed by Versa Press of East Peoria, Illinois.

Contents

Foreword: The Places Where the Stories Camp

My story is out walking around. My story is a forest person of the old times, one who wears clothing made from moss and a belt made out of ashwood withes. And here is the place where my story chooses to camp.

In rough English translation, those are the words Abenaki storytellers often used to begin the telling of a traditional tale. The story approaches the listener, not just as a collection of words, not as an abstraction, but as a living being, one who remembers and is about to share.

I have long been impressed by the memory of stories. I do not mean the way humans remember stories—impressive as that is. Complicated stories actually seem to be easier to remember than simple facts. It is as if our brains have been hot-wired to hold the form of a story more securely than almost anything else and the telling of stories can be found at the heart of every human culture.

In this case, however, when I speak of the memory of stories, I mean the way stories themselves remember the things that individuals (and nations) find it so easy to forget. Those lessons of moral conduct, of humility and of courage, of survival itself are held firm in the story's grasp. The old stories, those tales that have truly become tradition, are not just interesting for people to hear—they are as necessary as breath itself, the sacred breath that carries the words of life.

When we speak of "Native American" or "American Indian" cultures we are speaking of not just one single way of life, but generalizing about hundreds of extremely varied cultures stretching over a vast expanse. Unless we are out walking this land, we tend to forget the real geography of this continent we live on. One of the great mistakes made in the past by teachers and writers alike has been to see the Native peoples of America as simple "Indians," vanishing, irrelevant, locked into a distant past. (One of the true services of this book is to counter such stereotypes and provide access to a deeper understanding of a multiplicity of Native American cultures through the words of Native people themselves.) Yet there is one generalization that can be made about our more than 400 different American Indian nations. We all share a deep respect for the power, a power that often can only be described as sacred, of stories. Language, in the living shape of a song or a story, makes things happen.

It is for this reason that many Native people are uncomfortable with the words "myth" and "legend" being applied to our stories. For many people, myths and legends are seen as frivolous, untrue, parts of childhood meant to be left behind like a belief in "Never-Never Land." But our stories are, even when they are humorous, far from irrelevant. They are true in the deepest sense of the word, true because they are alive. True because they know more than we do. As a storyteller I am always telling people that I do not learn stories, I learn from stories. I do not just tell stories, I listen to them as they tell themselves to me, as I loan them my voice. So I find myself referring to that vast body of songs and stories, the oral (*and written*) literatures of the Americas, as *traditions.*

The coming of Europeans to the western hemisphere brought, among other things, a sustained assault upon Native cultures. Our cultures were often either ignored as irrelevant (or nonexistent) or attacked. Our living traditions, both oral and written, were threatened with purposeful destruction. Over 400 years ago, in Mexico, Spanish priests collected thousands or written books, the Codices of the Mayan and Aztec nations, piled them up, and burned them. In the United States, as recently as two decades ago, Native children were sent to boarding schools where the speaking of Native languages, the singing of traditional songs, was forbidden. Despite it all, though much was lost, much survived. It survived not just because of the tenacity of Native people but because of the necessity of those traditions.

And, interestingly enough, those traditions did not just survive in their original forms. If I might make another generalization about Native American cultures, it is this: Native American cultures have consistently displayed an ability to absorb and incorporate new things. (In terms of material culture, consider the way the horse—absent for thousands of years from the continent—became the heart of Plains cultures less than two generations after that beautiful animal's reintroduction by the Spanish.) Early on, as early as the European occupation of Peru, Native people began to write in European languages. The American Indian as a writer in Spanish, English, and French is not just a phenomenon of the twentieth century.

Today, when we speak of Native American literature we are speaking about both a deep oral tradition and a strong, varied body of written literature that has been recognized around the world. However, perhaps more than any other body of literature, contemporary

Native American writing is based upon, indebted to, and deeply aware of the original tribal traditions that went before. Story still remains the beating heart of American Indian literature.

It is especially because of the primacy and the importance of stories that Native American literature is of such value to teachers and this book is such an important guide. The form of story is such that it draws the listener or the reader in. It creates interest. The purpose of the story is to communicate on a number of levels. To teach. That dual role of the story as entertainer and teacher has never been more needed in the classroom.

The lessons taught by so many Native American stories, both traditional and contemporary, have never been more needed in our classrooms. The stories remember histories that others have forgotten. They teach us again the importance of community and generosity, the importance of the individual ,and the balancing virtues of courage and compassion, self-respect and self-control. The strength of women, the true values of family, the recognition that we human beings are not alone in the world but part of a complex and interdependent web of life are themes easily found—not once, but again and again.

There is so much to say, but it is better to hear it in the stories themselves. This book will be, I am certain, an extremely useful beginning point. It can tell you where to look if you want to find those places where, as my elders put it, "the stories camp." Come with open eyes, open ears, and, most of all, an open heart and the stories will welcome you into their lodge. I have spent most of my life on the story trail and I can assure you that it is a good journey. Wlipamkaani, nidobak. Travel well, my friends.

—Joseph Bruchac
June 1998 / Moon of Strawberries

Preface

Roots and Branches: A Resource of Native American Literature Themes, Lessons, and Bibliographies began with my increasing frustration over trying to make regional literatures available to my students. The project formally began in the spring of 1992 when I left my English teaching position at Simms High School for one year, having received the 1992–93 Christa McAuliffe Fellowship for Montana for my proposal, "Personal Connections in Time and Place Through Native American Literature: The Development of a Study of Native American Literature for Montana Students from Kindergarten through Twelfth Grade."

At the start, several educators suggested that a resource for using Native American literature would develop fairly easily since "there wasn't much out there." They were right. The lists in catalogs from major publishing companies and distributors featured limited selections of legitimate and culturally relevant texts. One catalog listed under "Native American" the Chinese American novel *The Woman Warrior*, by Maxine Hong Kingston. I also found that most teachers I surveyed were relying on popular storybooks and novels by non-Native authors. But once I began visiting the seven Montana tribal communities—Blackfeet, Crow, Flathead (Salish/Kootenai), Ft. Belknap (Assiniboine/Gros Ventre), Ft. Peck (Assiniboine/Sioux), Northern Cheyenne, and Rocky Boy (Chippewa/Cree)—I found lifetimes of volumes of oral and written resources. On my first visit, Blackfeet Tribal Education Director Harold Dusty Bull handed me a printed bibliography twenty pages thick and said, "Tell me what's in these books." That was the beginning of the bibliographies in *Roots and Branches*.

Although I have tried to establish an objective position throughout my research and writing, I must admit my own ethnic, cultural, geographical, and educational biases have influenced the philosophy, form, and content of this resource. Born and raised in the suburbs of Chicago, two generations removed from Norwegian immigrants, I had little previous personal experience with Native American cultures and peoples. For twenty-six years I have lived on the Eastern Front of the Montana Rocky Mountains, the ancestral home of the Blackfeet people and more recently the Métis, exiles from Canada. Here I have been teaching secondary language arts for the last twelve years to students of mixed heritages. A fourth have Native ancestry, predominantly Blackfeet, Sioux, Métis, and Chippewa/Cree.

In each community there were those who challenged the right of non-Indians, such as myself, to use their stories or cultural philosophies in public school classrooms, saying, "Story is vital to our cultural survival." Others, sometimes sitting at the same table, expressed their concerns that "the truth must be told about who we are!" I am grateful for the challenges because they have forced me to re-examine my own motives and values. Consequently, throughout my research, I have felt a tremendous responsibility to first of all respect tribal people, their children, their cultures, and their traditions, and to make every possible effort to avoid any further exploitation through this project.

Roots and Branches: A Resource of Native American Literature Themes, Lessons, and Bibliographies represents the voices of many. As I struggled to find a way to reflect those voices, it became clear that I only confused readers. Therefore, I wish to point out clearly here that when I use the first person throughout the text, I am in fact relying on many other voices who have helped me learn. Still, I can only speak from my own experience with students, with Montana Native people in particular, and with published historical and critical resources I have read. I have applied whatever experience that represents to texts included in this resource.

I am most reminded of my own limitations as well as the limitations within these pages whenever I reread Sherman Alexie's poem "Native American Literature" in *Old Shirts and New Skins*, especially when I read the following ten lines:

> Because you have seen the color of my bare skin
> does not mean you have memorized the shape of my ribcage.
>
> Because you have seen the spine of the mountain
> does not mean you made the climb.
>
> Because you stood waist-deep in the changing river
> does not mean you are equal to mc^2.
>
> Because you gave something a name
> does not mean your name is important.
>
> Because you sleep
> does not mean you see into my dreams.
>
> —Sherman Alexie

I am still non-Indian, granddaughter of Christian Norwegian and Swedish immigrants, having been indoctrinated primarily by the stereotypes in movies, television, and Western novels, and having been raised apart from traditional Indian cultures. In no way can I own their stories, nor can I claim to give them voice. In truth, I cannot *teach* Native American literatures. But I can affirm their right to be heard and read, and with the help of many other educators, I have made available sources for those stories within this text, *Roots and Branches*.

—Dorothea M. Susag
Simms High School
Simms, Montana

Acknowledgments

For the last six years, at the University of Montana, with tribal peoples from across the state, and with numerous educators and authors, I have been privileged to study North American tribal histories and cultures, Native American literatures, and the writing of language arts curricula. I am greatly indebted to those whose vital contributions have made this publication possible.

- The Department of Education and the Christa McAuliffe Fellowship Program, which provided the initial funds for study.

- Dr. Murton McCluskey, Joseph Bruchac, and Denise Juneau, who read and responded to a number of complete drafts, graciously answering my many phone calls; and Beverly Slapin, who provided expert attention and meticulous detail to the entire draft.

- The Montana Advisory Council for Indian Education and the Northern Cheyenne Tribal Council, who provided written letters of support; tribal elders, leaders, and tribal college personnel who encouraged me and entrusted me with materials they considered especially relevant for their children, as well as for children outside their communities: Minerva Allen, Tim Bernardis, Bob Biggard, Norma Bixby, Julie Cajune, LeRoy Comes Last, Judy Davis, Harold Dusty Bull, Elsie Geboe, Long Standing Bear Chief (Harold Gray), Kevin Howlett, Tony Incashola, Leonard Littlewolf, Dr. Joe MacDonald, Sharon Magee, Victor Miller, Peggy Nagel, Jennie Seminole Parker, Bob Parsley, Linda Pease, Margaret Perez, Dr. Janine Pease Pretty on Top, Anita Scheetz, Joyce Silverthorne, Loren Stiffarm, Ron Terriault, Dr. William Thackary, and Curley Youpee.

- Principals, teachers and students who graciously responded to my requests for information regarding what literatures are available and what they believe would benefit young people: Marge Abbott, Jeri Azure, Ron Belcourt, Marj Berlinger, Peggy Beswick, Laura Bleazard, Diane Boley, Jeanette.A. Borchert, Carol Capps, Bill Chambers, Bernadette Dimas, Silvia Denny, Deana Dolberg, Sandra Evenson, Carole Filler, Josephine Corcoran, Jay Eagleman, Megan Fite, Alan Gardipee, Pam Geboe, Stacy Gordon, Bonnie Granbois, Laura Hafer, Kathy Hess, Pam Jackson, Heidi Juel, Stan and Carol Juneau, Denise Juneau, Eileene Karge, Peggy Kimmet, Roberta Kipp, Laura Lake, Laura Lowe, Pat Littlebird, Linda Littlewolf, Sharon Magee, Karin Morrison, Myrna Mitchell, Tom

Mollgaard, Sandra Murie, Laurie Nelson, Elaine Neese, Herman and Randee Pipe, Avis Prentice, Tim Rosette, Frances Russette, Warren Schwartz, Mel Sergeant, Carol Single, Francine Small, Diane Spencer, Bill Stops, Rusty Tatsey, Daisy Three Irons, Ken and Theodora Weatherwax, and Wilma Windy Boy.

- The University of Montana professors who shared in the vision and guided me through the research and writing: Dr. William Bevis, noted authority on Western American and Montana literature; Dr. Beverly Chin, past president of NCTE and professor of English education; Dr. Richmond Clow, professor of Native American studies; Debra Earling, writer of fiction and poetry and professor of Native American literature; Dr. Lois Welch, former chair of the Creative Writing Department; and Dr. Bonnie Craig, director of the University of Montana's Native American Studies Program from 1991 to 1997, when cancer took her life.

- My colleagues in education, friends and relatives who provided invaluable encouragement, support, collaboration, and feedback time and again when I asked several to read—and reread—drafts of sections and chapters: Marge Abbott, Clara Beier, Jan Clinard, Margaret Eller, Megan Fite, Laurie Henthorne, Donna Miller, Sandy Nypen, Holly Pepprock, Dawn Sievers, Diane West-Mott, the Board of Simms High School, the administration and staff, my students at Simms, and the students of Poplar School who provided inspiration to me and written responses to many texts and lessons included in *Roots and Branches,* my own grandchildren, my mother, Louise Harrisville, my daughter and her husband, Lori and Hugh Maxwell, both educators, and my husband, Sylvan Susag, a career counselor in Poplar on the Fort Peck Reservation. For their encouragement and continuing support over the last six years, I am most grateful.

- The NCTE Editorial Board and editors Dawn Boyer, Michael Greer, and Pete Feely, who believed in such a project and contributed profoundly to its completion with their encouragement, advice, and direction; and Zarina Hock, NCTE staff editor, and Precision Graphics under the direction of Kirsten Dennison, for their meticulous reading and suggestions in the final preparation of the manuscript.

To these and to others I may have failed to mention who have also shared in the vision, to those who have contributed their own voices and translations to my rethinking and rewriting, and to those who believe in the undeniable right of all people to tell their own stories and the right of all children to hear and read the stories of their heritage, I dedicate this work.

Permissions

We gratefully acknowledge the permission to reproduce the following materials.

p. 3: "Just the Other Day" by Lizabeth Staber (Blackfeet). Used by permission of the author.

p. 4: Owl poem and drawing used by permission of William Darby.

p. 13: "Remember," from the book *She Had Some Horses* by Joy Harjo. Copyright 1982 by Joy Harjo. Used by permission of the publisher, Thunder's Mouth Press.

p. 16: "My Family" by Delia Spotted Bear, Physical Education Teacher at Pretty Eagle Catholic School, St. Xavier, MT. Used by permission of the author.

pp. 16–17: "The Bighorn River" by Len Plenty. Used by permission of the author.

p. 17: "A Circle Begins" by Harold Littlebird (Laguna/Santo Domingo Pueblo). Used by permission of the author.

pp. 17–18: "we are a people" by Lance Henson. Used by permission of the author.

pp. 28–29: "The Girl Who Loved the Sky" by Anita Endrezze, from *at the helm of twilight* (Broken Moon Press), 1992. Used by permission of the author.

pp. 32–33: "Sure You Can Ask Me a Personal Question" by Diane Burns. Used by permission of the author.

pp. 47–49: "Introduction to Native American Literature" by Sherman Alexie, from *Old Shirts and New Skins.* Used by permission of Kenneth Lincoln, General Editor of Series, UCLA.

p. 47: "Sending a Voice" by Kenneth Lincoln, from *Native American Renaissance.* Used by permission of the author.

pp. 93–94: Lakota cosmology reprinted from *Lakota Myth* by James R. Walker, edited by Elaine A. Jahner, by permission of the University of Nebraska Press. Copyright 1983 by the University of Nebraska Press.

pp. 240–241: Map entitled *Native North America* reprinted with permission from the map's author, Michael J. Caduto, © 1996, All Rights Reserved. The map is originally found on pages xiv and xv of *Keepers of Life: Discovering Plants Through Native American Stories and Earth*

Activities for Children by Michael J. Caduto and Joseph Bruchac (Golden, Colorado: Fulcrum Publishing, 1996).

pp. 242–245: Maps taken from *Native North American Literature.* Edited by Janet Witalec. Copyright © 1994, Gale Research, Inc. Reproduced by permission. All rights reserved.

p. 260: "Educational Philosophy of the Assiniboine and Gros Ventre Tribes" used by permission of Tribal Education Committee, Ft. Belknap Agency.

p. 261: Sioux philosophy used by permission of Sung' Gleska.

p. 262: "Blackfeet (The Pikuni Way)" written by Long Standing Bear Chief. Used by permission.

p. 263–264: Crow (Absorka) philosophy used by permission.

p. 264: Kootenai philosophy used by permission of Patricia Hewankorn, Director, Kootenai Culture Committee.

p. 264: Flathead Culture Committee Philosophy used by permission of Antoine Incashola.

p. 265–266: Cheyenne philosophy used by permission of Jennie Parker, Northern Cheyenne Tribal President.

Introduction

Roots in Story

Why teach Native American literatures? Eight years ago in my Freshman English class, a quiet and slight girl, with long hair, braided and banded, would softly move into her seat, near the front but off to one side. Day after day, her downcast eyes and firm-set mouth would say, "Leave me alone." If she spoke at all, it was in quiet, short responses. But when she wrote, she told stories of her brother's attempted suicide and stories of a nephew, just under two, who had smothered to death the previous summer. She told of her mother's drinking, of her eight siblings, of an absent father, and she sometimes told of her cousins—many of whom were also mixed bloods—living one hundred miles north on the Blackfeet Indian Reservation in Browning, Montana. Betsy wrote poetry, too. "Feelings on paper," she called it, feelings upon feelings, barbed and penetrating, filling page after page, no matter what the assignment.

As a sophomore, Betsy enrolled in our Montana Literature class. We sat in a circle, but her chair wanted to turn out. Still reluctant to share with the class, she found the seminar format threatening. But she wanted an A. So when her turn came to present her experience with Percy Bullchild's telling of the Blackfeet story, "Napi and the Sun's Leggings" in *The Last Best Place: A Montana Anthology,* she moved to stand behind the podium. From there she told us about Napi, the Blackfeet transformer and culture hero whom Creator Sun had entrusted to take care of life on Earth. Napi is "always roaming about for adventure or mostly for food" and always ends up "doing something foolish." In this particular story, Napi repeatedly tries to run away with a pair of "red-winged woodpecker feather fringed leggings," yet every morning he wakes to find himself back in the same tipi where he has first found the leggings, back in the tipi of Creator Sun who gives Napi a final warning: "There is a restriction on those red-winged woodpecker feather fringed leggings of mine and if that restriction isn't complied with, you shall find out the consequences. . . . Remember and take my advice to you, don't wear them just any time, unless your heart is all given to your Creator" (Bullchild 1990, 47). But Napi disregards Creator Sun's warning, and, for the sole purpose of admiring himself, he puts on the leggings. As soon as Napi's feet touch the ground, the dry grass begins to burn, and he can escape only when he jumps into the creek. At the end of her retelling, Betsy shared the most important values she found exhibited in this story—honesty and respect. Then, with wide eyes and a still cautious smile, she closed her presentation and said, "Percy Bullchild is my relative."

From that day I watched Betsy's head lift to smile and interact with her classmates, who carried their own varieties of mixed heritages. She was moving into an older new world, confirming an identity rooted in place and story. And the other students' responses to her "Indianness" grew more and more positive, evidence of their growth as well. From the stories they read of her Blackfeet people, they learned that Indian means much more than staggered falls down bar-front steps, much more than "eighteen money"* spent fast on friends and family, and much more than fatherless children with smudged faces. Each student began to realize that being Indian can mean valuing personal sacrifice, respect for others, and generosity. It can mean knowing the absolute necessity of community and the intimate connection to place, knowing the importance of law within ancient tribal texts, and knowing the actual interdependence of all things living. Being Indian can mean Blackfeet, Cheyenne, Crow, or any of more than 500 different Native societies in America today. All of the students began to realize that many of the strong Native cultural values they had found in story were present—or missing—from their own lives. At the end of the year, one of Betsy's classmates wrote, "These stories have certainly destroyed many images I've had of the Old West, images drawn by movies and books, invariably written by whites."

When Betsy was a senior, I heard about her telling Napi stories to her teammates on the volleyball bus. Voices and visions from her ancestral landscape—not generated and not taught, but affirmed in a public school classroom—had helped to provide her with a positive identity and with the spiritual strength to survive both her real and imagined fears. The Blackfeet stories she had read and heard in class had also proved the significance of her relationship with her aging Blackfeet grandmother. Last year, Betsy shared with me this poem she had read at her grandmother's funeral.

---

* Although the situation may differ from tribe to tribe, on the Ft. Peck and Blackfeet Reservations, "eighteen money" refers to claim money, lease money, per capita payments based on tribally-owned enterprises, or tribal money that is held in trust by the Bureau of Indian Affairs (BIA) until the person is eighteen.

Just the other day
  I met a woman
with so much life and vigor
I watched her sit for hours
hunched over buckskin beading
her coal black hair streaked
  with gray
her hands working patiently with
  the needle

Just the other day
  I met a woman
who entranced me with her Napi tales
her voice wise with age
  pulling me into the story
Just the other day
I held her hand
Singing Silent Night softly to her
till her eyelids heavy from fatigue
  slowly slid shut

Just the other day
I had to say good-bye
to a woman I had met not so long ago
my memories held locked away
inside my mind
my eyes puffy from tears
my soul hurting for our loss
my heart relieved for now,
there is no more pain in my
Grandma's soft brown eyes.

—Lizabeth Staber (Blackfeet)

Why teach Native American literatures? The answer is rooted in story. A few years ago, in preparation for reading a play about Norwegian immigrants, I asked my freshman students to talk with their parents and grandparents about their ethnic or national origins and about the circumstances of their ancestors' immigration to America. A few students argued, unwilling or afraid to communicate with either parents or grandparents, while others expressed their frustration with the assignment because they were certain no one at home would know about "immigration" or "ancestors," "places or stories." Eventually they accepted the assignment, and I prepared to assign parts for reading aloud when William, in the last seat, middle row, raised his hand. He asked, "Does Indian count?"

Does Indian count! Struck with the painful irony in his words, I stood speechless, overcome with contradictory emotions of shame, relief, and gratitude for the simple yet powerfully complex question that suddenly exploded into multiple voices and images before me. "Did the Indians' migratory patterns make them immigrants?" "Did the forced removal of Indians from their ancestral lands to prisoner-of-war camps and reservations make them immigrants?" "Do my ancestors' deaths from starvation and disease count?" "Do the 'places and stories' of my mother's people count?" "If Indians count, *how* do they count?" "Does my mother and her dark skin count?" "Do the boarding school experiences of my mother, my father, my grandparents and great grandparents count?" "Do I, sitting in the fourth seat, third row, with my less-than-average grades and my atypical thinking patterns, count?" "Does my confusion over my identity—white, brown, Scottish, Chippewa/Cree, son of the mountains and son of alcohol—count?" "Do my feelings of frustration, anger, shame, pride, hope, and joy count?"

Like nearly a fourth of our students in this small Montana community, over one hundred miles from the nearest reservation, William is Native American, a mixed-blood, of Turtle Mountain Chippewa/Cree ancestry. He has hidden his Native heritage and has denounced its value to his peers, hoping to avoid insult and ridicule from those who would associate him with "lazy, irresponsible, drunken savagery." But on this day—hoping not to hear the same answer he and his ancestors had heard for hundreds of years—William raised his hand and asked, "Does Indian count?"

Later in the school year, William, age 14, wrote and illustrated the following poem:

An Owl Hoots in the
night sitting on a branch watching over
our sick souls; and when we
die he reports to our family
that we are gone and
that he lifted us to heaven.

When I asked him to share with the class how he had heard this story—a story similar to one I had heard from a Chippewa/Cree woman the previous year, William smiled and said, "My mother told me, and her mother told her, and her mother told her, and . . . that's how I know this story."

At the end of the unit, we posted William's poem on the classroom wall with other students' poetry. The following week, in an essay response to reading *Mourning Dove: A Salishan Autobiography*, Amanda, age 16, commented, "another value of [Indian peoples] is their culture and the way their traditions are followed and respected. As I read [William's] poem, I realized that the spiritual aspect has never left the tribe's beliefs."

Why teach Native American literatures? In an Indian literature class at the University of Montana, I listened to Salish/German poet Debra Earling talk about the ways "education changes the story of your life." I wondered about our educational system in America and the ways that education has affected young people of Native heritage, especially those who are separated from their ancestral landscapes and communities. If their experiences in our public school classrooms have the power to change the stories of their lives, what happens to children who don't hear the stories of their own people? And if they do, what happens when their teachers and texts in the public schools regard those stories as inferior, obsolete, representing wrong values of property and government, and representing inadequate means for survival? What happens to children whose public education is rooted in an alien culture? How do the stories of their lives change? What do they learn to value, what do they learn to reject, and what do they learn about survival when they don't ever hear or read about the suffering, loss, and endurance of their own people? How do they establish positive identities for themselves when voices within their culture are ignored, twisted, and suppressed, and when voices outside their culture decide for them who they are and who they should become? What happens to the relationships among children from differing cultures within classrooms? Do the children from the dominant culture develop an understanding of and respect for the similarities as well as the differences among all peoples? Or do they learn to practice discrimination against all cultures different from their own? I know the answers to these questions—I see their faces at school each day.

Today more than ever before, many educators recognize the undeniable right of children to locate their identities in the stories and experiences of those who have gone before, and the right of all young people to experience the storied landscapes of surrounding peoples and cultures. Consequently, educators are requesting more literatures from multicultural resources. To meet this growing need, publishing companies are mass-producing textbooks and literatures by and about American Indian peoples.

However, this increased production and availability of resources has not eased the classroom teacher's selection process. Instead, the challenge and responsibility for presenting meaningful and appropriate Native American literatures to students of all ages and races has become more important, yet increasingly more difficult. So much of the new literature represents non-Native cultural voices and is written and promoted apart from any specific tribal or cultural context. Also, many of the new, as well as the older popular literatures, eclipse truths about Native American peoples and reinforce negative stereotypes, which deny the individuality and the humanity of Indian peoples. Whenever we use books and stories that fail to represent American Indian experiences honestly, we risk perpetuating a dangerously racist cultural isolationism.

I realize the power of those stereotypical images whenever I encourage my non-Native students to search for truths outside the boundaries of their history books, because they frequently grow tense and defensive. However, I have also watched that tension dissolve as they learn to expose and challenge the popular "Indian" stereotypes as well as the stereotypes they themselves live with every day. I have watched the shadow continue to fade whenever young people such as Betsy, William, and Amanda hear and read stories told and written by Native Americans themselves, especially those writers and storytellers from the Native students' own cultural heritages. And when students like Betsy and William bring their rooted stories into the classroom, I watch the shadow disappear. In the 1994 publication *Crossing the Mainstream: Multicultural Perspectives in Teaching Literature*, Eileen Iscoff Oliver provides an excellent, exhaustively researched rationale for the study of multicultural literatures by *all* students. She writes:

> Everyone—the many students of color across our country and everybody else—is entitled to know the history and pain and beauty of the world as it has been recorded by artists who come from all of the strands that make up American literary society. . . . May we read, learn, and grow from these experiences and teach our students to do the same. (Oliver 1994, 11)

Why teach Native American literatures? All our students, especially those from mixed family, cultural, or ethnic heritages, struggle to establish individual and unique identities. Nevertheless, by facilitating their growth and understanding of themselves and the worlds around them, teachers can help them confront life with personal dignity, with compassion for themselves and for others, and with hope for a meaningful future. Through Native American oral and written literatures, students can develop a sincere appreciation for the artistic expression and for the validity and serious complexity of each Native American's personal, cultural, and historical experience, while they also can learn to say with conviction, "Yes, Indian counts!"

Philosophy, Scope, and Challenge

In his introductory essay to *Native North American Literature*, Joseph Bruchac writes: "Clearly, the contemporary North American Native experience is a varied one, and the Native writers of Canada and the United States share in the complexity of that experience, just as they share in the richness of the many traditions which make up North American Native literature today. It is a tree with many branches, a tree that grows on the plains and in the mountains, in the deserts and in the cities, a tree which is, through it all, still rooted strong in this land" (Bruchac 1994, xiv). Out of respect for the "rooted" and complex experiences of Native people, *Roots and Branches*—a resource among many—has been written with the following philosophy in mind:

> To respect Native voices who speak from a tribal ethnic consciousness as well as from an awareness of the European American cultural impact on them and on their peoples, and to support each student's search for his or her cultural ties to ancient and contemporary writers and storytellers.

Roots and Branches is a resource of themes, lessons, and bibliographies from many cultures and regions. Although the length of the bibliographies prohibits an extensive list of recommended uses for the selections, suggestions for use with other literatures and with themes normally covered in language arts programs are incorporated in several annotations. Also, *Roots and Branches* recognizes various contexts from which these literatures have grown. The three maps in Appendix A provide an introduction to geographical contexts where teachers can find the current location of tribes and reservations as well as the approximate location at the time of European contact. The brief history of federal Indian policy in Appendix B provides a summary of significant dates, events, and their consequences for all people of Native American ancestry. This is especially important since most of the literatures from the last two hundred years reflect the impact of these polices on individual lives. The stereotypes defined in Appendix C are an essential context to recognize, because the proliferation of negative and unrealistic images, beginning with the first European contact, has impacted the lives of all Native Americans and has prevented non-Native people from knowing the truths about Native Americans as individuals. In Appendix D, the Montana tribal philosophies provide strong contradictions to the stereotypes defined in Appendix C. Although they are examples of spiritual and cultural contexts that can especially assist students who read Montana-based literatures, teachers and students in other areas may use them as examples of what they can discover in their own regions and communities. Since *Roots and Branches* began with the seven Montana tribal cultures and communities, a list of Montana regional publications is included in Appendix E. As a result of ancestral and forced migration patterns, of federal boarding school and relocation programs, and of non-Native encroachment into Native lands, the Montana peoples share cultures, stories, histories, and relatives with Native peoples from across America and Canada. Consequently, the list grew to encompass not only texts and themes from Montana and from the Northwest, North Central, and Plains regions, but from all over the North American continent.

Reading beyond my own cultural and literary boundaries, I found it necessary to investigate the critical landscapes and traditions of Native American cultures. Chapter 2, "Historical and Cultural Literary Contexts," represents the summary of my research and experience with these literatures and cultures. In no way can this summary speak for all Native American traditions, nor can it address all readers of Native American literatures. Instead, I hope that teachers and students who use it as a guideline will establish their own understandings and comparisons as they hear and read literatures from their surrounding Native cultures and landscapes.

There are limitations to this book. Since it cannot provide complete cultural contexts for each work, teachers have the responsibility to educate themselves and to encourage and support their students' own research as they use Native American literatures. In fact, the search is continual and critical. Whenever possible, research should begin with the important primary resources: individuals in local tribal communities, such as elders, Native educators, tribal education directors, tribal culture committees, tribal colleges, and Native American studies departments in regional colleges and universities. Students can listen to tribal leaders tell about the role of story in their communities, and teachers can invite oral historians, elders, and tribal storytellers into the classroom to teach students about their cultural philosophies as well as contemporary issues in their communities. When making connections with tribal peoples, educators should respect the right of all people to be reimbursed for their expertise. Watching Montana Native peoples give tobacco, beaded pins, blankets, and star quilts, as well as monetary gifts, I have observed the great respect they have for the practice of honoring individuals who share themselves for the benefit of the community.

A note about terminology is in order here. I have used the terms "Native American" and "Indian" interchangeably for two reasons. Many people regard "Indian" as a derogatory misnomer— "Columbus's mistake"—and they prefer to use the term "Native American," in an attempt to "set things right" and to demonstrate long-neglected respect. On the other hand, University of Montana professor Debra Earling maintains that Native people, having survived five hundred years of genocide, alienation, and discrimination, have given dignity to the term "Indian." Since most Native people regard themselves first as members of tribal nations and second as "Native American" or "Indian," I have made references in *Roots and Branches* to specific tribal affiliations of individual storytellers and writers whenever possible. However, accurate identification of nation names is also problematic because the French, Spanish, and English conquerors and the agents of the federal government mistranslated and misnamed them. Today, many of those misnomers, such as Sioux, Gros Ventres, and Crow, remain "legal" and familiar. As I attempted to resolve these issues for the purposes of this book, I relied on publishers' and distributors' designations, on references within the texts themselves, on whatever individual storytellers and writers called themselves, and on Native consultants. As a result of my effort to rely primarily on designations within or in association with individual texts, occasional spelling variations exist within this resource. I have also avoided assigning what some scholars might consider "culturally appropriate" nation names, especially when the texts or writers themselves suggest differences.

Roots and Branches does not pretend to be the ultimate scholarly work on Native American literature. In no way does it address all the issues that derive from teaching specific kinds of literatures, but readers will find in this book lists of works by individuals who have made major contributions to the critical study of Native American literatures.

For teachers across the continent reading this text, I hope it will stimulate the desire to walk through areas unfamiliar (and yes, scary) to them in order to broaden their own and their students' world views. I hope it will help teachers find ways to integrate Native American literary traditions into language arts classes, as well as provide access to resources that will increase teachers' and students' awareness of the Native American contributions to our national literary history. I also hope that other books will be written from a variety of geographical areas, specifically respecting their particular and unique tribal cultures.

Works Cited

Bruchac, Joseph. 1994. "A Living Tree with Many Roots: An Introduction to Native North American Literature." In *Native North American Literature*, ed. Janet Witalec. Detroit, MI: Gale Research, Inc.

Bullchild, Percy. 1990. "Napi and the Sun's Leggings." In *The Last Best Place: A Montana Anthology,* eds. William Kittredge and Annick Smith. Helena: The Montana Historical Society Press.

Oliver, Eileen Iscoff. 1994. *Crossing the Mainstream: Multicultural Perspectives in Teaching Literature.* Urbana, IL: National Council of Teachers of English.

1
Themes, Rationales, and Subthemes

How can teachers in public-school classrooms bring together literatures from diverse Native and non-Native cultures? Despite the multiple perspectives between cultures and among individuals within cultures, we all share the experience of being human, needing survival and security, affection, belonging, and, at the highest level, self-actualization. A thematic approach to teaching literature provides opportunities for students to recognize such similarities between themselves and other human beings from different cultural circumstances. At the same time, the thematic approach can facilitate our students' understanding of the diverse and sometimes contradictory underlying assumptions that inform the stories they hear and the literatures they read. It is important to remember, though, that the following themes are not intended to separate literatures into finite categories or tidy boxes where certain books "fit." With their prevailing concept of interconnectedness, Native literatures especially resist such structures. The themes in this resource merely represent a pattern of organization that teachers from various cultures might use to help their students cross the barriers of time and culture.

Theme: Remembering the Old Ways

Central to all Native American cultures is *story.* Riding on the storyteller's breath, through image, word, and silence, is a vision—circling through the imagination and spirit of listeners to unite them all in "the old ways," a common experience of living value. Central to the concept of story is the practical action of remembering, keeping in mind or remaining aware of the values most necessary for survival. According to Joseph Bruchac, in his introductory essay to *Native American Stories,* the old ways, the "knowledge that native people obtained from thousands of years of living and seeking balance," was taught in "two very powerful ways. The first way was through experience, the second through oral tradition, especially through the telling of stories" (Bruchac 1991).

Although the vocabulary, values, and means of transmission may differ, the old ways concept can apply to all peoples and cultures with which our students might identify. Possessing spiritual and social values and visions, cultural communities "remember," translate, and transmit those traditions through the spoken and written word. However, new challenges facing each generation require that such traditions be clarified and reevaluated for their usefulness. Too often, though, non-Native individuals and institutions have suppressed Native voices and then presumed the right to perform the task of clarifying and reevaluating the old ways for Native people. This practice has resulted in serious misconceptions and consequent educational practices that have perpetuated distorted images of Native Americans for hundreds of years. For example, in classrooms across the continent, many teachers limit their teaching about Native Americans to the study of petroglyphs (the early writings or descriptive art of indigenous peoples) and to the study of Native uses of animals, herbs, and roots. Calling these "the old ways," the way Indians "used" to live, these teachers emphasize the Indians' sole reliance on nature for survival, a practice that many contemporary people, both Native and non-Native, regard as primitive and obsolete. In many of these same classrooms, teachers use Native stories and cultural practices to communicate the notion of culture as artifact, interesting as history but literally dead.

But literatures and personal testimonies from contemporary Native Americans demonstrate the contradiction of such views. In his Foreword to Bruchac's *Native American Stories*, N. Scott Momaday discusses the relevance of the "storyteller and his art."

> In general, stories are true to human experience. Indeed, the truth of human experience is their principal information. This is to say that stories tend to support and confirm our perceptions of the world and of the creatures within it. Even the most fantastic story is rooted in our common experience; otherwise, it would have no meaning for us. . . . In the presence of these stories we have an affirmation of the human spirit. It is a just and wondrous celebration. (Momaday 1991)

The following women featured in the 1993 publication, *Women of the Native Struggle: Portraits and Testimony of Native American Women*, remember their old ways and prove the relevance of traditional values for life today.

> People should go right down to their own roots and learn from there, learn from their own beginnings.—Olivia Pourir, Lakota (Farley 1993, 66)

> (Quoting a holy man) Every step you take on Earth should be a prayer.—Charmaine White Face, Oglala Lakota (Farley 1993, 60)

> We do not separate our spirituality from reality; they are the same. In our Lakota beliefs and ways, medicine people are chosen by the spirits.—White Face (Farley 1993, 68)

> [T]here was reciprocal respect of other people's ways. . . . You didn't take their way or force your own way on them. I think that is the greatest example of how to live in a multicultural world.—Donna Chavis, Lumbee (Farley 1993, 71)

> This is home. This is the land here. As a mother, it is important for me to have my children here . . . they are going to know their center . . . the whole connection—the community, the history, the stories. . . . They have roots and hopefully they will have wings to go along with those roots.—Chavis (Farley 1993, 85)

Many of the voices included in *Women of the Native Struggle* discuss beliefs and traditions that are similar to each other. Nevertheless, teachers and students must respect connections to specific cultures whenever they read these testimonies and use stories reflecting the old ways. This is especially important because these ways are still being communicated in all cultures through written literatures, through ceremonies, and through oral tradition—the primary vehicle for transmitting culture, for sharing values, for explaining natural phenomena, and for teaching survival skills.

Why should young people from differing cultures study the theme "Remembering the Old Ways"? Public schools today must prepare students to live in a technologically complex world where communication systems, labor force requirements, and family structures continually change. Today, many young adult Americans leave home to establish new values and new traditions, moving as often as every five years. Divorce is also more common today; according to one source, "the most widely cited recent estimates of future divorce risk are well over 50%" (Weiten and Lloyd 1994, 283). As a result Americans of all ages—including over 70 percent of our students—stand to experience fragmentation, loneliness, and alienation from each other. Even ten years after a divorce, "children appeared to be even more vulnerable [than their parents], often harboring internal fears of betrayal and rejection that carried into their own intimate relationships in adolescence and early adulthood" (Wallerstein and Blakeslee 1990, 11). Our earth also suffers from centuries of abuse, and the hope of a living and supportive environment for future generations is threatened. In response to the current situation, many traditional Native American people are saying that now is the time when the old ways are needed to restore harmony and balance within all creation.

> We recognize our relationship to the past and to our future because they are the same thing. This is a cyclic way of viewing things. . . . Our view is very different from what has become the industrial or North American world view. America is a country that was founded on and continues to be rooted in a frontier mentality. "The West" is a state of mind—a belief that you can always move forward and there will always be a new frontier to go to. . . . We must learn to live in a

society that is based not on conquest but on survival. This is not just an Indian issue; it is an issue that relates to all of us.—Winona LaDuke, Mississippi Band Anishinabe (Farley 1993, 98)

Along with traditional Native people, many scholars, political, economic, and religious leaders, and social scientists today are suggesting that despite our differences, we must realize our interdependent relationship to the rest of creation. The holistic, interdependent and cyclical, universal, and very personal world depicted in the following poem by Joy Harjo (Creek) is not a new idea—it is the old way of many Native American cultures.

Remember

Remember the sky that you were born under,
know each of the star's stories.
Remember the moon, know who she is.
Remember the sun's birth at dawn is the
strongest point of time. Remember sundown
and the giving away to night.
Remember your birth, how your mother struggled
to give you form and breath. You are evidence of
her life, and her mother's, and hers.
Remember your father. He is your life, also.
Remember the earth whose skin you are:
red earth, black earth, yellow earth, white earth
brown earth, we are earth.
Remember the plants, trees, animal life who all have their
tribes, their families, their histories, too. Talk to them,
listen to them. They are alive poems.
Remember the wind. Remember her voice. She knows the
origin of this universe.
Remember you are all people and all people are you.
Remember you are the universe and this universe is you.
Remember that all is in motion, is growing, is you.
Remember that language comes from this.
Remember the dance language is, that life is.
Remember.

—Joy Harjo

The following is a list of traditional lessons and values exhibited in many of the selections that are listed in this resource.

- a respect for and trust in the wisdom of elders
- a respect for the power of the elements
- a respect for the interdependent relationship between human beings and things of the earth
- the value of the contributions of even the smallest ones

- the values of wisdom, courage, bravery, respect and compassion for others, personal sacrifice, humility, and commitment to relatives and to community
- the value of the artist to a community
- the value of using ingenuity to solve problems
- the value of creating well-being among all people and being responsible for preserving the life of the people
- the value of stories, the way they are linked to the landscape, and the way they remain the substance and life of the people
- an appreciation for the consequences of foolish and self-indulgent behavior, disobedience, pride, jealousy, anger, competitiveness, and excess
- the importance of gratitude and ceremony
- the importance of being satisfied with who we are, what we have, and what we can do
- the importance of being wise and cautious
- the importance of understanding the ways conflicts must be resolved before people can live at peace with one another
- the importance of an intimate and vital relationship between young people and their elders
- the importance of the spiritual connections among all aspects of life
- the importance of being a unique individual while maintaining a responsibility for the community

Thanks to storytellers, writers, publishers, and teachers who have shared their gifts of story, Native and non-Native teachers and students today may also participate in this storytelling tradition and benefit from Native insights into human nature and the surrounding universe. In her book *Tonweya and the Eagles,* Rosebud Yellow Robe (Lakota) tells the growing-up experiences of her father, Chief Chauncey Yellow Robe. She includes a few of his favorite "age-old and well-loved stories, some frightening, some sad, some funny," as well as the following words of wisdom:

> People all over the world have their own way of life, but through their stories we find that we can understand them and live with them. Do not isolate yourselves, you will learn from others. (Yellow Robe 1992, 116)

Through the gift of Native American story, children and young adults today can learn to overcome fragmentation and alienation as they participate in the old ways. By reading these literatures and listening to traditional stories, children can learn to experience positive connections with others and to actively care about the relationships between themselves and their environments.

Subthemes: Remembering the Old Ways

Although the following suggested subthemes may be used at any grade level, the following order represents an increasing level of conceptual and literary sophistication.

Origin of Natural Phenomena Stories: stories about natural phenomena such as warm winter winds, sunflowers, and the Big Dipper

Tribal Creation Stories: stories about transformer–culture heroes such as Iktomi, Gluscabi, Napi, and Coyote, who find homes for their people, who help human beings get along, and who use their power to make the world safe

Tribal Culture Hero Stories: stories of trickster/transformers such as Iktomi, Gluscabi, Napi, Coyote, Ve'Ho, Old Man Coyote, Scewene, Raven, and Nanabosho, who not only create but suffer from the dangers of too much pride and foolish and self-indulgent behavior

Specific Tribal Culture Hero Stories: stories of a particular culture's trickster/transformer figure

Historical Stories: biographies, memoirs of historical figures, and stories about historical events, which emphasize the strength of ancestors to meet challenges

Poetry, Legends, and Longer Contemporary and Traditional Stories: stories about both internal and external conflicts, which are resolved when personal, communal, and spiritual values of the old ways are remembered and practiced

Theme: At Home Within Circles

As soon as the new class of freshmen walks through my door every September, I realize the importance of "circles" in life. Having left the security of buildings many of them have known for eight years, having moved into a new school where seniors taunt, jab, step on, and slander them in order to establish their power, these freshmen create circles of peers, who will surround and defend them against all such dangers. In response to the Individuals with Disabilities Education Act, many schools are practicing Responsible Inclusion, where students with special needs are brought into the circles of general classrooms. Even more practice Cooperative Learning, where students work together to achieve common goals. But many students in these same classrooms have forgotten the importance of other necessary circles in their lives. Few have more than one family meal—without the television—per week. Few ever converse with grandparents, and few participate regularly in religious worship or ceremony. At the "grown-up" age of fourteen, many have also left behind the daily rituals of love's circles—hugging and kissing—and teachers have learned to practice keeping their distance to protect themselves from charges of abuse or molestation.

Traditional Native stories, as well as contemporary Native literatures, affirm the importance of family and home, even as they recognize the ways these families may differ. Janine Pease-Pretty on Top (Crow), President of the Little Bighorn College, says:

> But you know Crows measure wealth a little differently than non-Indians. . . . Wealth is measured by one's relatedness, one's family, and one's clan. To be alone, that would be abject poverty to a Crow. (*Contrary Warriors* 1985)

Public school teachers can use Native American literature to validate the unique importance of each child's family and extended family, to validate a home within a particular landscape, within a spiritual and earthly environment. While a student at Haskell Indian Junior College in Lawrence, Kansas, Delia Spotted Bear (Crow) wrote the following poem about her separate, but still-present, family at home in Montana.

My Family

My mom is by the table, beading a belt.
My dad is sitting, watching the television.
My two brothers are playing basketball outside.
My oldest sister is out on a date.

My second-oldest sister is reading a book.
My little sister is out visiting our cousins.
I'm asleep on the couch!
I'm able to sleep
because I know my family is all around me

—Delia Spotted Bear

Traditional Native stories also stress the importance of viewing the natural world as friend or relative. Our young people already know the meaning of the words *environment* and *recycle*, whether it's pop cans, plastic bags, or trees—they know. Public service messages on television, Boy Scout campaigns to collect newspapers, and the efforts of parents and teachers have stimulated an awareness of their obligation to protect the environment. But Native stories and contemporary literatures can provide opportunities for teachers to extend environmental awareness in young people, where they can develop a sensitivity and responsibility which goes beyond mere obligation to establish an ethical framework for problem-solving and decision-making activities. The following poem demonstrates such respect for the intimate interdependency between humans and nature.

The Bighorn River

The Bighorn River flows
through the reservation.
As it goes, it meets the
Little Bighorn. They are like
a big brother and a little
brother together.

The sound of it makes
the reservation special.
It seems as if it protects
the reservation with happiness
and care. The reservation
knows it has a close friend
and that's the river.

The river wants to flow
to all the four winds but
knows it can just flow one way
with the same wind.

—Len Plenty (Crow)

Selections emphasizing the importance of grandmothers and grandfathers, of fields and drums, of rivers and flying eagles in the circle of the world, of ancestors and their continued presence, and selections that represent reminiscences of communal activities can be used to teach this theme.

A Circle Begins

in the surround of snow-touched mountains
a circle begins
in a meadow by a snow melt creek
where hands weave a house of thin green saplings
        it is a way of song
        a way of breathing
a pure womb to center oneself through sweat
a way of blessing and being blessed
a circle of humility, prayer and asking
and there are no clocks to measure time
but the beating of our singing hearts

—Harold Littlebird (Laguna Pueblo)

Harold Littlebird's poem, "A Circle Begins" and Lance Henson's "we are a people" both capture the experience of the individual being centered within landscape, within community, within ceremony, and within the past, present, and future.

we are a people

days pass easy over these ancient hills
i wander near a moccasin path overgrown with
rusted cans and weeds
i stand in the forest at sunset waiting for
a song from the rising wind

it is this way forever in this place
there is no distance between the name
of my race
and the owl calling

> nor the badgers gentle plodding
> we are a people born under symbols
> that rise from the dust to touch us
> that pass through the cedars where
> our old ones sleep
> to tell us of their dreams
>
> —Lance Henson (Cheyenne)

Through this literature, teachers can facilitate the growth of their students into responsible, caring adults. When students hear poems and stories expressing respect for parents and grandparents, respect for surrounding landscapes, the value of gifts from relatives, and the importance of even the smallest person's responsibility to the community, students from all cultures begin to share similar stories and to write poems in honor of grandparents. As teachers share Native American poems and stories, young people can learn when to trust, how to cooperate, and how they can help create a community where all members may feel secure.

Subthemes: At Home Within Circles

Circles of Relatives: poetry and essays that emphasize the important presence of grandmothers, grandfathers, and ancestors in the lives of young people

Circles in Landscapes: poetry, essays, and stories that exhibit circular symbols such as drums, dances, wheels, fields, birds in flight, and seasons

Circles in Gifts: poetry and stories about the importance of gifts and "returning the gifts"

Circles in Life: poetry, stories, and novels that emphasize the cycle of life in the community and the way Native people work together

Circles in History: memoirs and biographies about nineteenth and twentieth century individuals who lived in community

Circles in Literature: stories by contemporary writers, such as Momaday, Vizenor, Welch, Bruchac, and Erdrich, that exhibit the interaction between oral cultural and literary traditions and Western literary themes, motifs, and symbols

Theme: Change and Growth

All of us who teach have watched our students experience various conflicts with families, peers, teachers, coaches. We have also observed the negative effects of serious conflicts we might never witness: after gym class, Brian teases Amy about the size of her breasts; an older teenager, carrying beer in his pickup, offers Robert a ride home from practice; Yvonne, at thirteen, is pregnant; two brothers lose their father in a plane crash, and five years later their mother dies of cancer; Jerry has practiced with the basketball team every night after school, but he never plays more than 45 seconds in a game.

One way we address these conflicts in the language arts class is to provide units on the themes "Growing Up," "Rites of Passage," or "Change and Growth," where students read stories and poems featuring protagonists who resolve such conflicts within themselves and with others. But students' responses to these literatures vary dramatically, depending on gender, race, culture, and/or different family situations. This is especially true with literatures about Native Americans by non-Native authors, since many of the popular storybooks and novels reinforce negative stereotypes, denying the individuality and humanity of Indian peoples. When we explore texts such as *The Indian in the Cupboard*, *The Education of Little Tree*, and *Soun Tetoken: Nez Perce Boy*, by non-Native authors, and compare them with texts by Native authors, we can see how the cultural biases of authors can influence their characters' motivations and behaviors. Texts by Native authors, with more realistic Native characters and situations, can help students develop a knowledge of various Native American artistic expressions and personal and historical experiences, which counter negative stereotypes. These texts can also provide opportunities for students to understand themselves and their conflicts.

First published in 1980, *The Indian in the Cupboard*, by English writer Lynne Reid Banks, is one of the most popular "Indian" books today. The white boy, Omri, changes and grows through his experiences with "Little Bear," a plastic toy who comes alive. From regarding these little figures as curiosities, as extensions of himself and of his own imagination, Omri grows to respect their right to a life of their own. But the book presents serious problems for Native readers and for non-Native children who don't know much about the Iroquois culture. According to *The Indian in the Cupboard*, a real Indian exists only in the past, values scalping and war, and needs to be taught language, morals, and responsibility—by the white boy. This Indian inspires fear in white men, and he eats and moves like a predatory animal who can't survive without the help of a white man (Banks 1988).

Lakota writer Virginia Driving Hawk Sneve portrays a very different picture of Native children. Set in South Dakota, Sneve's *The Chichi Hoohoo Bogeyman* (written in 1975) is, like *The Indian in the Cupboard*, a contemporary story, but the protagonists are real Native children, three cousins, who encounter a "weird creature" while exploring an old fort. They name it after the figures that the Hopi, Sioux, and European Americans might use to scare children into obedience. ("Better watch out, or the Bogeyman will get you," my uncle would say.) They eventually learn from their grandfather that this creature is a person, "a deaf mute—[who] can't hear or speak and is retarded." It is a story of adventure, of loyalty to peers, of the danger-ous consequences of disobedience, of the effects of negative stereo-types on Indian children, and of the strength of traditional Hopi and Sioux values and beliefs. In Sneve's book, the three girls come into conflict with each other and with their parents and grandparents, but by the end of the story they have changed and grown to understand the importance of responsibility, of honesty, and of compassion for those who are different (Sneve 1993).

Ken Thomasma's book *Soun Tetoken: Nez Perce Boy,* published in 1984, portrays change and growth in a six-year-old Nez Perce boy who is adopted by Chief Joseph's brother. But the story is also typical of many "Indian" stories by non-Native writers. In a polarized world of Indian versus White, Soun has no conflicts with other human beings, unless they are white. After the Noble Savage stereotype, Soun proves his courage and bravery in the face of bears, wolves, and rushing waters, accomplishing extraordinary feats at an unusually young age. The most serious problem for young readers is that this book, like others by Thomasma, fails to portray real people with whom they can identify and instead perpetuates the belief that Indi-ans are artifacts (Thomasma 1984).

The 1992 publication *Morning Girl,* by Michael Dorris (Modoc), is also regarded as historical fiction. Providing strong contrast with Thomasma's books, it is a story about the lives of two Taino children on a Bahamian island in 1492. Twelve-year-old Morning Girl is "always doing things in her dreams, swimming or searching on the beach for unbroken shells or figuring out a good place to fish." Star Boy, her brother, sees "everything so upside down from [her]." These opposing views result in conflicts between the two children, normal conflicts. "[Star Boy] messed up the niceness for me. Just being him-self, he was too loud: making jokes when he should be serious, talk-ing when he should listen, running when he should sit. . . ." In a world many children will recognize as similar to their own, Morning Girl and Star Boy change and grow as they explore the secrets of nature, pretend to see the world as rocks and fish, safely hide from a storm, miss the new baby sister "who had never come home," disap-point their parents and each other. At the end, they welcome Colum-bus and his men, "the strangers . . . who had decorated their faces with fur and wore shiny rocks on their heads". Dorris doesn't pre-tend that Columbus's arrival was positive; he knows his readers are aware of "the rest of the story" (Dorris 1992).

The Education of Little Tree by Forrest Carter, first published in 1976, was promoted as an autobiography of an orphan who learns the ways of Cherokee Indians from his grandparents in Tennessee. There is much controversy over the social and racial heritage of the author. Research suggests, and his wife has stated publicly, that he was not Cherokee at all but a former Ku Klux Klan member. "According to those who knew him before he died in 1979, the author was really Asa (Ace) Carter, a former speechwriter for Alabama Governor George Wallace and a notorious white-supremacist leader" (*Newsweek* 1991). But more importantly, the characters in *The Education of Little Tree* betray the non-Native voice. There is a scene on a bus where white people ridicule Little Tree and his family. Little Tree remains ignorant, assuming that the giggling of white people on the bus represents "friendly" attitudes. A Blackfeet educator commented about this picture: "No Indian child I know would misunderstand the laughter of white people; we learn very early to recognize ridicule." Throughout the text, the young boy never expresses anger toward those who discriminate against him, but as he grows, he develops the ability to perfectly communicate with nature and Mother Earth, escaping the realities most Indian children today experience (Carter 1991).

By contrast, the autobiographical essays of Zitkala-Ša (Gertrude Simmons Bonnin, Yankton Sioux) contain stories that more realistically represent the experiences of five generations of Native children. Moreover, in *American Indian Stories*, first published in 1900 in *The Atlantic Monthly,* the child behaves like children today from many different cultures. In the first essay, the child argues with her Yankton mother and rudely ignores her warnings about the white men who want to take the child to boarding school. Her mother says, "Don't believe a word they say! Their words are sweet, but, my child, their deeds are bitter."

A thousand miles from home, the child soon realizes the challenges this change presents, and readers can identify with her natural response. When loud bells replace the quiet sunrise, and scissors dare to "gnaw" her braids, the child refuses to "submit" and hides under her bed until she is "dragged out . . . kicking and scratching" and is "tied fast in a chair." Alone in the night she "[moans] for [her] mother." When a "dear classmate" dies, she grows "bitter" and censures the white caretaker "for cruel neglect." When she is brought in from play for "some misconduct," having "disregarded a rule which seemed needlessly binding," she is "sent into the kitchen to mash the turnips for dinner in a large glass jar." With "fire in [her] heart," she works her "vengeance" in "hot rage" and breaks the jar. Despite these experiences with forced assimilation at the eastern school, Zitkala-Ša values the education she receives, and "against [her] mother's will," she continues her schooling to become a teacher.

While the three essays in *American Indian Stories* portray a child disrespectfully resisting adult controls, they also prove that stirring memories of a mother's traditional ways, memories of a Dakota landscape, memories of Iktomi tales around the campfire and their lessons in the ways of deceivers, and an education in reading, writing, and European American ways, can all help the boarding school "captive" change and grow. From the child who disobeys her mother and seeks bitter and "triumphant revenge," she grows to desire reconciliation with her mother and a reasonable "new way of solving the problem" (Zitkala-Ša 1985).

The above texts illustrate challenges and growth experiences which cross many cultures because they represent what it means to be human, but the way these young people grow through these challenges may be more culturally specific. Throughout the world, distinct cultural communities also practice formal ceremonies or rites of passage, such as graduations and marriages, that symbolically represent change and growth. In the Lakota tradition, the Hanbleceya or vision quest is a ceremony for boys, and the Ball-Throwing Ceremony is traditional for girls. Formal ceremonies, such as the Jewish bar mitzvah or the Christian confirmation or baptism, might not accompany all change experiences, but family and peer communities recognize the symbolic significance of events such as first hunt, first win, first love. Still, young people's most significant experiences with change and growth will occur when they can value their own identities, especially within their cultural communities and surrounding landscapes. The following excerpt from Kimberly Kai Rapada's essay demonstrates the growth she achieved when she realized the importance of personal, familial, and cultural pride.

> I didn't need the looks on the outside; it didn't matter. I had what counted, what was inside. . . . Now, if there is a hurdle of any sort, if I don't necessarily fit the society's role, I fight for what I believe to be equal. Like Billy Mills and Chief Joseph, I want the Native American people, including my family, to be proud of me; but more importantly, I would like to be proud of myself. (Rapada 1992, 19)

Although these rituals and experiences might change from generation to generation, they represent necessary stages of change and growth in the lives of all people. Stories, novels, and autobiographies listed under this theme feature situations in which children and young adults can experience growth when they encounter problems and find resolutions to conflicts within themselves and with others.

**Subthemes:
Change and
Growth**

Grief Stories: poems and stories in which young people encounter personal rejection, moving away, or the loss or death of a relative

Vision Quests: both traditional and contemporary stories of young men and women who experience visions and learn the value in personal sacrifice

Hunting Stories: stories about young men who learn how to hunt from fathers and grandfathers

Lessons in the Wisdom of Elders: stories and novels that demonstrate the sometimes tragic consequences of ignoring, and the wisdom in following, the advice of the elders

Transformation Stories: trickster/transformer or culture hero figures in traditional and contemporary stories

Theme: Between Two Worlds

At a time when it is vital that different groups find common ground for the establishment of positive communication and resulting peace, it is also valuable to focus on the differences and conflicts between people and within individuals. The Assiniboine tell a story called "Bandit the Raccoon," which Minerva Allen includes in the Bilingual Materials for children on the Ft. Belknap Reservation.

One day Bandit and some children go to town, where a storekeeper gives Bandit a banana. The next day Bandit returns without the children, and he takes another banana. But because he is alone, because he is different, not a child, he is arrested and jailed for stealing. And here the story ends: "Bandit looked like a bandit alright, standing behind the bars. But he was only a raccoon."

Like so many traditional Native American stories, "Bandit the Raccoon" carries meanings for all grade levels while addressing a central issue—racial and cultural prejudice and discrimination. Coming from his native culture and now living as a "minority" in an alien culture, Bandit exists between two worlds. Misunderstanding the rules, he suffers serious consequences when the storekeeper, a member of the dominant culture, delivers mixed messages. In the following essay, Murray Stonechild (Cree) similarly explores the tensions of living between two worlds.

Being Indian today is what you as an Indian make of it. You can live the traditional ways of yesterday or you can blend in with today's white society. But remember, you cannot wash the color of your skin away. But you can wash the pride of being Indian away, only if you as an Indian want to.

To me, being Indian is the same, but being in a different environment. You "have to" get an education today. Yesterday, you "had to" fill your quiver with arrows. Today, you "have to" fill your head with knowledge. Yesterday, you "had to" hunt and gather food. You "had to" set up camp and have strong, steady poles. Today, you "have to" get a job, pay bills, buy food, rent or buy a home.

But today it's much easier. You have welfare, food stamps, handouts. And you have alcohol. Yet, it's much harder. If you can survive in today's society and maintain your *soul* self, and if you can do these things and know who you are as a person, you are a true warrior. (Stonechild 1992, 13)

Despite two hundred years of nationwide efforts to establish a "melting pot" society and to force assimilation into the dominant Western European culture, America remains multicultural and multiracial, a composite of diverse minorities. Within these minorities, individuals search for personal identities while they encounter insensitivity, intolerance, and hostility from the dominant culture. Hirschfelder and Singer, in *Rising Voices*, regard these conflicts as "harsh realities," which begin as soon as children are old enough to watch television and read books, where they are confronted with distorted messages about Native Americans in advertisements, movies, clothing, and toys.

Brian Willis, a sixteen-year-old Mississippi Choctaw, describes his experience with the "between two worlds" conflict in his essay, "A World Within a World."

> I live in a world within a world. My world consists of a proud Indian heritage. The other world is full of high technology, futuristic ideas, and huge corporations. My world is called the reservation. It may not have fine hotels and penthouses, but who needs these things on a reservation? On the reservation, everyone is equal in some way or another. We have the same color skin, the same language, and the same beliefs. (Willis 1992, 57)

It is not only minority children who suffer the consequences of such a polarized world. When adults of any culture move, divorce, remarry, and combine families, children experience the conflicts of living between two worlds. Even in the best situations, these children also may receive messages that teach them to feel shame when they feel a natural affection for the absent parent or for their previous home. Believing they must reject one world for another, they ask, "Who do I belong to?" and "Where do I fit in?" and they carry their loss and accompanying anger into adulthood.

Many writers and storytellers from the late nineteenth century, as well as contemporary authors, articulate the two-world conflict experienced by both adults and young people. However, not all of them carry the tension and its negative consequences into adulthood. Brian Willis, at the end of "A World Within a World," suggests a *traditional* resolution to the conflict:

> As the Choctaw tribe heads into the coming years, we may leave the reservation, but we cannot relinquish our heritage. My heritage is something that will remain important to me until the day I die. (Willis 1992, 57)

Rather than escape or surrender, Willis affirms the primacy of traditional values as he and other Native American young people continue to live between two worlds.

The value in focusing on the "between two worlds" theme is clear. When teachers use stories and poems featuring this theme, and when they establish an atmosphere where all experience is regarded as valuable and real, young people can learn to develop insight into their own lives while they work towards positive conflict resolution.

Subthemes: Between Two Worlds

Home and School: stories and poems that represent cultural adaptation experiences for Indian children

Old Ways and New Stories: stories that portray Native Americans in their initial experiences with the encroachment, technology, behavior, and value systems of European Americans

Worlds within a World: stories and poems where the dangers which accompany the clash between differing value systems and ways of life are recognized and resolved

School, Home and Away: stories about boarding school experiences and the effects on individuals and communities

Who Am I?: novels, stories, and poems which articulate the "two world" conflicts between relatives, peers, communities, cultures, races, and generations, and which demonstrate the impact of those conflicts on the individual's search for a personal identity

Theme: Cultural and Personal Loss and Survival

One of the most common stereotypes of Native people is the "vanishing American." The following comments and statistics represent small shadows of the geographical and cultural disintegrations—and staggering genocide—that have contributed to this stereotype.

In the 1830s, just one of many Indian Removals resulted in deaths of up to 8,000 Cherokee men, women, and children on the "Trail of Tears." (Champagne 1994, 150)

Between 1836 and 1870, the Mandan and Hidatsa in central North Dakota lost "as much as 90 percent of their population, leaving only a few hundred survivors." (Champagne 1994, 154)

[Between 1850 and 1880,] California militia and self-appointed vigilantes indiscriminately [hunted] down and [killed] thousands of peaceful California Indian men, women, and children. . . . In less than 30 years the Indian population in California [declined] from over 100,000 in 1850 to just 16,000. (Champagne 1994, 176)

In 1887, approximately 140 million acres were owned in joint tenure by the Indians of the United States. The Allotment Act [Dawes Act] set up procedures which resulted in the transfer of some 90 million acres from Indian to white owners in the next forty-five years. (McNickle 1973, 83)

They made us many promises, more than I can remember . . . they kept but one. They promised to take our land, and they took it."—an old Lakota Sioux warrior (*Reservations* 1995, 45)

> Sometimes at evening I sit, looking out on the big Missouri. The Sun sets, and dusk steals over the water. In the shadows I seem again to see our Indian village . . . and in the river's roar I hear the yells of the warriors, the laughter of little children as of old. It is but an old woman's dream. Again I see but shadows and hear only the roar of the river; and tears come into my eyes. Our Indian life, I know, is gone forever.—Buffalo Bird Woman, Hidatsa (Nabokov 1978, 231)

By 1900, the wanton destruction of buffalo, bear, deer, and fish, forests, and rivers and the epidemics of disease, alcoholism, and poverty all contributed to the belief by non-Native people that Native peoples were the "vanishing Americans." In truth, genocide had done its work. According to Elliot West, in *The Way to the West: Essays on the Central Plains*, "During the four hundred years after 1500, some say, the aboriginal population of North America dropped by more than ninety-five percent, while others say sixty or seventy percent. Whichever is accurate, this was the greatest die off in the human record" (West, 86). From the estimated Indian population of 10 to 20 million in 1492, only 237,196 remained in 1900.

But the theme of cultural and personal loss and survival, which is especially present throughout contemporary literatures, proves the fallacy in the "vanishing" stereotype. Refusing to be silenced, storytellers and poets like Elizabeth Cook-Lynn live to "'consecrate' history and event, survival and joy and sorrow, the significance of ancestors and the unborn" (Cook-Lynn 1987, 59). They recount the memories of ancient cultural ways and trace the journeys of so many Native people who are fighting to preserve sacred ancestral lands. Most importantly, it is the storytellers and the poets who bear witness to the tenacity and power of the human spirit.

The history of Indian loss—and survival—is not limited to collective stories of massacres and lost homelands. Indian parents and grandparents also suffered the very personal loss of children. From the late nineteenth century to the mid-twentieth century, children were separated from their families and communities and taken to Indian boarding schools, sometimes for as long as ten years and across thousands of miles, for the sake of "civilizing" them. For generation after generation, the old ways, cultural values and beliefs—and language—together with the meanings of "belonging" and "home," were lost. A character in Linda Hogan's *Mean Spirit* says, "they have gone to school and returned with lives full of holes" (Hogan 1990, 217). Patricia Riley, in her introduction to the "Schooldays" section of *Growing Up Native American*, describes this common denominator of all Native peoples:

> Punished for speaking their native languages, ill fed and brutally treated, these children often emerged emotionally and physically scarred. Personal courage, memories of family and home, and love

for one another allowed these young Native Americans to endure and resist the efforts of those who meant to destroy their tribal identities. (Riley 1993, 116)

Despite the recoveries Native communities have experienced, writers like Paula Gunn Allen (Laguna/Sioux) and James Welch (Blackfeet/Gros Ventre) testify to the continuing power of genocide and cultural and personal loss, while their words demonstrate the still stronger will to survive and prevail. "The impact of genocide in the minds of American Indian poets and writers cannot be exaggerated. It is an all-pervasive feature of the consciousness of every American Indian" (Allen 1982, 39).

With the following very personal yet historical confrontation of loss, James Welch begins his nonfiction work *Killing Custer,* a narrative of the Battle of the Little Bighorn from the Indian perspective. Here he wanders into the landscape and memory of his great-grandmother, Red Paint Woman, a survivor of "Baker's Massacre" on the Marias River. There, 173 of Heavy Runner's "friendly" band—women, children, old men, and those already dying of smallpox—"traveled to the Sand Hills, the resting place of departed souls" (Welch 1994, 42).

> I remember wondering, as I wandered across the wasted flat [in the valley of the Marias River to the backup of the Tiber Dam reservoir], what the village must have looked like on January 22, 1870, the day before the [Marias Massacre or Baker's Massacre]. . . . Normally, there would have been a few children outside playing with buffalo-rib sleds or small bows and spears. . . . But it was a camp of death already. Smallpox, the white scabs disease, the white man's gift, had visited the Pikuni camps that winter. (Welch 1994, 42–44)

Continuing his story, Welch succeeds in "killing" the myths of Custer and his comrades and enemies, and with dark irony bears witness to the surviving spirit of Indian people and the universal condition of all humanity.

> The outcome of the Indian wars was never in doubt. It is a tribute to the Indians' spirit that they resisted as long as they did. Custer's Last Stand has gone down in history as an example of what savagery the Indians were capable of; the massacre on the Marias is a better example of what man is capable of doing to man. (Welch 1994, 47)

The last lines of James Welch's historical narrative profoundly demonstrate the prevailing strength of spirit despite the odds: "Before he died, Black Elk called up a rain shower out of a blue sky in an effort to nourish the roots of the withered sacred tree. The Indian spirit was, and remains, hard to break" (Welch 1994, 286).

The theme of cultural and personal loss and survival is universal. When fifty students in a consolidated rural high school in Montana were surveyed, the results proved these students also lived "lives full of holes." Over 70 percent were not living with both their natural parents; with no standard other than gut feelings, most could not explain how they knew what was right and wrong; most rarely ate meals with the whole family together and without the entertainment of television; most had no idea of their ethnic heritage, and of those who did know, few could tell stories about ancestors even two generations removed. Those with Native American heritages were reluctant to admit that fact out loud. Some had difficulty pronouncing the tribal name. These were contemporary young people who could write page after page about what disturbed them: loneliness, personal rejection, physical and mental abuse, premarital sex, sexual harassment, drugs, terrorism, the deaths of children and relatives, war, and the power of those who would control them. Like young people today from all cultural backgrounds, these students deserved to read and hear the stories of how others experienced loss and how they survived.

To be sure, most Native American writers are telling stories that reflect the impact of their common histories on past and present lives. But they are also telling the stories of personal and communal loss and survival that are common to us all, stories and poems representing what it means to be human. The literary expressions of these poets vary in tone from joy to irony, to passion, to anger, to bitterness, such as in "The Girl Who Loved the Sky" by Yaqui poet Anita Endrezze. After experiencing the childhood joy of "best friends," the speaker suffers such profound sorrow and loss that she finally sees "the world clearly," holding a flame of "bitter" awareness.

Outside the second grade room,
the jacaranda tree blossomed
into purple lanterns . . .
Inside, the room smelled like glue.
The desks were made of yellowed wood,
the tops littered with eraser rubbings.
. . . There, I learned
how to make butter by shaking a jar
until the pale cream clotted
into one sweet mass . . . And there,

I met a blind girl who thought the sky
tasted like cold metal when it rained
and whose eyes were always covered
with the bruised petals of her lids.

She loved the formless sky, defined
only by sounds, or the cool umbrellas
of clouds. On hot, still days
we listened to the sky falling
like chalk dust. We heard the noon
whistle of the pig-mash factory,
smelled the sourness of home-bound men.

I had no father; she had no eyes;
we were best friends. The other girls
drew shaky hopscotch squares
on the dusty asphalt . . .
Alone, we sat in the canvas swings,
our shoes digging into the sand, then pushing,
until we flew high over their heads . . .

I was born blind, she said, an act of nature.
Sure, I thought, like birds born
without wings, trees without roots.
I didn't understand. The day she moved
I saw the world clearly: the sky
backed away from me like a departing father.
I sat under the jacaranda, catching
the petals in my palm, enclosing them
until my fist was another lantern
hiding a small and bitter flame.

—Anita Endrezze

Despite a history that has resulted in victimization and genocide for millions of Native peoples, writers today are refusing to admit defeat and to accept the image of "Indian as artifact." Instead, they continue to insist on their right to define for themselves who they are as they restructure their lives from the fragments of the past and the present. Many, like James Welch, Anita Endrezze, and Linda Hogan, tell their own stories of cultural and personal loss and survival, which can benefit all young people; these are stories of spirits that "remain hard to break," stories of people who "come together for a healing."

The sharp smell of burning sage added to their comfort. . . . The people were silent. They were small in the world and they knew it. Their human woes were small. Their time was short. They didn't want to live their lives eaten up with grief. . . . When it was all dark the singing began. . . . The people took faith, took heart, in the sounds and the sparks, and the occasional cool brush of air that entered the room like a hand, touching every person on the shoulder or the head or on the skin of a hand. (Hogan 1990, 216)

Subthemes: Cultural and Personal Loss and Survival

Era or Time Period: for example, Patricia Riley's *Growing Up Native American,* has four sections: "Going Forward, Looking Back," which includes the concept of living in two worlds while maintaining an awareness and connection with original language and culture; "Nineteenth Century"; "Schooldays"; and "Twentieth Century"

Specific Geographical Areas, Cultural Systems, or Historical Events

Separation from Relatives, Landscapes, Cultures, Pride, Self and Spirit: stories featuring separation and its subsequent effects, such as loneliness, abuse, death, disease, alcoholism, poverty, and suicide

Means of Survival: stories highlighting the awareness of ancestors and values, reconciliation and home, a sense of the spiritual, and humor

Specific Native Cultural or Literary Traditions: images and sound patterns; heroes; integration of oral tradition, historical events, and the present; and the trickster and transformer motif in contemporary texts

Theme: Lifeways and Stereotypes

Each of us, no matter what our cultural or racial background, has a way of viewing and interpreting the meaning of our surroundings. It is our world view, our lifeway, our bias, functioning as a pair of permanently tinted glasses which we resist removing unless strongly encouraged or provoked. Culturally and racially determined, our world view defines our relationship to the universe as a whole. It also defines the values of all things material, spiritual, animate, and inanimate, for ourselves and for others as well.

Frequently, our world view results in ethnocentrism, the attitude of regarding our own culture as central, superior *or* inferior to other cultures. Although this may positively manifest itself in a personal and communal pride, a negative side of ethnocentrism can result in evaluation, judgment, and rejection of different cultures and races. This is racism, which Ardy Bowker (Eastern Cherokee) describes as being "perpetuated through a system of unequal power relationships in private and public institutions and is manifested in the form of prejudice, discrimination, and stereotyping" (Bowker 1993).

So what is the relationship between world view, ethnocentrism, and stereotypes? Stereotyping may be defined in several ways, but in all cases, stereotyping frequently occurs as a result of our ethnocentrism, when we need to describe cultures and individuals outside ourselves while we continue to wear our tinted glasses. Stereotyping occurs when our own bias or world view outlines the shape of another person or group or culture. Stereotyping occurs when we permanently lock people into the position or image we see, and, according to one dictionary, stereotyping occurs when members of a group develop and maintain a simplified and standardized conception or image of themselves or others, and "invest that image with special meaning" (*Random House* 1967). We might also say that stereotyping occurs when someone else tells "*my* story about me." Another way of talking about stereotype is to consider it *myth,* "an unproved collective belief that is accepted uncritically and is used to justify a social institution" (*Random House* 1967). A myth is not entirely false and not entirely true, but it reveals much about the values of those who believe the myth or rely on the stereotype.

Why and how should intermediate level students, as well as older students, read and learn about stereotypes? "Some stereotypes have no basis in fact, while others may be based at least on a small element of truth. Unfortunately, stereotyping of American Indians, which began at the onset of European contact with indigenous populations, has led to many inaccurate and misleading generalizations that are present in contemporary American society" (Bowker 1993, 30). The most visible stereotypes of Native Americans include noble savage, heathen, wild, princess or squaw, nomadic, redskin, uncivilized savage, childlike, anti-education, undisciplined children, white man's helper, and vanishing American. (Appendix D provides definitions and sources for each.)

One of our most important tasks as teachers is to continually search for truths and to facilitate and empower our students as they search for truths about themselves, their own cultures, and the worlds outside themselves. *The Chichi Hoohoo Bogeyman* demonstrates the effect of limited truths, of stereotypes, on Native children. In the following excerpt, Cindy tells her Sioux cousins why she behaved so badly, embarrassing them at a movie they had just seen:

> ". . . That was a stupid movie. Everybody in it was stupid—especially the Indians. Indians are always stupid and dumb in movies. That's why everyone thinks Indians should act that way in real life." Cindy got up from the cot, stuck one finger behind her head, hopped around in a fake war dance and rapidly patted her mouth with her other hand. "When I grow up I'm going to be real smart and use only big words when I talk. Nobody will dare call me a dumb Injun." (Sneve 1993, 34)

Stereotypes are not perpetuated in movies alone; many popular books and stories about Native Americans rely on several different stereotypes of Native peoples. These stereotypes often arise from social, political, and economic situations in which certain individuals or groups stand to benefit from the perpetuation of such images. For example, many popular stories about Indians feature a singular Indian hero, such as Chief Joseph, who unsuccessfully struggles alone against insurmountable odds. When the hero ultimately surrenders or dies, the European American belief in the superiority of a particular kind of civilization and Manifest Destiny appear to prevail. The stories non-Natives tell, about who Native Americans were or are, can reinforce the non-Natives' beliefs about themselves and the world around them. The stories may also represent the non-Natives' desire to atone for the sins of cultural destruction and genocide, by portraying characters who fall because they are innocent and unsophisticated—in other words, primitive.

Children and young adults within our classrooms and communities also repeat such stereotypes. Whooping and hollering three-year-olds beg grandfathers to make them bows and arrows. Older children taunt each other with names like "savage" and "squaw," and teens and adults tell "Indian" jokes. Others who have developed compassion for minorities believe Native Americans and their cultures "were" far superior to the "money-hungry murdering Americans." Michael Dorris summarizes the situation: "On occasion [Indians] are presented as marauding, blood-thirsty savages, bogeys from the nightmares of 'pioneers' who invaded their lands and feared for the consequences. At other times they seem preconcupiscent angels, pure of heart, mindlessly ecological, brave and true. And worst of all, they are often merely cute, the special property of small children" (Dorris 1982, vii). Ardy Bowker (Eastern Cherokee), in her book *Sisters in the Blood*, provides one of the best discussions of "Racism and Stereotyping in Native America," and the impact of stereotypes on Native American women in particular. Bowker also discusses the way stereotypes are used to describe situations, such as "They all drop out of school," "They all get a monthly check from the federal government," or "They are all drunks" (Bowker 1993, 30). Yet most of the children and young adults who use and accept these stereotypes as truth probably don't know one Indian person well enough to be invited into his home. Moreover, as long as the stereotypes are so prevalent and available, they have no need to search beyond what they already know and believe.

By contrasting popular books and stories by Native and non-Native writers, teachers can help students appreciate the way individual voices address and counter racial and cultural stereotypes that have objectified Native American peoples. One such voice is the speaker in the following poem by Diane Burns (Anishinabe/Chemehuevi) in which the speaker responds to ignorant non-Indians who want to fit her into a stereotypical racial and cultural category. Native adults who have traveled outside their home communities into multi-ethnic cities have heard, and know by heart, the stereotype-invested questions that lie underneath each of the lines. The last two lines reveal the speaker's frustration and her assertion of her personal identity.

Sure You Can Ask Me A Personal Question

How do you do?
    No, I am not Chinese.
No, not Spanish.
    No, I am American Indi—uh, Native American.
No, not from India.
    No, not Apache.
No, not Navajo.
    No, not Sioux.
No, we are not extinct.
    Yes, Indin.
Oh?
    So that's where you got those high cheekbones.
Your great grandmother, huh?
    An Indian Princess, huh?

Hair down to there?
Let me guess. Cherokee?
Oh, so you've had an Indian friend?
That close?
Oh, so you've had an Indian servant?
That much?
Yeah, it was awful what you guys did to us.
It's real decent of you to apologize.
No, I don't know where you can get peyote.
No, I don't know where you can get Navajo rugs real cheap.
No, I didn't make this. I bought it at Bloomingdale's.
Thank you. I like your hair too.
I don't know if anyone knows whether or not Cher is really Indian.
No, I didn't make it rain tonight.
Yeah. Uh-huh. Spirituality.
Uh-huh. Yeah. Spirituality. Uh-huh. Mother Earth.
Yeah. Uh-huh. Uh-huh. Spirituality.
No, I didn't major in archery.
Yeah, a lot of us drink too much.
Some of us can't drink enough.
This ain't no stoic look.
This is my face.

—Diane Burns

When teachers understand the origins of stereotypes, they can better help young people of all ages to grow in their ability and willingness to regard themselves and others as unique individuals, and to distinguish between lifeways and stereotypes.

Works Cited

Allen, Paula Gunn. 1982. "Answering the Deer." *American Indian Culture and Research Journal* 6.3: 39.

Banks, Lynne Reid. 1988. *The Indian in the Cupboard.* Santa Barbara, CA: ABC-Clio.

Bowker, Ardy. 1993. *Sisters in the Blood: The Education of Women in Native America.* Bozeman: Center for Bilingual/Multicultural Education, Montana State University.

Bruchac, Joseph, ed. 1983. *Songs From this Earth on Turtle's Back.* Greenfield Center, NY: The Greenfield Review Press.

Bruchac, Joseph. 1991. *Native American Stories.* Golden, CO: Fulcrum Publishing.

Burns, Diane. 1983. "Sure You Can Ask Me a Personal Question." In *Songs from this Earth on Turtle's Back,* ed. Joseph Bruchac. Greenfield Center, NY: The Greenfield Review Press.

Carter, Forrest. 1991. *The Education of Little Tree.* Albuquerque: University of New Mexico Press.

Champagne, Duane. 1994. *Chronology of Native North American History.* Detroit, MI: Gale Research Inc.

Contrary Warriors: A Story of the Crow Tribe. 1985. Rattlesnake Productions. Videocassette.

Cook-Lynn, Elizabeth. 1987. "You May Consider Speaking about Your Art." In *I Tell You Now: Autobiographical Essays by Native American Writers,* eds. Brian Swann and Arnold Krupat. Lincoln: University of Nebraska Press.

Dorris, Michael. 1982. Foreword to *American Indian Stereotypes in the World of Children: A Reader and Bibliography,* ed. Arlene B. Hirschfelder. Metuchen, NJ: The Scarecrow Press, Inc.

Dorris, Michael. 1992. *Morning Girl.* New York: Hyperion Books for Children.

Endrezze, Anita. 1992. *at the helm of twilight.* Seattle, WA: Broken Moon Press.

Farley, Ronnie, ed. 1993. *Women of the Native Struggle: Portraits and Testimony of Native American Women.* New York: Orion Books.

Harjo, Joy. 1997. *She Had Some Horses.* New York: Thunder's Mouth Press.

Henson, Lance. 1992. *A Cheyenne Sketchbook: Selected Poems 1970–1991.* Greenfield Center, NY: The Greenfield Review Press.

Hirschfelder, Arlene B., and Beverly R. Singer, eds. 1992. *Rising Voices— Writings of Young Native Americans.* New York: Charles Scribner's Sons.

Hogan, Linda. 1990. *Mean Spirit.* New York: Ivy Books.

Littlebird, Harold. 1983. "A Circle Begins." In *Songs From this Earth on Turtle's Back,* ed. Joseph Bruchac. Greenfield Center, NY: The Greenfield Review Press.

McNickle, D'Arcy. 1973. *Native American Tribalism.* New York: Oxford University Press.

Momaday, N. Scott. 1990. Foreword to *Native American Stories,* ed. Joseph Bruchac. Golden, CO: Fulcrum Publishing.

Nabokov, Peter ed. 1978. *Native American Testimony.* New York: Harper & Row.

"New Age Fable from an Old School Bigot?" 1991. *Newsweek,* Oct. 14, p. 62.

Plenty, Len. 1992. "The Bighorn River." In *Rising Voices—Writings of Young Native Americans,* eds. Arlene B. Hirschfelder and Beverly R. Singer. New York: Charles Scribner's Sons.

The Random House Dictionary of the English Language, Unabridged Edition. 1967.

Rapada, Kimberly Kai. "My Role as a Native American" In *Rising Voices— Writings of Young Native Americans,* eds. Arlene B. Hirschfelder and Beverly R. Singer. New York: Charles Scribner's Sons.

The Reservations. 1995. The American Indians Series. Alexandria, VA: Time-Life Books.

Riley, Patricia, ed. 1993. *Growing Up Native American: An Anthology.* New York: Wm. Morrow.

Sneve, Virginia Driving Hawk. 1993. *The Chichi Hoohoo Bogeyman.* Lincoln: University of Nebraska Press.

Spotted Bear, Delia. 1992. "My Family." In *Rising Voices—Writings of Young Native Americans,* eds. Arlene B. Hirschfelder and Beverly R. Singer. New York: Charles Scribner's Sons.

Stonechild, Murray. "To Be an Indian." In *Rising Voices—Writings of Young Native Americans,* eds. Arlene B. Hirschfelder and Beverly R. Singer. New York: Charles Scribner's Sons.

Thomasma, Ken. 1984. *Soun Tetoken: Nez Perce Boy.* Jackson, WY: Grandview.

Wallerstein, Judith, and Sandra Blakeslee. 1990. *Second Chances: Men, Women, Children a Decade After Divorce.* New York: Ticknor & Fields.

Weiten, Wayne, and Margaret A. Lloyd. 1994. *Psychology Applied to Modern Life: Adjustment in the '90s.* Pacific Grove, CA: Brooks/Cole.

Welch, James, with Paul Stekler. 1994. *Killing Custer: The Battle of the Little Bighorn and the Fate of the Plains Indians.* New York: W.W. Norton.

West, Elliot. 1995. *The Way to the West: Essays on the Central Plains.* Albuquerque: University of New Mexico Press.

Willis, Brian. "A World Within a World." In *Rising Voices—Writings of Young Native Americans,* eds. Arlene B. Hirschfelder and Beverly R. Singer. New York: Charles Scribner's Sons.

Yellow Robe, Rosebud. 1992. *Tonweya and the Eagles and Other Lakota Tales.* New York: Penguin.

Zitkala-Ša. [1900] 1985. *American Indian Stories.* Lincoln: University of Nebraska Press.

2

Historical and Cultural Literary Contexts

What is Native American literature? Although some have tried—major publishing houses included—the definition of Native American literature cannot be reduced to myth, mysticism, or historical artifact, evidence of "the way Indians used to live." In truth, traditional oral and contemporary written Indian literatures, in the plural, reflect the diversity of over five hundred tribal cultures, with a variety of literary traditions within each of those cultures. These literatures also demonstrate the influences and consequences of intertribal contact and European American culture contact, expressing the individual lives that stem from these various cultural and historical experiences. According to Gerald Vizenor, "Native American literatures embrace the memories of creation stories, the tragic wisdom of native ceremonies, trickster narratives, and the outcome of chance and other occurrences in the most diverse cultures in the world" (Vizenor 1995).

Despite the diverse experiences and traditions, both older and more contemporary Indian literatures do display similar characteristics and visions. "Intelligent analysis becomes a matter of identifying smaller assumptions that underlie our own culture and its literature and art," writes noted poet and literary critic Paula Gunn Allen in her essay "The Sacred Hoop: A Contemporary Perspective." Especially important are those assumptions that are "peculiar to the locale, idiom, and psyche of the writer" (Allen 1983, 3). Allen compares and contrasts some Western European traditions with what she regards as the more predominant Native literary traditions (Allen 1992). Allen's critical work has provided a cultural and literary context for literatures, especially those rooted in Plains Indian cultures. Still, the following list and discussion of elements can represent no more than my own experience with the literatures mentioned, the work of Paula Gunn Allen, and the works of contemporary literary critics I have read.

Cultural and Literary Elements in Native and Western European Literatures

1. Underlying assumptions about the universe
2. Definition and practice of power
3. Meaning and function of symbol
4. Literary purposes
5. Classification of genres
6. Definition of "hero"
7. Organizational patterns
8. Recurring motifs in Native American literatures
9. Themes of loss and survival

Keeping in mind my need to generalize because of the limitations of time, space, and experience, I hope the following will facilitate teachers' and students' understanding as they read and explore the Native American literatures listed in this resource.

Underlying Assumptions about the Universe

Western and tribal traditions may hold different underlying assumptions about the universe. Very generally speaking, the Western European universe, primarily based on the Judeo-Christian world view, consists of polarized categories—good or bad, masculine or feminine, civilized or savage, superior or inferior, with a definite line drawn between spiritual and material realities. The Western European world view is also based on the medieval "Great Chain of Being" concept, with God at the top and animals at the bottom. Furthermore, the Western European universe, like those of the Hopi and certain other Indian cultures, embraces a linear view of history, in which cultures and peoples can progress toward the establishment of "new worlds." In contrast, Dakota educator Dr. Debbie LaCroix, in workshops given at NCTE conferences and conventions, uses a circle to describe the universe of her people. Within this circle, "all have an equal place on the Sacred Hoop, the circle of life, and all have spirit." Individuals are responsible for working toward a sense of harmony and balance with all creation. In this universe, individuals "compete to be stronger, to become wise, to become more centered than on the previous day."

In Linda Hogan's novel *Mean Spirit,* Michael Horse, "the last person in Indian Territory [Oklahoma] to live in a tepee," reads aloud from his written "gospel according to Horse" (*written* because today, "they won't believe it unless they see it in writing"):

> Live gently with the land. We are one with the land. We are part of everything in our world, part of the roundness and cycles of life. And all life is sacred. . . . Restore your self and voice. Remake your spirit, so that it is in harmony with the rest of nature and the universe. Keep peace with all your sisters and brothers. Humans whose minds are healthy desire such peace and justice. (Hogan 1990, 362)

In his book *Other Destinies*, Choctaw/Cherokee/Irish writer Louis Owens describes a way of looking at the world that Native American writers offer—a way that is "new to Western culture":

> It is a holistic, ecological perspective, one that places essential value upon the totality of existence, making humanity equal to all elements but superior to none and giving humankind crucial responsibility for the care of the world we inhabit. (Owens 1992, 29)

In these Indian worlds, the significance and consequences of the past circle into the present, and voices of ancestors speak through poets today who continue to search for harmony with all Creation. Since the European colonization of the western hemisphere, Native American cultures and peoples have experienced dramatic changes over the years as they have both resisted and adapted to the European American culture. Nevertheless, many American Indian writers today stand firm in the faith that their Native cultural heritages can never be destroyed.

Reading works by writers such as James Welch and Linda Hogan, non-Native students frequently are confused when ravens speak, the dead walk, and dreamers wake with magical stones in hand. However, when these students examine their assumptions about the universe, they can begin to understand and accept the realities of worlds and views different from their own.

Definition and Practice of Power

Western Europeans frequently define power in economic, historical, and political terms; it is the force by which individuals impose their will upon others. This power is frequently viewed negatively, especially today when many people regard powerful institutions as corrupt and evil. By contrast, Native power may be described as a benevolent living force that circulates through human beings so all life in this world might continue. In novels by Louise Erdrich, Leslie Silko, and N. Scott Momaday, the characters move into community, frequently rejecting the Western European concept of temporal power and the "American Dream" of individual freedom and material success. This is also true in the novels of James Welch and D'Arcy McNickle. Writing about McNickle's work, William Bevis observes:

> [T]he free individual without context is utterly lost. . . . No "free individual" who achieves white success in these six books is really admired, and certainly the free "mode of life" they have "chosen" is not preferred to tribal context. (Bevis 1990, 102)

Because this Native power is viewed as being connected to word and thought, traditional and contemporary Indian peoples have placed great value in their choice and use of words. The important value of noninterference is also related to this Native idea of power, especially with respect to education. Rather than *directly* using power to impose their will or opinions regarding desirable and undesirable behaviors upon others, many Native people have traditionally used story to educate their children and to communicate *indirectly* their beliefs to those outside their cultures. For example, when Frank B. Linderman asks Pretty-shield (Crow) her people's opinion of Sitting Bull, she says:

> I was about twenty-eight or thirty years old when I saw Sitting-bull here at this very place. I will tell you what happened on that day, and then you may write down your own answers to your own questions. (Linderman 1972, 196)

Trusting that individuals will make decisions most appropriate for themselves, Indian people such as Pretty-shield also allow others to suffer and learn from the consequences of inappropriate decisions.

Meaning and Function of Symbol

In the Western European tradition, a symbol suggests other meanings in addition to its literal meaning. Generally, a symbol stands for something greater than itself; a cross stands for Christ or the Crucifixion, a flag stands for a country or state. By contrast, in Lame Deer's Cheyenne universe, the physical aspect of the symbol is as valid and important as the reality it represents (Lame Deer 1972). Bevis discusses this issue in the novels of Welch and McNickle. Whereas non-Native peoples are "accustomed to using nature, abstracting it, confining it to [their] purposes," in these novels, "Nature is not a symbol, subordinate to the human need for understanding. Animals have their own rights in life and art. . . . Native American nature is urban . . . at the *center* of action and power, in complex and unpredictable and various relationships" (Bevis 1990, 112–13).

Two examples from Linda Hogan's *Mean Spirit* also serve to illustrate what looks like symbol but is, in fact, spiritual power. Joe Billy (Osage) holds a medicine bundle with dry parchment-like covering, and closes his eyes:

> He heard what he thought were warnings stirring beneath the surface of his skin, beneath the floors of his house.
> In the morning, his wife opened the door to the study to find her husband asleep in the chair. . . .
> [I]nside [the leather pouch] Martha could see that something was moving. The sight of it bumping and turning in Joe Billy's hands startled her and she drew in such a frightened breath that Joe Billy woke and looked from her blue eyes to the moving bundle that he held.
> "What's in there?" Martha asked.
> He blinked at her and all he could really say was, "It's the older world, wanting out." (Hogan 1990, 138)

For Joe Billy's people, as well as for the Blackfeet in James Welch's novels, the sacred medicine bundle itself carries the power to structure and maintain their universe. In *Mean Spirit*, following the persistent visits of death and fire, the narrator observes a gathering of Indians and whites at a Fourth of July celebration:

> They were in a trap, a circle of fear, and they could not leave. Money held them. It became a living force. One way or another, if they had it or if they didn't, it held them like the caged parrots a vendor was selling. . . . They were crowded in their cages. They all faced south toward the deep, wet jungle, their homeland. (Hogan 1990, 293)

In this instance, the Native narrator views money as a spiritual power, a very real living force.

Literary Purposes

From a formalist critical perspective, the written work may be regarded as an entity unto itself; in the mimetic view expressed in *Hamlet*, "the purpose of playing . . . is to hold . . . the mirror up to Nature." This purpose is also true of Native literatures. In his Foreword to *Keepers of the Earth*, N. Scott Momaday says, "stories are true to human experience. Indeed, the truth of human experience is their principal information" (Momaday 1988).

In general, both Native and non-Native written literatures are more private than public, engaging individuals, not communities; other Western European and Native traditions also value the role and scope of self-expression. However, traditional Native stories usually are regarded within the tribal community as being "told by," not "invented or created by," their storytellers. Also, Native stories have many roles: some teach, some are ceremonial, some carry history, and some are told purely for entertainment. Through the act of traditional Indian storytelling, listeners can learn values and behaviors important to the community while they are also entertained, with storyteller and listeners participating together in the storytelling. Thus, stories themselves act as unifying factors. Ceremonial stories, as well as popular stories, bring listeners into harmony and balance with the entire community, as the children learn to practice the social and spiritual ways of their elders. In this way, stories actually define a community, a people as a whole; this is the sacred nature of story. It is for this reason that tribal people might own their stories, and believe that "something is lost when the stories leave our community." As teachers familiar with America's *public* literature, including television, movies, radio, and videotape in which little attention is paid to who "owns" the stories, we need to be sensitized to the different role that story plays in Native cultures. Culture committee members in one Montana community asked me to make sure that readers of *Roots and Branches* understood the following:

> Be careful about using stories *out of time*, because many tribes have particular seasons when some stories must not be told; respect the *integrity or value of the story* for the community; learn about *why we*

have stories—because someone cared enough to share and to carry on; remember that *stories belong to people—they are the personal collective history and memory of a people;* tell the history of Native people *accurately,* and always remember that these stories represent a *diversity of people.*

Whenever teachers use traditional Native stories, they should explain their vital role in maintaining a particular tribe's integrity, and they should emphasize the difference between reading a stranger's story and hearing it from an elder.

Although this integrative purpose of literature may be more obvious in the oral tradition, many Indian poets today express a respect and responsibility for their communities. Also, many contemporary Indian literary works feature characters who move into communal balance and harmony as they search for identity. After reading Sherman Alexie's *The Lone Ranger and Tonto Fistfight in Heaven,* one of my seniors remarked, "I really liked the book, but sometimes I felt like an outsider. I didn't know enough about his world to understand the 'inside' jokes and stories." According to Louis Owens in *Other Destinies,* without this knowledge, non-Native readers find themselves "outside the text," whereas the Indian reader is the "privileged" or integrated audience (Owens 1992, 29). Owens suggests that Indian writers today are pulling both Indian and non-Indian readers into community, demanding that they know something about the mythology and literary history of Native Americans.

Classification of Genres

Directly linked to the purposes of literature is the classification of genres. For traditional Native literatures especially, the Western European terms "fiction" and "non-fiction" are somewhat meaningless, because traditional stories are regarded as true. Traditional Native literatures may be classified according to function and cultural context instead of by form and style. Also, each traditional category may include what Western Europeans might call "poetry" and "prose." Having been influenced by both Native and Western European literary traditions, contemporary writers such as Leslie Marmon Silko and N. Scott Momaday blend poetry and prose into one narrative, even as they write novels, short stories, poetry, or drama.

One traditional Native American cycle features the popular and intensely complex trickster/transformer or culture hero. Known by different names, genders, and behaviors, this hero and antihero (in Western European terms) can take on the forms of animals and humans, depending on the particular tribal tradition. To the Sioux, he is Iktomi, the spider; to the Southwest Plateau Indians and the Salish, he is Coyote; to the Crow, he is Old Man Coyote; to Indians in the Northwest, he is Raven; to the Blackfeet, he is Old Man and Napi; to the Abenaki, he is Gluscabi; to the Cree in Montana and Canada, he is

Wisahkecahk; to the Cheyenne, he is VeHo; and to the Gros Ventres, he is Nee Ot. Representing a wide range of possible human actions, the trickster is capable of much good, but he or she also may exhibit the most undesirable human behaviors. With mischief in mind, the hero may overreach, deceive, and manipulate others to get what he wants. Sometimes, he earns his just reward and brings ridicule on himself in the end. Through the stories, listeners learn how to imitate positive and creative behaviors, to understand the power or good that they may access, while they also learn to recognize their own deceitful and fraudulent behaviors. Listeners may also learn to avoid stupidity—and even death—by being watchful and wary of those who might deceive them.

Early twentieth-century and contemporary Indian writers, such as N. Scott Momaday, Zitkala-Ša, Gerald Vizenor, James Welch, Joseph Bruchac, D'Arcy McNickle, Louise Erdrich, and Debra Earling, frequently incorporate the trickster and his wide range of behaviors in poetry, stories, and novels. Brigit Hans, in her introduction to *The Hawk is Hungry and Other Stories* by twentieth-century writer D'Arcy McNickle, includes McNickle's explanation of the continuing importance of Coyote to the Salish people:

> Indian story telling presents a contrasting view of man's role in the historical process: the coyote tales are especially good for this. Coyote is rarely a hero, or if he starts out to be a hero invariably he ends up a scoundrel or he finds himself outsmarted. There are no mounting crises and no gratifying denouements. Life is an arrangement of reciprocal expectations and obligations, and no one is allowed to set himself up as a power unto himself. (Hans 1992)

In his critical analysis of N. Scott Momaday's *House Made of Dawn* and the character of Tosamah, the Priest of the Sun, Louis Owens writes:

> Tosamah mocks, ridicules, and challenges every fixed meaning or static definition. . . . Like the traditional trickster, [he] is in dialogue with himself, embodies contradictions, challenges authority, mocks and tricks us into self-knowledge. (Owens 1992)

Quoting Momaday, Owens also writes that "Tosamah serves at times as the author's 'mouthpiece'." The same is true with Gerald Vizenor's fiction, where "the author/trickster [attacks] terminal creeds and [loosens] the shrouds of identities" (Owens 1992, 254).

Definition of "Hero"

The traditional Western European hero is self-reliant and male, resolving conflicts in order to achieve communal and individual goals. Stories written by non-Indians about Indians frequently feature a singular hero, such as Chief Joseph, Chief Seattle, Crazy Horse, or Sitting Bull. These heroes unsuccessfully struggle alone against insurmountable odds. When they ultimately surrender or die, the European American values of a particular civilization's superiority and Manifest Destiny appear to prevail. Rather than communicating the Indian peoples' image of who they were or are, these stories simply reinforce the value system of the non-Indian writers.

On the other hand, the protagonists in Indian literatures frequently exhibit values necessary for the survival of the community. Indian writers such as Charles Eastman, Wooden Leg, and Prettyshield tell stories about Chief Joseph, Crazy Horse, and Sitting Bull that differ significantly from those told by Susan Jeffers or published by Troll Publications. The protagonists or heroes in Welch's *Winter in the Blood,* Silko's *Ceremony,* McNickle's *Runner in the Sun,* Ella Deloria's *Waterlily,* and Momaday's *House Made of Dawn,* learn the negative effects of individualism and instead move into community and into the common tribal understanding of a ritual tradition. Bevis calls this process "homing in," or becoming connected to place; "'knowledge' is formed and validated tribally," and "the protagonist ends *where* he began" (Bevis 1990, 103–107). At the end of *Fools Crow* by James Welch, the hero finds himself surrounded by and completed with images from his community: "Red Paint's hand, the rhythm of the drum, his vision of the other world, Feather Woman, and drops of water on the bare earth that countless feet had trampled smooth over the winter." As an adult, Fools Crow is now responsible, "burdened with the knowledge of his people, their lives and the lives of their children" (Welch 1986, 390). In Hogan's *Mean Spirit,* Belle thinks to herself, "bees [are] like Indians, with a circular dance, working together for the survival of the next generations" (Hogan 1990, 312). Ella Deloria, an early twentieth-century Dakota linguist and ethnologist and the author of *Dakota Texts,* suggests that growing up, to the traditional Dakota people, means assuming one's individual responsibilities within the home and community (Deloria 1992). In contrast, many non-Natives may describe themselves as grown up when they have disconnected, have become independent, have left home to "seek a fortune."

Organizational Patterns

The organizational pattern of Indian oral and written literatures differs from the Western European tradition of unity in linear time, place, and action. Instead of a plot characterized by rising action, climax, and falling action, Indian stories are frequently cyclical and episodic, with varying times, settings, and points of view. Language and image may suggest multiple directions and interpretations. *Love Medicine* by Louise Erdrich reads like a collection of gossip with words and stories from several narrative voices. In Leslie Silko's *Ceremony,* scenes move from the time of World War II, to before the war and after the war, then into the realm of the extraordinary with ancient stories of Tayo's Laguna Pueblo. In each chapter of N. Scott Momaday's *The Way to Rainy Mountain,* the elements of legend, history, and the personal are brought together to create a whole in which "The imaginative experience and the historical express equally the traditions of man's reality" (Momaday 1969, 4). These lead readers or listeners into holistic experiences that bring together all of their characters' related experiences to create new meaning or understanding.

Recurring Motifs in Native American Literatures

Though all cultures and literatures may communicate similar archetypal patterns, it is valuable to look at several recurring motifs that pervade both traditional and contemporary Indian literatures.

Everyone and Everything Is Related

In the collection *Growing up Native American,* Louis Owens writes about the Yahoo River and the Great Horned Owl:

> [F]rom the Yahoo we must have learned to feel water as a presence, a constant, a secret source of both dream and nightmare . . . the Great Horned owls called in drumming voices, vague warnings of death somewhere. (Riley 1993, 275)

In *Other Destinies,* Owens writes about the Blackfeet world of James Welch's *Fools Crow:*

> [T]here is no disjunction between the real and the magical, no sense that the magical is metaphorical. In the world Welch recovers, Raven talks to men and women, the sacred and the profane interpenetrate irresistibly, and this is reality. (Owens 1992, 165)

The Reality and Power of Dreams

The dream motif appears throughout Native literatures, such as in Joseph Bruchac's contemporary stories, in children's literature, and in the as-told-to autobiography *Plenty Coups, Chief of the Crows* by Frank B. Linderman. In this book Chief Plenty Coups describes a dream he once had in which he saw the future disappearance of the buffalo and their replacement with domestic cattle. Trusting his dream and its foreshadowing of the inevitable non-Indian presence in Crow territory, Plenty Coups fought with the white man, providing scouts, warriors, and supplies to the military in order to safeguard the land and culture of his people (Linderman 1962). Today the Crow people are one of the few tribes still living in the lands of their ancestors. Pretty-shield (Crow) also tells a story about a woman she once knew who had a dream that saved her people. In the dream, a woman-mouse tells the woman that a Lakota war party will attack soon if the people don't return to the place they have come from (Linderman 1972). The story not only demonstrates the Crow trust in dreams and the voices of animal-people, but it also reveals the importance of women in Crow society.

The Real Presence of Ancestors and the Importance of Memory

In the introduction to her collection of prose and poetry, Elizabeth Woody (Yakama/Warm Springs/Wasco/Navajo) explains what her ancestors mean to her:

> It was United States government policy, until just a few years ago, to eradicate all Indian languages. It was illegal to teach them in schools. I am part of the generation in which this language massacre reached its final stage: I learned only English. But those older languages are active in my brain. Waking to the aroma of coffee, I listened as a child to the Indian words of my grandmother and great-aunt in the morning. I also heard the softness of their walk and the song accompanying them from the birds in the junipers. Such simple pleasures elude me to this day, but the memory returns stronger as I grow older. Even though I've had to become proficient in a language and speaking style entirely different from that of my Sahaptin-Wasco-Diné ancestors, I believe the language I use in my poetry comes from the deep well of these ancient American languages. Listening to the older aspects of myself in my relatives, I was initiated into a life's work with words. (Woody 1994, 14-15)

The Sacred Nature of Children and the Importance of Elders

Pretty-shield (Crow) tells Linderman, "my grandchildren are like the dry earth when rain falls upon it" (Linderman 1972, 133). Lame Deer (Lakota) says: "In their own homes Indian children are surrounded with relatives as with a warm blanket" (Lame Deer 1972). And as the sacred cornmeal is sprinkled "by the door of your classroom," the speaker in the poem, "For Misty Starting School," by Luci Tapahonso (Navajo), asks the child to "remember now, where this cornmeal is from / remember now, you are no different . . . / remember now, you are no different / blessing us / leaving us" (Tapahonso 1987). In his introduction to *The Way to Rainy Mountain*, N. Scott Momaday (Kiowa) describes his return to his grandmother's grave.

> Her name was Aho, and she belonged to the last culture to evolve in North America. . . . Now that I can have her only in memory, I see my grandmother in the several postures that were peculiar to her: standing at the wood stove on a winter morning and turning meat in a great iron skillet; sitting at the south window, bent above her beadwork, and afterwards, when her vision failed, looking down for a long time into the fold of her hands; going out upon a cane, very slowly as she did when the weight of age came upon her; praying. I remember her

most often at prayer. She made long, rambling prayers out of suffering and hope, having seen many things. (Momaday 1969, 10)

The Importance of Play and Humor

Humor is prominent in stories and poetry by storytellers and poets such as Joseph Bruchac, Sherman Alexie, D'Arcy McNickle, Diane Burns, Luci Tapahonso, and Pretty-shield. Taking a satirical view of the colonized Native world, the novel *Dead Voices*, or "published stories," by Gerald Vizenor, portrays trickster "exterminators" who practice chemical warfare against fleas, trickster hunters who pretend to be like the animals and then move in for the kill, and trickster fur traders. Writing with dark irony in *The Lone Ranger and Tonto Fistfight in Heaven,* Sherman Alexie describes a vision and contrasting ways of measuring time:

> The buffalo come to join us and their hooves shake the earth, knock all the white people from their beds, send their plates crashing to the floor. We dance in circles growing larger and larger until we are standing on the shore, watching all the ships returning to Europe. All the white hands are waving good-bye and we continue to dance, dance until the ships fall off the horizon, dance until we are so tall and strong that the sun is nearly jealous. *We dance that way.* (Alexie 1994, 17)

> At the Tribal Council meeting last night, Judas WildShoe gave a watch he found to the tribal chairman.
> "A white man artifact, a sin," the chairman said, put the watch in his pouch.
> I remember watches. They measured time in seconds, minutes, hours. They measured time exactly, coldly. I measure time with my breath, the sound of my hands across my own skin.
> I make mistakes. (Alexie 1994, 109)

Themes of Loss and Survival

There is a very important characteristic of written Indian literature that resembles the protest literature of other marginalized peoples and yet differs from that of American Indian oral traditions. Appearing in even the earliest written works, it is the theme of dispossession and displacement, of loss, and of cultural and personal decay manifested in high rates of unemployment, abuse, alcoholism, and suicide. Frequently characters experience breakdowns in communication while they search for significance and identity to defy the stereotypes that relegate Indian to artifact. To recover losses their ancestors experienced, writers today may romanticize a cultural past they personally have never known. Nevertheless, they express an indomitable struggle to survive as individuals and as nations. According to James Welch, these writers "proudly describe their own cultures, with an underlying realization and sadness that they are being swallowed up by the dominant culture, rather than being accepted by it." Still, they insist on "their unalienable right to bang at the gates" (Welch 1994, 7). The power to recreate community exists within this writing as it works to renew and protect a living tradition.

What is Native American literature? The above discussion may function as one approach to this question, especially with respect to Plains tribal cultures. In defining any literature, we must answer the question "What does it do?" With Native American literatures, we can say that they express the storytellers' and writers' own historical and cultural heritages.

Three contemporary writers, Kenneth Lincoln, professor of American literature and Native American studies at UCLA, Wendy Rose (Hopi/Miwok), and Sherman Alexie (Spokane/Coeur d'Alene), have voiced their definitions:

> There is no *genre* of "Indian Literature," because we are all different. There is only literature written by people who are Indian and who, therefore, infuse their work with their own lives the same way you do. (Rose 1981, 402)

> Grounded Indian literature is tribal; its fulcrum is a sense of relatedness. To Indians tribe means family. . . . Tribe means an earth sense of self. . . . Tribe means ancestral history, the remembered presence of grandmothers and grandfathers gone before. . . . Tribe means spiritual balance through inherited rituals. . . . Tribe means the basics of human community shared, lean to fat. . . . And given four hundred sad years of Indian dispossession, tribe often means nonwhite inversions of the American mainstream, a contrary ethnicity and dark pride, even to a people's disadvantage. (Lincoln 1983, 8)

In the following poem from Sherman Alexie's *Old Shirts and New Skins* (1993), the speaker tells his listeners what Native American literature will and will not do. Insisting that no one can ever truly tell or completely understand another's story, Alexie provides his definition of the genre, which bears the scars of what Kenneth Lincoln calls, "four hundred sad years of Indian dispossession."

Introduction to Native American Literature

Somewhere in America a television explodes

& here you are again (again)
asking me to explain broken glass.

You scour the reservation landfill
through the debris of so many lives:
old guitar, basketball on fire, pair of shoes.
All you bring me is an empty bottle.

Am I the garbageman of your dreams?

*

Listen:

it will not save you
or talk you down from the ledge
of a personal building.

It will not kill you
or throw you facedown to the floor
& pull the trigger twice.

It believes a roomful of monkeys
in a roomful of typewriters
would eventually produce a roomful
of poetry about missing the jungle.

You will forget
more than you remember:
that is why we all dream slowly.

Often, you need change of scenery.
It will give you one black & white photograph.

Sometimes, it whispers
into anonymous corner bars
& talks too much about the color
of its eyes & skin & hair.

It believes a piece of coal
shoved up its own ass
will emerge years later
as a perfectly imperfect diamond.

Sometimes, it screams
the English language near freeways
until trucks jackknife & stop all traffic
while the city runs over itself.

Often, you ask forgiveness.
It will give you a 10% discount.

*

Because you have seen the color of my bare skin
does not mean you have memorized the shape of my ribcage.

Because you have seen the spine of the mountain
does not mean you made the climb.

Because you stood waist-deep in the changing river
does not mean you were equal to mc^2.

Because you gave something a name
does not mean your name is important.

*

Because you sleep
does not mean you see into my dreams.

*

Send it a letter: the address will keep changing.
Give it a phone call: busy signal
Knock on its door: you'll hear voices.
Look in its windows: shadows dance through the blinds.

In the end, it will pick you up from the pavement
& take you to the tribal cafe for breakfast.

It will read you the menu.
It will not pay your half of the bill.

—Sherman Alexie

Works Cited

Alexie, Sherman. 1993. *Old Shirts and New Skins.* Los Angeles: University of California.

Alexie, Sherman. 1994. *The Lone Ranger and Tonto Fistfight in Heaven.* New York: HarperCollins Publishers, Inc.

Allen, Paula Gunn. 1982. "Answering the Deer." *American Indian Culture and Research Journal,* 6.3: 39.

Allen, Paul Gunn. 1992. "The Sacred Hoop: A Contemporary Perspective." In *Studies in American Literature.* New York: Modern Language Association of America.

America's Fascinating Indian Heritage. 1978. Pleasantville, NY: The Reader's Digest Association, Inc.

Bevis, William. 1990. "McNickle: Homing In." In *Ten Tough Trips: Montana Writers and the West.* Seattle: University of Washington Press.

Bowker, Ardy. 1993. *Sisters in the Blood: The Education of Women in Native America.* Bozeman: Center for Bilingual/Multicultural Education, Montana State University.

Bruchac, Joseph. 1994. "A Living Tree with Many Roots: An Introduction to Native North American Literature." In *Native North American Literature,* ed. Janet Witalec. Detroit, MI: Gale Research, Inc.

Bruchac, Joseph, ed. 1983. *Songs from this Earth on Turtle's Back.* Greenfield Center, NY: Greenfield Review Press.

Byler, Mary Gloyne. 1987. "Taking Another Look." In *Through Indian Eyes: The Native Experience in Books for Children,* eds. Beverly Slapin and Doris Seale. Philadelphia, PA: New Society Publishers.

Caduto, Michael, and Joseph Bruchac, eds. 1988. *Keepers of the Earth: Native American Stories and Environmental Activities for Children.* Golden, CO: Fulcrum Publishing.

Champagne, Duane. 1994. *Chronology of Native North American History.* Detroit, MI: Gale Research, Inc.

Contrary Warriors: A Story of the Crow Tribe, 1985. Rattlesnake Productions. Videocassette.

Cook-Lynn, Elizabeth. 1987. "You May Consider Speaking about Your Art." In *I Tell You Now: Autobiographical Essays by Native American Writers*, eds. Brian Swann and Arnold Krupat. Lincoln: University of Nebraska Press.

Deloria, Ella Cara. 1992. *Dakota Texts*. Vermillion, SD: Dakota Press.

Dorris, Michael A. 1982. Foreword to *American Indian Stereotypes in the World of Children: A Reader and Bibliography*, ed. Arlene B. Hirschfelder. Metuchen, NJ: The Scarecrow Press, Inc.

Endrezze, Anita. 1992. *at the helm of twilight*. Seattle, WA: Broken Moon Press.

Hans, Brigit. 1992. Introduction to *The Hawk Is Hungry and Other Stories*, by D'Arcy McNickle. Tucson: University of Arizona Press.

Henson, Lance. 1992. *A Cheyenne Sketchbook: Selected Poems 1970-1991*. Greenfield Center, NY: The Greenfield Review Press.

Hirschfelder, Arlene, and Beverly R. Singer, eds. 1982. *Rising Voices— Writings of Young Native Americans*. New York: Charles Scribner's Sons.

Hogan, Linda. 1990. *Mean Spirit*. New York: Ivy Books.

Jennings, Francis. 1976. *The Invasion of America—Indians, Colonialism, and the Cant of Conquest*. New York: W.W. Norton and Company.

Lame Deer, John (Fire), and Richard Erdoes. 1972. *Lame Deer, Seeker of Visions*. New York: Washington Square Press.

Lincoln, Kenneth. 1983. "Sending a Voice." In *Native American Renaissance*. Berkeley: University of California Press.

Linderman, Frank B. 1962. *Plenty Coups: Chief of the Crows*. Lincoln: University of Nebraska Press.

Linderman, Frank B. 1972. *Pretty-shield: Medicine Woman of the Crows*. Lincoln: University of Nebraska Press.

McNickle, D'Arcy. 1973. *Native American Tribalism*. New York: Oxford University Press.

Momaday, N. Scott. 1969. *The Way to Rainy Mountain*. Albuquerque: University of New Mexico Press.

Momaday, N. Scott. 1988. Foreword to *Keepers of the Earth: Native American Stories and Environmental Activities for Children*, eds. Michael Caduto and Joseph Bruchac. Golden, CO: Fulcrum Publishing.

Nabokov, Peter, ed. 1991. *Native American Testimony*. New York: Penguin.

Owens, Louis. 1992. *Other Destinies: Understanding the American Indian Novel*. Norman: University of Oklahoma Press.

The Random House Dictionary of the English Language, The Unabridged Edition, 1967.

Reyhner, Jon, and Jeannie Eder. 1992. "A History of Indian Education." In *Teaching American Indian Students,* edited by Jon Reyhner. Norman: University of Oklahoma Press.

Riley, Patricia, ed. 1993. *Growing Up Native American: An Anthology.* New York: Wm. Morrow & Co.

Rose, Wendy. 1981. "American Indian Poets and Publishing." *Book Forum* 5(3): 402.

Sheehan, Bernard. 1973. *Seeds of Extinction—Jeffersonian Philanthropy and the American Indian.* New York: W.W. Norton and Company.

Tapahonso, Luci. 1987. *A Breeze Swept Through.* Albuquerque, NM: West End Press.

The Reservations. 1995. The American Indians Series. Alexandria, Virginia: Time-Life Books.

Vizenor, Gerald. 1992. *Dead Voices: Natural Agonies in the New World.* Norman: University of Oklahoma Press.

Vizenor, Gerald, ed. 1995. *Native American Literature: A Brief Introduction and Anthology.* HarperCollins Literary Mosaic Series. Berkeley, CA: HarperCollins College Publishers.

Welch, James. 1986. *Fools Crow.* New York: Viking Penguin.

Welch, James. 1994. "Introduction." *Ploughshares,* 20.1 (Spring): 7.

Woody, Elizabeth. 1994. *Seven Hands, Seven Hearts.* Portland, OR: The Eighth Mountain Press.

3
Secondary Level Units, Lessons, and Activities

Representing a variety of structures and approaches, most of the following units, lessons, and activities have been used with high school students and in teacher development workshops. More developed descriptions of specific selections may be found in Chapters 4, 5, and 6, but each plan includes goals, suggested resources, a variety of activities, and references to related themes. The plans also offer diverse biographical, geographical, and historical background materials to show some of the possibilities for teaching the works in context. I hope teachers might find the suggestions useful as they develop similar units featuring literatures from other landscapes and cultures.

Contents

I. 9-Week Unit: Commitment to Relatives and to Community

Developed by Donna Miller and Dorothea Susag

Themes: Remembering the Old Ways; At Home within Circles; Between Two Worlds; Change and Growth

Grade Level: S

This unit uses Indian literature to model the importance of family members and cultural values in the determination of personal identity. Students discover answers to "who am I" or "who are we" questions through a study of and response to family relationships and cultural influences.

Goals

- To understand the concept of culture and to examine students' cultural systems
- To become aware of the ways values motivate behavior and shape culture
- To realize the values and consequences of a personal commitment to community and to affirm individual and family values
- To recognize the way cultural rituals and ceremonies create and perpetuate community
- To become aware of and to challenge stereotypes of American Indians, European Americans, and elderly people
- To experience contemporary Native American literature in three genres: novel, short story, and poetry
- To practice oral storytelling, oral reading, and writing in response to Native American literature

Resources

Byler, Mary Gloyne. 1992. "American Indian Authors for Young Readers: An Annotated Bibliography." In *Through Indian Eyes: The Native Experience in Books for Children,* eds. Beverly Slapin and Doris Seale. Philadelphia, PA: New Society Publishers.

Ruoff, A. LaVonne Brown. 1990. Preface to *American Indian Literatures: An Introduction, Bibliographic Review, and Selected Bibliography.* New York: Modern Language Association of America.

Surviving Columbus: The Story of the Pueblo People. 1992. Albuquerque, NM: KNME-TV, PBS. Videocassette.

Hidden Places: Ancient Places. 1980. Montana Committee for the Humanities. Videocassette.

McNickle, D'Arcy. 1987. *Runner in the Sun.* Albuquerque: University of New Mexico Press.

The Lakota: One Nation on the Plains. 1976–1978. University of Mid America. Videocassette.

Deloria, Ella. 1988. *Waterlily.* Lincoln: University of Nebraska Press.

Transitions: The Death of the Mother Tongue. 1991. Native Voices Public Television Workshop. Bozeman: Montana State University. Videocassette.

Earling, Debra. 1990. "Perma Red." In *The Last Best Place: An Anthology of Montana Literature,* eds. William Kittredge and Annick Smith. Helena: Montana Historical Society Press.

Selected poetry from Bruchac, Joseph, ed. 1983. *Songs from this Earth on Turtle's Back.* New York: Greenfield Review Press.

Allen, Paula Gunn. "Grandmother"
BigEagle, Duane. "My Grandfather Was a Quantum Physicist"
Brant, Beth. "For All My Grandmothers"
Burns, Diane. "Sure You Can Ask Me A Personal Question"
Goose, Mary. "Just an Old Man"
Hale, Janet Campbell. "Where Have All the Indians Gone?"
  and "Walls of Ice"
Harjo, Joy. "Remember"
Kenny, Maurice. "Corn-Planter"
Young Bear, Ray A. "Grandmother"

Prereading Activities

1. Discuss ways we might distinguish between people from a variety of ethnic backgrounds, including African American, Norwegian, Italian, and Native American. Students write their definitions of an Indian, and the teacher will compile them (without names) for the purpose of discussion at the beginning and at the end of the unit. For assistance, teachers can rely on Mary Gloyne Byler's definition in Slapin and Seale's *Through Indian Eyes:* "There is more to being an American Indian—Apache, Seneca, Hopi, or whatever tribe—than can be acquired through an act of will, a course of study, or discovering an Indian ancestor somewhere in the family tree. It is not an intellectual choice. In short, being Indian is growing up Indian: it is a way of life, a way of thinking and being" (Byler 1992, 289). A. LaVonne Brown Ruoff, in *American Indian Literatures,* provides a complex definition from the Bylaws of the National Indian Education Association (Ruoff 1990, vi).

2. Watch the video *Surviving Columbus* or the video *Hidden Places: Ancient Places,* produced by Montana Committee for the Humanities, 1980. *Hidden Places* is a thirty-minute film that describes the dry canyon lands of the American Southwest, where Indian cultures flourished thousands of years before Columbus's voyages. The host visits the Great Gallery of Barrier Canyon in Utah, the Hueco Tanks in Texas, and the Catholic mission church in Zuni Pueblo, New Mexico.

Selection 1: *Runner in the Sun* by D'Arcy McNickle

Journal Activities (for each day's reading, approximately 20 pages per night)

1. Each chapter has a title; explain how this title suits the chapter's subject, or sketch an event, character, landscape, or symbol from the chapter.

2. Note any incidents in which a character behaves responsibly or irresponsibly toward his or her community and define that behavior. How would you respond to that character and his or her actions?

3. Keep a page in your journal on which to record a list of all vocabulary words and their definitions; add any words to the list that are unfamiliar to you as you read.

4. Look for aspects of the precontact environment of the Pueblo Indians that resemble behaviors, beliefs, or traditions of your own culture.

Postreading Activity

In the role of Quail, write journal entries spanning one week, reporting all that you have learned about the beliefs and values shaping this culture. Include in your entries your observations regarding how these values dictate or motivate community behaviors.

Questions for Further Consideration

1. Research the etymology or the connotations and denotations of the word *salt*. Based on this research, how effective is the author's naming of his protagonist?

2. How has Salt learned to balance his individual desires with the welfare of his people?

3. Because Flute Man and Dark Dealer desire personal power and advantage, they are feared. Think of someone you know with similar desires. Write an entry in your diary exploring reasons you might fear that person.

4. To what extent does this book contradict negative stereotypes of Native Americans? List five common stereotypes and then use specific events or personal characteristics that demonstrate the contradiction.

Transition Activity

Watch the video *The Lakota: One Nation on the Plains*, produced by the University of Mid America, 1976–1978 and available through the Montana Committee for the Humanities. With N. Scott Momaday narrating, this video describes the movement of the Plains Indians across the Great Plains. It focuses on a case study of the Lakota, their migration into the region in the eighteenth century, and their adaptation to the new environment.

Selection 2:
Waterlily **by**
Ella Deloria

Reading Activities

1. Keep a log of each day's reading and give each chapter a title. Note incidents in which characters behave responsibly toward community and describe that behavior.

2. After each reading, ask an "I wonder why?" question that may be answered through class discussion or library research, and keep one journal page for definitions of vocabulary words that are new to you.

Chapter 2:   Choose a custom or ritual and compare it with a behavior or custom in your world.

Chapter 5:   Choose an example of good manners and compare it with similar behavior in your family.

Chapter 6:   Work with the teacher to create two typed pages of "Cliffs Notes" for this chapter, and then work in groups of two or three to create your own "Cliffs Notes" for subsequent chapters. They will be compiled in a booklet for each student. Denise Juneau, an English teacher in Browning, Montana, has used this strategy with more lengthy books in her high school classes to facilitate students' independent learning. "Cliffs Notes" should include main characters; setting (time and place); chapter summary of lessons, incidents, ceremonies, and researched definitions for terms not defined in text; and identification of the crisis and resolution within chapters.

Chapter 7:   Define gender roles in this culture and compare them with those of your culture.

Chapter 8:   You are the natural child of Rainbow and you have never experienced the Hunka ceremony that is held for Waterlily. How would you feel and how would you act toward your parents and Waterlily? Do you believe the adults' explanations to natural children are adequate or fair? Write a letter to Rainbow and tell him how you feel.

Chapter 9–15:   Work in seven groups for three days to create "Cliffs Notes" for these chapters.

Questions for Discussion with Groups

Chapter 9:   Is self-mutilation justified in this situation? Why might a people discontinue this practice?

Chapter 10:   How are white men defined?

Chapter 11:   Why is the Sun Dance so important to the Dakota people?

Chapter 12:   What is the value of the Grandmother in Dakota culture?

Chapter 13:   Was Waterlily's decision to marry Sacred Horse a wise decision? How would you evaluate this decision?

Chapter 14: Under what circumstances have you felt as lonely as Waterlily? How did you cope with that loneliness?

Chapter 15: What was the impact of diseases such as small-pox on tribal people in North America?

Chapters 16 and 17: Take one external conflict and examine how it causes an internal conflict for Waterlily. How is each major conflict in the novel resolved at the end?

Postreading Activity

In cooperative groups, create Venn diagrams that compare the characters Salt and Waterlily, the personal sacrifices of Salt and Waterlily, the roles the elderly play in each novel, one important ceremony or ritual from each culture, the gender role definitions from each culture, important values from each culture, and the ways kinship obligations control the lives of Salt and Waterlily.

Transition Activity

Watch the 30-minute videotape *Transitions,* produced by Native Voices Public Television Workshop and available through the Montana Committee for the Humanities. This film, by Blackfeet producers, explores the relationship among language, thought, and culture, and examines the impact of language loss in Native American communities.

**Selection 3:
"Perma Red" by
Debra Earling**

Prereading Activity

Respond in groups or in writing to the following questions: How do we know who we are? Is who we are determined by what others think of us? Why do some people prefer being alone to being with others? Why is it hard to ignore what others think of us? Can we control what others think about us?

Assignment 1

Read the opening six paragraphs of "Perma Red." In groups, answer the following questions: How does Louise feel? What are the images, the words and phrases, that communicate the mood of this section? What is the effect of this imagery on Louise, the protagonist?

Assignment 2

As you complete the reading, respond in your log to the following questions.

1. What do you think Louise wants? What is she afraid of?
2. How does the author describe the community on the reservation? How does Louise feel about herself in relation to that community? How is this a story of living in two worlds?

3. How did the story affect you? Were you angry, sad, indifferent? Were you sympathetic with Louise? Explain your answer.

4. Do Louise and her relatives remind you of anyone you know, anyone you have ever seen, or a similar experience?

5. Identify a passage in the story that captures an important message or idea and explain why you chose that passage.

6. Does the title fit the story? How? Explain your answer.

7. Why does Louise leave the reservation if home is where she really wants to be?

8. What is missing in the story that we must fill in as we read it?

9. What factors contribute to Louise's confusion? To what or whom does she feel responsibility?

10. What is the relationship between the nature images and an individual struggling with her identity in this story?

Assignment 3

Research the following questions in workshop groups.

1. Who are the Salish people?

2. What is the history of the Flathead Reservation?

3. What was federal policy regarding Indians during the time of this story, the 1940s?

4. What is the significance of sweet grass to the Salish people?

Postreading Activities

Writing: Write the next chapter of Louise's story or write letters of advice from Salt and Waterlily to Louise.

Storytelling: "Perma Red" is Debra Earling's story of a facet of family history. Think of your own story. Locate the story in a place, recall vivid images, real or invented, and tell your own story that captures a part of your life. Share your story orally with the rest of the class.

Selection 4: Poetry   *Prereading Activity*

Write a journal entry recalling an experience with a grandparent or an elderly person.

Reading Activity

In cooperative groups, select poems from the list given in the "Resources" for this unit, and create a visual representation of theme or subject in the poem, such as a collage, original artwork, shadow boxes, or dramatization. As a group, read and present the poem to the rest of the class.

Postreading Activity

Write a poem to a grandparent or elder.

Closing Activities

1. In small groups and using the various cultures you have encountered in this unit, as well as your own culture, as models create a list of at least five factors usually contributing to cultural and personal identity. Be prepared to share these lists orally with the entire class. Then, as a large group, select the five or six most important factors. In small groups, select one of those factors and explore in depth how it applies to each of three selections discussed in this unit.

2. Select one of your social groups—school, family, friends, church, nation—and define your personal responsibilities within that group in a short essay, poem, or short story.

II. 2-Week Unit: World View, Myth, and Bias in America's Ethnic and Cultural Roots

Themes: Lifeways and Stereotypes; Remembering the Old Ways; Between Two Worlds.

Early in the year we examine the concept of *myth*, exploring the many possible truths behind myths to discover who we were as peoples and who we are today. Although not many young people realize it, this is an important activity because their values and beliefs have been shaped by the stories they have grown up knowing, by the education they have received, and by the landscape within which they have lived. All of these contexts have contributed to their world views as individuals, as members of families, and as members of communities. Teachers may adapt the assignments to similar selections from other texts.

Goals

- To develop an understanding of the concept of personal and cultural world views
- To develop strategies for critically examining the origin and characteristics of myth
- To develop an awareness of the diversities, similarities, and values in various Native American cultural and story traditions
- To develop an awareness of racist and biased language and its impact on readers over centuries
- To develop strategies for examining messages for racial and cultural bias

Resources

Slapin, Beverly, and Doris Seale. 1992. "The Bloody Trail of Columbus Day." In *Through Indian Eyes: The Native Experience in Books for Children,* 7–8. Philadelphia: New Society Publishers.

Bruchac, Joseph (Abenaki). 1991. "Gluscabi and the Game Animals." In *Native American Stories,* 109–113. Golden, CO: Fulcrum Publishing.

Mourning Dove (Okanagan). 1990. "Coyote and the Wood-Tick." In *Coyote Stories,* 163–170. Lincoln: University of Nebraska Press.

Rides at the Door, Darnell Davis (Blackfeet). 1979. "The Magic Leggings." In *Napi Stories,* 15–16. Browning, MT: Blackfeet Heritage Program.

Deloria, Ella C. (Dakota). 1992. "Iktomi Tricks the Pheasants." In *Dakota Texts,* 9–11. Vermillion, SD: Dakota Press.

Smith, John. 1984. "General History of Virginia." In *American Literature, Yellow Level,* 14–19. Evanston, IL: McDougal, Littell.

Bradford, William. 1984. "Of Plymouth Plantation." In *American Literature, Yellow Level,* 21–24. Evanston, IL: McDougal, Littell.

Brant, Beth. 1992. "Grandmothers of a New World." In *Through Indian Eyes: The Native Experience in Books for Children,* eds. Beverly Slapin and Doris Seale, 102–110. Philadelphia: New Society Publishers.

Pocahontas. 1996. Burbank, CA: Walt Disney Home Video. Distributed by Buena Vista Home Video. Videocassette.

Surviving Columbus: The Story of the Pueblo People. 1992. Albuquerque, NM: KNME-TV, PBS. Videocassette.

"The Nations of the Northeast." 1994. *The Native Americans* Series. Atlanta, GA: TBS Productions. Videocassette.

Green, Rayna. 1975. "The Pocahontas Perplex: The Image of Indian Women in American Culture." *The Massachusetts Review,* 16(4): 698–714.

Washburn, Wilcomb E. 1964. *The Indian and the White Man.* Garden City, NY: Anchor.

Jennings, Francis. 1976. *The Invasion of America: Indians, Colonialism, and the Cant of Conquest.* New York: W.W. Norton.

Steinbeck, John. 1966. *America and Americans.* New York: Viking.

Prereading Activities

1. Define world view using material from the "lifeways and stereotypes" theme. After discussing various cultural world views, write your own world view.

2. List facts about Columbus Day that you believe are true.

Selection 1

Read "The Bloody Trail of Columbus Day" by Beverly Slapin and Doris Seale. Written from a Native perspective, this selection reveals some seldom-heard facts about Spanish genocidal policies and the Taino and Arawak peoples' powerful resistance.

Reading Activity

1. List facts from this reading that are consistent with what you know is true.

2. List facts from this reading that differ from what you previously knew.

3. Explain the differences between the two and the way world view might influence the presentation of facts.

Selection 2

Use trickster/transformer stories in Native literatures from Chapter 2, especially those from the Abenaki, Blackfeet, Dakota, and Salish.

Selection 3

Tell traditional stories such as "Gluscabi and the Game Animals," "Coyote and Wood-Tick," "The Magic Leggings," and "Iktomi Tricks the Pheasants," providing geographical and cultural background.

Questions for Further Consideration

1. How would you define *oral tradition* as represented in this literature?

2. What are the characteristics and values of tribal cultures represented by this literature?

3. Where have you seen these characters in people or situations around you or within you?

Selections 4 and 5   Read "The General History of Virginia" by John Smith and "Of Plymouth Plantation" by William Bradford.

Reading Activities

1. Write two questions of your own for the class to consider: one question that is answered in the text and an "I wonder why" question.

2. Examine the textbook for editor's bias, which may be communicated in several ways: the choice of materials to include in the text, the background information provided, the kinds of questions asked at the end of each selection, and the introductory material before each selection. For example, in the introduction to "The General History of Virginia," the editors call this "John Smith's most important work." It is important to discuss the implications of the words *most important*, especially after examining John Smith's perception of Indian people as communicated in this text. Bias is also strong in selections by Custer and Catlin in the textbook's Original Land unit and in the textbook writers' choice of a few poems from the Native tradition.

3. Examine more carefully the section in the text in which Smith describes an Indian leader as "a great grim fellow . . . with a hellish voice, and a rattle in his hand . . . with strange gestures . . . [and then] three more such like devils came rushing in with the like antique tricks."

4. In workshop groups, consider the implications of words such as *grim, hellish, rattle, strange, devils, rushing, antique,* and *tricks* in responding to the following questions:

   a. What might readers conclude about Indians or about John Smith, the writer?

   b. What are the implications for a Christian audience, for an audience that had never met Indian people, and for an Indian audience?

Postreading Activities

1. You are a member of John Smith's company and you have heard about Bradford's settlement in Plymouth. Write a letter to Bradford informing him about the hazards and benefits of settlement in the New World.

2. Compare Bradford and Smith according to subject matter, tone, style of writing, and bias.

Selection 6   In "Grandmothers of a New World," Beth Brant discusses the legend about John Smith and Pocahontas as related in accounts based on John Smith's story. Then she counters Smith's account with another Pocahontas story that is based on Brant's understanding of Pamunkey practices and on her belief in the traditional strength and influence of Native women. Brant suggests, "John Smith's so-called rescue was, in fact, a mock execution—a traditional ritual often held after capture of enemies."

Postreading Activities

1. Watch the same scene from Disney's *Pocahontas* and be prepared to discuss how the messages in the film might influence the beliefs and behaviors of both Native and non-Native people today.
2. In six workshop groups, build cases to defend or prosecute Brant, Disney, or Smith for deceiving audiences for personal gain.

Selections 7 and 8   View 30 minutes each from *Surviving Columbus* and "The Nations of the Northeast," in which Native Americans from the Southwest and Northeast tell stories of their ancestors and the coming of the Europeans.

Viewing Activity

While watching the films, keep a list of observable details (what people say and do, the music, and the setting) and a list of your interpretations of what those details might communicate about Pueblo culture or Northeastern tribal cultures.

Selection 9   Read "Pocahontas Perplex: The Image of Indian Women in American Culture" by Rayna Green.

Reading Activity

Write answers to the following questions and be prepared to discuss them in workshop groups.

1. What are Green's subject, opinion, and thesis?
2. How does this fit in with the discussion of myth and world view?

Selection 10   "Document 5 of Personal Relations: Captain John Smith" was published in *The Indian and the White Man* by Wilcomb E. Washburn as part of a series on Documents in American History. Two of John Smith's men, Walter Russell and Anas Todkill, wrote the following passage, which includes remarks of Wahunsonacoch (Powhatan) regarding John Smith. Russell and Todkill noted what the Indian leader had said regarding Smith and his company.

I knowe the difference of peace and warre better then any in my
Countrie. But now I am old, and ere long must die . . . my two sisters,
and their two daughters, are distinctly each others successours. I
wish their experiences no lesse then mine, and your love to them, no
lesse then MINE TO YOU . . . you are come to destroy my Countrie,
so much affrighteth all my people, as they dare not visit you. What
will it availe you to take that perforce, you may quietly have with
love, or to destroy them that provide you food. . . . Think you I am so
simple not to knowe it is better to eate good meate, lie well, and
sleepe quietly with my women and children, laugh, and be merrie
with you, have copper, hatchets, or what I want being your friend;
then bee forced to flie from al, to lie cold in the woods, feed upon
acorns roots and such trash, and be so hunted by you that I can neither rest eat nor sleepe . . . and if a twig but breake, everie one crie,
there comes Captaine Smith. (14–18)

Postreading Activity

Characterize Powhatan based on this speech. What do you learn
about what he values, how he feels about John Smith's company?
How does this compare with your previous views or the films you
have seen?

Selection 11   Read from *The Invasion of America* by Francis Jennings regarding the
word *savage* and Smith's use of the word after the 1622 "massacre" of
Jamestown. Jennings suggests Smith used such strongly racist language
for two reasons: the language justified further attacks on the Indians,
which would then facilitate the colony's physical and economic expansion in the "New World," and Smith may have been looking for a scape-
goat for the deaths of at least 6,000 settlers due to starvation during the
period 1607–1622, when only 347 had died at the hands of Indians.

Reading Activity

In pairs, write summaries of each paragraph in the reading and be
prepared to share your summaries with the rest of the class.

Selection 12:   Originally appearing as text in a photo essay, this essay has since
"America and   been published in the February 1998 *Literary Cavalcade* magazine pro-
Americans" by   duced by Scholastic. In it, Steinbeck lists over fifty myths Americans
John Steinbeck   believe about themselves and then he provides evidence that contradicts each myth. For example, we view ourselves as a nation of "do-
it-yourselfers" but we don't know enough to look in the gas tank
when our car quits running. "We say we value home, but the average
American moves every five years." The essay demonstrates the complex nature of popular belief. Students can apply the following three-
part strategy for understanding myths as preparation for the next
research activity and closing activities.

1. What is a truth in this myth?
2. What are other truths behind this myth that might contradict the myth?
3. What does this myth reveal about those who believe it?

Research Activity

Students are given a variety of resources in which they might uncover more truths about nine common myths of Indian peoples and settlers that Jennings discusses and refutes in *The Invasion of America*. Students should also have access to some of the historical and cultural resources listed in Chapter 4 of *Roots and Branches*, as well as information from the "Brief Summary of Federal Indian Policy" and the descriptions and explanations of popular stereotypes in Appendices B and C.

- Myth: Indians were a savage and barbaric menace.
- Myth: The New World was uninhabited.
- Myth: Europe discovered this land.
- Myth: Europe came to settle (rather than exploit).
- Myth: Indians were inferior and uncivilized.
- Myth: Indians were nomadic.
- Myth: European colonists fought only defensive wars.
- Myth: The land was "free" because the Indians did not own the land.
- Myth: Traits of the two cultures were incompatible.

Closing Activities

A. This assignment provides opportunities for students to practice research and documentation skills, higher-level thinking skills, and dramatic skills. Each of nine groups is given one myth from the preceding list.

1. You have been given a myth, which you will research and explain using the three-part strategy for explaining myths.

    Example: Myth: The New World was uninhabited.

    a. What is a truth in this myth?

    America was uninhabited by Europeans.

    b. What is another truth behind this myth that might contradict the myth?

    America was inhabited by an estimated 15 to 30 million indigenous people.

    c. What does this myth reveal about those who believe it?

    Belief indicates ethnocentricity, which denies the humanity of others from different cultures and races.

2. As a group, you may use any of the materials we have read in this class to help you understand and explain this myth.

3. You must use material from Jennings and at least two other resources.

4. Write the correct MLA citation for each of your resources.

5. Objective: In 5 minutes, present to the class your understanding of the myth, using creative drama, visual aids such as posters, music, illustrations, or an oral presentation.

B. This assignment makes use of students' spatial abilities and appeals to visual learners. The assignment provides opportunities for cooperation between art and English classes and for the inclusion of art specialists.

1. Select a myth and explore it to find all possible truths. Be sure to look for contradictory truths.

2. Using newspapers, magazines, headlines, pictures, photographs, and drawings, create a group collage that communicates various aspects of your myth.

3. Find a published poem that addresses the issues in your collage.

4. Be prepared to present your collage, explaining what you have accomplished, and to read the poem. You may use music to accompany your presentation.

In both of the above assignments, on tests, in journals, in classroom discussions, and in other activities, the students exhibited a markedly increased respect for Indian peoples and their history of suffering and survival despite European American encroachment. They demonstrated a growing awareness of the way bias affects meaning and an understanding of the importance of examining primary sources to discover hidden or different truths. They learned to question information in even the most "sacred" classroom materials: history and literature textbooks.

III. 5-Day Lesson: Oratory of Resistance and Revolution in American Literature

Themes: Cultural and Personal Loss and Survival; Between Two Worlds

This lesson extends the study of Patrick Henry's speech to demonstrate the ways Native Americans also resisted oppression through rhetoric and action. Through reading and hearing the speeches of Tecumseh and Pushmataha, students develop a new respect for the Native Americans' politically effective and poetic use of language.

Goals

- To develop an awareness of both Native and non-Native movements to resist oppression and domination by external forces between 1776 and 1820

- To develop an understanding of the similarities and differences between individuals and their rhetoric of resistance in America during the later eighteenth and early nineteenth centuries

- To develop an understanding of the impact of popular stereotypes on our perception of history

- To develop an appreciation for the way the speeches of these Native orators contradict the stereotypes of early Indian people as savage and uncivilized

- To practice applying a formal strategy for analyzing and evaluating oral communication using occasion, audience, purpose, response, and a variety of rhetorical or literary devices

Resources

Patrick Henry's "Speech to the Virginia Convention," 1776, in support of the revolution against Britain. Henry's speech appears in most American Literature anthologies.

Vanderwerth, W. C. 1989. *Indian Oratory: Famous Speeches by Noted Indian Chieftains,* Norman: University of Oklahoma Press.

Tecumseh's "Speech to Choctaws and Chickasaws," Spring 1811 (61–68), a plea for the Choctaws and Chickasaws to join in a common effort with the British against the Americans.

Pushmataha's "Speech to Choctaws and Chickasaws," Spring 1811 (70–76), a response to Tecumseh's plea and for continued allegiance to America. (Although he supported Andrew Jackson, his people fell victim to Jackson's removal policy in the 1830s.)

It is important to make a comment about translations and the possible influence on the texts of the transcribers and translators, even with Patrick Henry's speech, because none of these speeches are recorded today, word for word.

Postreading Activity

After hearing and discussing each speech, create a grid and then compare the speeches.

	Patrick Henry	Tecumseh	Pushmataha
Occasion			
Audience			
Purpose			
Response			
Rhetorical devices			

After this lesson, students admit their surprise at the language and persuasive skills of the Indian orators, finding strong similarities between the three speeches.

Closing Activities

1. Write a persuasive paper or deliver a speech that makes use of the elements of style and purpose you have observed in the three speeches.

2. Imagine yourself in the audience of Henry or Tecumseh and Pushmataha. Tell your story and give your impression of the speech to your children and grandchildren who have survived the removal to Indian territory west of the Mississippi.

3. Draw a map and time line, including population figures before and after, to trace the removal and relocation of one of the tribes.

IV. 4-Week Unit: Introduction to Native American Literature

Themes: Remembering the Old Ways; Between Two Worlds; Cultural and Personal Loss and Survival

This unit gives students the opportunity to read and study the culture and history of a particular tribe, its literary traditions, and the contemporary writers who are rooted in that tradition. Students also learn that storytelling is fun and educational, and they appreciate the values and cultural characteristics the stories reveal.

Goals

- To learn from the history and traditions of surrounding cultures
- To develop an awareness of the diversities and similarities in Native American cultures
- To explore the literary, historical, and geographical connections between past and present storytellers
- To experience listening and telling stories in situations that might resemble Native American traditions

Prereading Activity

Listen to a storyteller from a local tribal community. When a Blackfeet oral historian and storyteller visited our school, he spoke to several smaller groups throughout the school, and then he spoke to an adult class in the evening. Before he came, we discussed the respectful way the students should receive his oral presentation: Make no recordings or videos, take no notes, carry no books or pencils (which might distract while listening), and do not interrupt with questions until he is finished speaking and asks for questions. The students who were prepared in this way demonstrated respect, whereas others who had not participated in the preparatory discussions turned to visiting with their peers during the presentation.

Selections

Listen to "The Coming of Stories" (Seneca), "Tunka-Shila, Grandfather Rock" (Lakota), and "Gluscabi and the Game Animals" (Abenaki), told by Joseph Bruchac in *Keepers of the Earth: Native American Stories* (audio cassettes, Fulcrum Publishing, 1992), after briefly examining the geographical and historical background of the Seneca, Lakota, and Abenaki people.

Discuss the tradition and purpose of storytelling in traditional Native communities such as these, the ways stories hold Native communities together, and the ways these same stories can apply to our lives today.

Selections

From available materials, each student selects at least three writers and texts from a particular culture. The following lists represent the students' selections from one class.

Salish/Kootenai/Coeur d'Alene

Hale, Janet Campbell. 1985. *The Jailing of Cecelia Capture.* Albuquerque: University of New Mexico Press.

———. 1991. *The Owl's Song.* New York: Bantam Books.

Selected poetry of Janet Campbell Hale.

Lesley, Craig. 1989. *River Song.* New York: Dell.

Walker, Deward E., Jr. 1980. *Myths of Idaho Indians.* Moscow: University of Idaho Press.

Salish

Earling, Debra. Selected stories and poems from *Ploughshares, Talking Leaves, Dancing on the Rim of the World,* and *The Last Best Place.*

McNickle, D'Arcy. 1991. *Runner in the Sun.* Albuquerque: University of New Mexico Press.

———. 1992. *The Hawk Is Hungry.* Tucson: University of Arizona.

Mourning Dove. 1990. *Coyote Stories.* Lincoln: University of Nebraska Press.

Blackfeet

Bullchild, Percy. 1985. *The Sun Came Down.* San Francisco: Harper and Row.

Welch, James. 1974. *Winter in the Blood.* Caledonia, VA: RR Donnelley.

———.1979. *The Death of Jim Loney.* New York: Penguin.

Blackfeet/Blood

Fraser, Frances. [1959] 1990. *The Bear Who Stole the Chinook.* Vancouver, BC: Douglas and McIntyre.

Hungry Wolf, Beverly. 1982. *The Ways of My Grandmothers.* New York: Quill.

Welch, James. 1986. *Fools Crow.* New York: Viking Penguin.

Crow

Lowie, Robert H. 1993. *Myths and Traditions of the Crow Indians.* Lincoln: University of Nebraska Press.

Feather Earring, Monica, Fred Turnsback, Philamine Old Coyote, and Lela M. Puffening. 1978. *Prairie Legends.* Billings: Montana Council for Indian Education.

Medicine Crow, Joseph. 1992. *From the Heart of the Crow Country: The Crow Indians' Own Stories.* New York: Orion.

Dakota

Allen, Paula Gunn, ed. 1989. *Spider Woman's Granddaughters.* New York: Fawcett Columbine.

Deloria, Ella Cara. 1988. *Waterlily.* Lincoln: University of Nebraska Press.

Standing Bear, Luther. 1934. *Stories of the Sioux.* Lincoln: University of Nebraska Press.

Zitkala-Ša. [1900] 1985. *American Indian Stories.* Lincoln: University of Nebraska Press.

———. [1901] 1985. *Old Indian Legends.* Lincoln: University of Nebraska Press.

Reading Activities

1. Keep a daily journal of reading, pages, dates, and titles of stories or chapters.
2. Come to class with a question about the reading for class discussion.
3. Keep a log of your own memories that the reading evokes.

Postreading Activities

1. Without notes, tell a traditional story you have read.
2. Write a definition of the trickster/transformer figure for the particular culture you are reading, and use examples from the stories to support your definition.
3. Read at least one novel or memoir that is based in the same culture as the stories.
4. Tell a 15-minute story from your own heritage, a story from your own experience, or an original story related to the readings. You may use music or props to help you tell the story.
5. Illustrate your presentation with video, original drawing, photographs, paintings, or posters.
6. Prepare a 20- to 30-minute presentation to the class that communicates what you have learned about the storytellers you have read, the stories and central characters, the ways contemporary writers use old stories in the new stories, and the history and geographical locations of the tribes or reservations.

V. 6-Day Unit: Bias and Stereotype in Literature about Native Americans

Theme: Lifeways and Stereotypes

The following unit has been used in workshops for teachers, both on and off reservations, but students in a critical thinking elective have also participated in the unit. Even the students who consider themselves most conscious of the effects of prejudice and stereotyping are surprised by the pervasive generalizing that exists in literatures they commonly read or use in classrooms.

Goals

- To increase awareness of the ways our own world views influence our understanding of others
- To increase awareness of the presence and effects of bias and stereotypes
- To respect the integrity of tribal cultures and peoples and to affirm the right of all people to define themselves in their own voices
- To respect the diversity of all tribal cultures and to promote cross-cultural understanding

Possible Resources

Caldwell-Wood, N., and L. Mitten. 1992. "*I* Is Not for *Indian:* The Portrayal of Native Americans in Books for Young People." *Multicultural Review,* 1.2 (April): 26–33.

Hirschfelder, A. 1982. *American Indian Stereotypes in the World of Children: A Reader and Bibliography.* Metuchen, NJ: Scarecrow Press.

McCann, D. 1993."Native Americans in Books for the Young." In *Teaching Multicultural Literature in Grades K–8,* ed. V. Harris. Norwood, MA: Christopher Gordon Publishers.

McCluskey, Murton L. (Blackfeet). 1993. *Evaluating American Indian Textbooks and Other Materials for the Classroom.* Helena: Montana Office of Public Instruction.

Slapin, Beverly. 1990. *Basic Skills Caucasian Americans Workbook.* Berkeley, CA: Oyate.

Slapin, Beverly, and Doris Seale (Santee/Cree). [1987] 1992. "How to Tell the Difference." In *Through Indian Eyes: The Native Experience in Books for Children.* Philadelphia, PA: New Society Publishers.

Stedman, R. 1982. *Shadows of the Indian: Stereotypes in American Culture.* Norman: University of Oklahoma Press

Stutzman, E. 1993. *American Indian Stereotypes: The Truth Behind the Hype, An Indian Education Curriculum Unit.* ERIC Document ED364396.

Prereading Questions

1. What difference does it make who writes the stories as long as they tell the "truth"?

2. If you were assigned to write an *autobiography* (not a *biography*) about 1 month in the life of the person on your right, what kind of problems would you encounter?

3. What might get in the way of your telling his or her story as your own, of your writing an accurate or truthful account of your neighbor's life?

Introduce the unit by explaining that students will be examining selections from literatures that were written by people trying to describe the lives of others.

Selection 1   Read aloud from *Basic Skills Caucasian Americans Workbook,* "Note from Publisher" and "Caucasian American Clothing and Fashion." More may be read if time permits.

Slapin's book is satire, based on an actual workbook about Native Americans. What if this text were the only way white children could learn about their ancestors and the only way people of color were to learn about white people?

Question for Discussion

What is a world view? Each of us has a way of viewing and interpreting the meaning of the world around us. Culturally and racially determined, our world view defines our relationship to the universe, and it defines—for us—the values of all things. Some possible world views are as follows:

- A view of humans as dependent on the harmonious and benevolent forces in the universe.

- A view of humans as the center of the universe, surrounded by a vast space in which we carry out our desires, build what we wish, control nature as we can, and tear it all down and start again.

- A view of humans as having a balanced relationship with everything in the universe.

- A belief that a loving God controls all that happens and that everything that happens works for good.

- A belief that no one can be trusted because all people generally have their own selfish interests in mind and cannot be trusted to care about others.

- A belief that there is nothing after this life, and so we need to get whatever we can out of each day because that is all there is.

Activities

1. Students write their own world views and then discuss the possible impact of this world view on their lives as well as on the lives of those around them.

2. Native educators Debra Earling (Salish) and Tyler Medicine Horse (Crow/Sioux) have asked students to draw or write a definition of an Indian and keep the definition for later use. This is a useful activity because it forces people to confront their own biases and recognize the ways they participate in stereotyping others on the basis of race.

Question for Discussion

What is ethnocentrism? The perspective of viewing one's own culture as central and superior to other cultures. Although this may positively manifest itself in a personal and communal pride, ethnocentrism often results in evaluation, judgment, and rejection of different cultures and races.

Selection 2   Read from a tribal cultural world view such as the Pikuni way, included in Appendix D of *Roots and Branches.* Students learn about a world view that appears very different from those exhibited in the texts students will examine later.

1. What is bias? Where I stand in relation to the rest of you, and what I see, hear, and smell represents my bias, point of view, an image filtered through a particular cultural experience, one side of a choice.

2. Is it possible to be unbiased? Students begin to realize how difficult it is for us to escape our own biases. They also admit that even history texts are biased.

3. What is a stereotype? An exaggerated and negative generalization, another group's story about me, our own bias or world view, generally placed on another person or group or culture, a way of permanently locking people into a position.

4. Can a stereotype be positive?

5. Can a positive stereotype produce negative consequences?

6. How does stereotyping limit individuals? Possible responses: We internalize it and believe it. We assume the stereotype represents the whole group. Indian children who believe the stereotype begin to doubt their own abilities. It limits our understanding of the diversity of other peoples. It victimizes those who are stereotyped by limiting the possibility of their individual growth or experience. In the presence of pervasive stereotyping, Indian children begin to believe they have no voice, and educators in Native communities comment that in the presence of non-Indians, they remain silent or they demonstrate their anger by doing violence against themselves, each other, or the non-Indian community.

Transitional Activity   Students examine the sources of specific stereotypes about Indian peoples, using those explained in Appendix C of *Roots and Branches,* and discuss the books they have read that might exhibit some of these stereotypes. Examples:

Brother Eagle, Sister Sky by Susan Jeffers

Peter Pan ("What Makes the Red Man Red?") by J. M. Barrie

Little House on the Prairie series by Laura Ingalls Wilder

The Indian in the Cupboard series by Lynne Reid Banks

John Smith and Pocahontas by John Smith

Double Life of Pocahontas by Jean Fritz

The Education of Little Tree by Forrest Carter

Annie and the Old One by Miska Miles

Knots on a Counting Rope by Bill Martin, Jr. and John Archambault

The Sign of the Beaver by Elizabeth George Speare

When the Legends Die by Hal Borland

The Light in the Forest by Conrad Richter

Only Earth and Sky Last Forever by Nathaniel Benchley

George Catlin readings from *The Last Best Place*

Names of sports teams

All Indians represented as Plains Indians

1995 Disney film *Pocahontas*

Complete publication information for most of these examples appears in Chapter 7 of this book.

Selection 3 Slapin and Seale's "How to Tell the Difference" in *Through Indian Eyes: The Native Experience in Books for Children* includes examples and 25 criteria for evaluating books for racial bias and stereotype.

Selections On an overhead, show excerpts from popular literatures, using Slapin and Seale's criteria for locating possible stereotypes.

Brother Eagle, Sister Sky by Susan Jeffers (New York: Dial, 1991), cover and last page.

"Journals of Exploration" by George Catlin in *Last Best Place*, eds. William Kittredge and Annick Smith (Helena: The Montana Historical Society Press), pp. 181–82.

Return of the Indian in the Cupboard by Lynne Reid Banks (New York: Doubleday, 1986), pp. 34–35 and 158–59.

The Education of Little Tree by Forrest Carter (Albuquerque: University of New Mexico Press, 1991), pp. 2–3.

Assignment

To pairs of students, distribute a marking pen and two overheads with printed pages from the following books. It is important to use primary-level materials because the need to generalize for younger children often creates very strong stereotypes that are easier to recognize. Using the overhead, students identify and share the evidence of stereotypes and non-Native biases with the rest of the class.

The Light in the Forest by Conrad Richter (New York: Knopf, 1953), Acknowledgments.

Little House on the Prairie by Laura Ingalls Wilder (New York: Harper & Row, 1971), pp. 136–137.

The Double Life of Pocahontas by Jean Fritz (New York: Putnam, 1983), pp. 12–13.

Soun Tetoken: Nez Perce Boy by Ken Thomasma (Jackson, WY: Grandview, 1984), pp. 26–27 and 106–107.

Sitting Bull by Jane Fleischer (Mahwah, NJ: Troll Associates), pp. 30–31.

Anpao: An American Odyssey by Jamake Highwater (Philadelphia: Lippincott, 1977), p. 20.

When the Legends Die by Hal Borland (Philadelphia: Lippincott, 1963), p. 25.

Only Earth and Sky Last Forever by Ken Benchley (New York: Harper Trophy, 1972), pp. 108–109.

Julie of the Wolves by Jean Craighead George (New York: Harper & Row, 1972), pp. 8–9.

The Indian in the Cupboard by Lynne Reid Banks (New York: Avon, 1980), pp. 20–21.

Alligators All Around by Maurice Sendak (New York: Harper & Row, 1962), letter "I."

Little Chief by Syd Hoff (New York: Harper & Bros., 1961), pp. 60–62.

Sanapia, Comanche Medicine Woman by David E. Jones (Prospect Heights, IL: Waveland Press, 1972), pp. 18–19.

Closure

Read aloud from the following poems and definitions from the end of Chapter 2 of *Roots and Branches*, which address the issues of cultural and personal identity, bias and stereotype, and their effect on both Indian and non-Indian individuals and communities.

"Introduction to Native American Literature" by Sherman Alexie

Definition of Tribal Literature from "Sending a Voice" by Kenneth Lincoln

"Sure You Can Ask Me a Personal Question" by Diane Burns

Closing Activities

1. Compare your present attitudes about Native American peoples, or about being Native American, with those of your peers or with the attitudes you had before beginning this unit.

2. Tell your own story about the pain of prejudice and stereotyping.

Other Activities

1. Examine possible reasons for the perpetuation of stereotype and bias (we think it is true if it is in print, we need to generalize because of limited information, we need to simplify for younger learners, we fear losing our central or "superior" position, we need to control our environment, or we need to make someone else responsible for our problems).

2. Look at truths behind bias, stereotype, and myth: the historical source of the stereotype, the different truths that contradict the stereotype, what the stereotype tells us about those who believe it and what they think is important, and the power individuals achieve when they stereotype.

3. Ask students to identify times they have been stereotyped or have been the object of name-calling because of their membership in a targeted group. How did it feel? What happens to people when they are stereotyped?

4. Talk about the importance of respecting the right of all people to tell their own stories about who they are.

5. Learn about tribal cultures and the way they influenced individual behaviors such as gift-giving and hospitality toward others, especially strangers.

6. Examine evidence of frontier settlers' attitudes toward Indians and discuss the Indians' attitudes toward settlers and the U.S. government, which broke the treaties.

7. For older students: Create a scenario in which students experience discrimination and judgment based on external characteristics alone (style of shoes, color of eyes, hair length).

VI. 5-Day Lesson: *The Way to Rainy Mountain* by N. Scott Momaday: A Journey into Human Reality through Imagination and History

Themes: Remembering the Old Ways; At Home within Circles

This lesson has been used in an adult Native American literature class, in a Western literature class for seniors, and in workshops for teachers, where they begin to recognize the presence of multiple meanings in a literary text. The lesson also uses several aspects of intelligence: linguistic, spatial, interpersonal, intrapersonal, and kinesthetic.

Goals

- To develop a respect for the integrity of the present and historical lives of Native American peoples represented by this literature
- To become acquainted with the Kiowa literary and cultural tradition through video, prose writing, poetry, and personal artistic expression
- To explore the multiple and very individual meanings in selected chapters of *Rainy Mountain*
- To experience the way N. Scott Momaday's writing demonstrates the integration of the past, present, and future, the landscape, and history and imagination to create a concrete human reality
- To develop the skills of listening, critical thinking, and oral and graphic expression
- To demonstrate positive attitudes toward oneself, people of other cultures, and environment

Resources

Lee, Francis, and James Bruchac, eds. 1996. *Reclaiming the Vision, Past, Present, and Future: Native Voices for the Eighth Generation.* Greenfield Center, NY: Greenfield Review Press.

McNickle, D'Arcy (Salish). 1973. *Native American Tribalism: Indian Survivals and Renewals.* London: Oxford University Press.

Momaday, N. Scott. [1969] 1996. *The Way to Rainy Mountain.* Tucson: University of Arizona Press.

Momaday, N. Scott. 1983. "The Delight Song of Tsoai-talee." In *Songs from this Earth on Turtle's Back,* ed. Joseph Bruchac, 157–162. New York: Greenfield Review Press.

N. Scott Momaday, Storyteller. 1989. Native American Audio Library. Santa Fe, NM: Sunset Productions.

"N. Scott Momaday." 1994. In *Native North American Literature,* ed. Janet Witalec, 432–448. Detroit, MI: Gale Research.

"The People of the Great Plains (Part One)." 1994. *The Native Americans* Series. Atlanta, GA: TBS Productions. Videocassette.

Winner of the Pulitzer prize for his novel *House Made of Dawn*, published in 1968, N. Scott Momaday is an essayist, poet, storyteller, lecturer, and novelist with a strong interest in the graphic arts. In the 1960s, he retraced the ancient Kiowa migration from the Rockies in Montana through the Black Hills and across the Plains. After the death of his grandmother in 1965, he made the journey to her home and to Rainy Mountain. This is the story that introduces *The Way to Rainy Mountain*, a novel that spans 300 years of Kiowa history and features Kiowa tradition and myth as the focus, the central place from which all other stories grow.

In each of the 24 two-page chapters, the storyteller shares three stories—a traditional story, a historical story, and a contemporary experience—that are connected to each other as well as to the preceding and following chapters. But unlike the more predictable, abstract thematic connections European Americans may make, within the chapters in *Rainy Mountain*, the stories merge and diverge on concrete images such as fire, antelope, buffalo, arrows, horses, and words.

The following lesson places readers in communities of nine people. Each is responsible for keeping a part of the story; at the same time he or she must share it orally with the group in order to solve a problem.

Prereading Activities

1. Show selected excerpts from "The People of the Great Plains (Part One)," in which contemporary Native voices define the Plains Indian people and their relationship to the land, using photographs of tribal heroes from a variety of Plains tribes.

2. Establish the personal and communal landscape of *The Way to Rainy Mountain*:

   a. First paragraph from "Introduction"

   b. Biographical sketch of N. Scott Momaday

   c. The estimated placement of Kiowas at the time of contact using D'Arcy McNickle's maps from *Native American Tribalism: Indian Survivals and Renewals*.

Reading Activity

Divide students into groups of nine and arrange them in circles. Distribute the nine paragraphs to each group, a different one to each student, with all groups having the same nine paragraphs from the first three chapters of *Rainy Mountain*. Each group is to establish a logical order for the readings by arranging paragraphs into three chapters, with three paragraphs in each chapter, and establish a rationale for its choices. Each student owns the paragraph he or she has received and may not pass it to another to read. While reading paragraphs aloud, students may want to rearrange the way the group is sitting or standing.

This problem-solving exercise provides the opportunity for participants to read aloud and to listen to each other, to explore the different possibilities for experiencing and understanding Momaday's story, and to demonstrate the ways our own particular views make other possibilities difficult to conceive. Taking about an hour, groups respond to this activity in a variety of ways. Because they are not used to listening carefully and would rather read, they grow frustrated when they must depend on hearing the story read aloud several times. Sometimes a strong leader will emerge and convince the other eight members to relinquish their stories, taking the separate paragraphs to his or her desk to arrange them. It also takes awhile for students to decide to get up and move to another spot in the circle. The most successful groups are those with Native people who are not looking for sequential order and who understand the circular structure that moves from myth into history into the personal and present, and then returns to myth, which begins each chapter. Also, the most successful groups stand up and read over and over, around the circle each time, so the entire story becomes a part of each participant.

Postreading Activities

1. Students from each group share, with the entire class, the order and rationales for their stories, and the entire class may react to the experience.

2. Show "The People of the Great Plains (Part One)," about the "era of history called Dog Days," and about the way "everything was possessed of personality in differing forms."

3. Look at one chapter and answer the following questions:

   a. What is a significant image in each of the three readings?

   b. What genre of literature might each of the three sections represent?

   c. In what ways are the three readings connected in each chapter?

   d. What conclusions might be drawn about Momaday's writing style, the world view portrayed in this writing, the relationship between the spiritual and material, and the relationship between the historical and the imaginary?

Closing Activities

1. While listening to a recording of N. Scott Momaday reading his poem "The Delight Song of Tsoai-talee," one student may draw on butcher paper or on the white board with colored markers while others watch, or all students may draw at their desks and then share with the group what they drew.

2. Each student selects a concrete object from his or her own landscape and writes a poem, telling the story and describing his or her personal connections with that object.

VII. James Welch's *Fools Crow*

Themes: Remembering the Old Ways; Between Two Worlds; Cultural and Personal Loss and Survival

This unit has been used in an elective Western literature course and in an evening Native American literature class. The students had previously experienced traditional Blackfeet stories from the collections of Percy Bullchild and Francis Fraser, and some had listened to a traditional Blackfeet storyteller. Although this novel is being used in American literature classes across the country, *Fools Crow* is an important text for Montana students. For example, our school is situated near the place where Fools Crow traveled towards his vision, near Fort Shaw where the soldiers who attacked Heavy Runner's camp were stationed, and about one hundred miles south of the sight of the Massacre on the Marias, the climax of the novel and a significant and tragic event in the history of Montana's Blackfeet people.

Goals

- To become aware, through the reading of *Fools Crow*, of the impact of Western settlement on the Blackfeet people and of the ways the Blackfeet survived culturally and personally

- To become acquainted with the Blackfeet literary, cultural, and historical tradition and experience by listening to the author discuss his work and through research and personal interviews

- To experience the genre of historical fiction and Welch's style of writing

- To experience the way James Welch's writing demonstrates the integration of dream and concrete reality, the incorporation of traditional story, traditional vocabulary, and the trickster/transformer figure in a contemporary text

Resources

Authentic Music of the American Indian. Compact Disc Digital Audio. CD 312. Legacy International, Box 6999, Beverly Hills, CA 90212.

Bennett, Ben. 1982. *Death, Too, for The-Heavy-Runner.* Missoula, MT: Mountain Press. Currently out of print, but available in libraries.

Ewers, John C. 1958. *The Blackfeet: Raiders on the Northwestern Plains.* Norman: University of Oklahoma Press

"Fools Crow by James Welch." 1994. Week Six, Audio Cassette. *Big Sky Radio,* hosted by Lowell Jaeger and Paul Zalis. 247 First Avenue East, Kalispell, MT 59901 (406-758-5713).

"James Welch." 1994. In *Native North American Literature,* edited by Janet Witalec, 659–68. Detroit, MI: Gale Research. Pages 664–65 are from a telephone interview with Welch conducted by Kenn Robbins and students in a creative writing class at the University of South Dakota, 1989. The interview was first printed in 1990 in *The South Dakota Review,* 28.1 (Spring): 103–10.

Long Standing Bear Chief, a.k.a. Harold Gray (Blackfoot). 1992. *Ni-Kso-Ko-Wa: Blackfoot Spirituality, Traditions, Values and Beliefs.* Browning, MT: Spirit Talk Press.

Montana Indians: Their History and Location. 1995. Helena: Montana Office of Public Instruction.

Schultz, James Willard. 1962. *Blackfeet and Buffalo: Memories of Life Among the Indians.* Norman: University of Oklahoma Press.

Welch, James. 1986. *Fools Crow.* New York: Viking Penguin.

Welch, James, with Paul Stekler. 1994. *Killing Custer: The Battle of the Little Bighorn and the Fate of the Indians*, 25–47. New York: W.W. Norton.

Background: The Blackfeet Reservation

Name

The name *Blackfeet* is controversial. Harold Gray, in *Ni-Kso-Ko-Wa: Blackfoot Spirituality, Traditions, Values and Beliefs*, says the proper name is *Siksika* (*Blackfoot* in English), but they are actually the Pikuni. The Blackfoot are the people who are located in Alberta, as are the Bloods. *Blackfeet* refers to the color of moccasins, darkened by prairie-fire ashes. Actually, the federal government insisted that the tribe should be called Blackfeet in 1935 because non-Indian people were commonly referring to them as Blackfeet and because "there are more than one of you."

Location

North: bound by United States–Canada border

South: 52 miles south to Birch Creek

East: an imaginary line starting near the junction of Cut Bank Creek and the Marias River and extending north

West: foothills of the Rockies

Browning, Montana, has been the headquarters of Blackfeet Indian Agency since 1894

Land Status

716,865 individually allotted acres

272,464 tribally owned lands

536,247 fee title or state lands

136 acres of government land

1,525,712 total acres (35 percent owned by non-Indians)

Population

7,179 Indians living on or near Blackfeet Reservation

6,094 Indians living off reservation

13,273 enrolled tribal members

2,500 non-Indians on reservation

Historical Background

- Ancestors of Algonquian linguistic orientation: Blackfeet (Siksika), Kainah or Bloods, and Piegans.
- Located until 1730 in the present Saskatchewan.
- Moved southward to follow the buffalo and other game, traveling in bands of 20–30 people, with a chief who decided the band's movement and settled disputes.
- Occupied lands from the Continental Divide, to the Montana–Dakota borders, to the Yellowstone River, and to Edmonton, Alberta Canada.
- Before 1800, they had little contact with other tribes or European Americans.
- Traded for tools, utensils, and weapons with Cree and Assiniboine and the Hudson's Bay Company.
- Probably obtained horses from the Shoshone.
- Dominated the area until 1800 with horses and guns, establishing a reputation as warriors and demanding the respect of other tribes and settlers.
- 1851: The Fort Laramie Treaty established an area for Blackfeet without their representation.
- 1855: Designed to stop warfare, the government treaty with the Blackfeet, called "Lame Bull's Treaty," provided for use of the original reservation as a common hunting territory.
- 1865, 1868: Although treaties negotiated for lands south of Missouri were not ratified by Congress, non-Indian homesteaders came anyway.
- January 23, 1870: Baker Massacre resulted in the deaths of 173 Piegans, primarily women and children of Heavy Runner's band, who were ill with smallpox.
- 1873, 1874: By presidential order and congressional act, the southern boundary was moved 200 miles north, taking away the land between the Marias River and the Sun River. Land to the south was opened to settlement. Remaining Blackfeet were forced to accept reservation living and a dependence on rationing for survival.
- Winter 1883–84: 600 Blackfeet starved to death because of the scarcity of buffalo and insufficient U.S. government provisions; other sources indicate the date was winter of 1882.

■ 1888: White Calf and Three Sons ceded additional lands to the U.S. government for survival needs. In return, the Blackfeet got tools, equipment and cattle for farming and ranching.

■ 1888: Sweetgrass Hills Treaty established separate boundaries for the Blackfeet, Fort Belknap, and Fort Peck Reservations.

■ 1895: A treaty was initiated by the U.S. government to secure minerals and land from the area that is now Glacier National Park. George Bird Grinnell, considered a friend of the Blackfeet, was part of this commission. In 1910, when minerals were not found, the area became part of Glacier National Park from the Continental Divide to the reservation.

■ 1895: Dawes Act: tribal people were selling allotted lands just to survive until 1907, when Woodrow Wilson returned all surplus lands to the tribe.

■ By the 1920s, two-thirds of Blackfeet people were directly dependent on the federal government.

■ 1935: Blackfeet Indian Tribe organization under the Indian Reorganization Act:

Established the tribe as a political entity.

Established the tribe as a business corporation in which all tribal members share.

Established the nine-member tribal council.

Membership consists of people "of Indian blood whose names appear on the official census rolls of the tribe as of January 1, 1935 . . . and all children born to any blood members." The constitution requires one-fourth or more Blackfeet blood quantum for membership in tribe.

■ 1921: Discovery of oil provided some economic hope.

■ 1964: A flood ripped down Two Medicine River, killing 30 Blackfeet and leaving hundreds homeless.

Prereading Activity

Because contemporary Indian writers often incorporate the trickster and his or her wide range of behaviors in poetry, stories, and novels, it is important to preface the reading of a novel such as *Fools Crow* with a discussion of the trickster/transformer figure, using the material from Chapter 2 in *Roots and Branches*.

Reading Activities and Assignments

1. Come to class every day with a question regarding an idea, a literary motif, symbol, or character that you think the other students should think about.

2. Keep a reading log that includes your responses to each of the questions or activities listed under each day's reading assignment.

Chapters 1–4

Begin a list of Blackfeet values communicated through this literature. What are the setting, situation, point of view of the narrator? Know the Blackfeet names for animals and their English equivalents. Using physical characteristics of three animals that are not part of Welch's landscape, create new names. Research the names for animals in the Blackfeet language. Look for evidences of the trickster/transformer figure in the narration, characters, and events.

Chapters 5–6

Be able to explain a vow and its value to the Blackfeet. Begin a list of White Man's Dog's characteristics.

Chapters 7–8

Identify and be able to explain an external conflict.

Chapter 9

Find a line that sounds wise to you. Write it down and describe what it means to you.

Chapter 10

How might the Blackfeet define a man? How might they define a woman? Research the ceremony of the Sun Dance or interview a person from a tribal community.

Chapter 11

Why did the Blackfeet war against the Crows? Using the history of federal Indian policy in Appendix B of *Roots and Branches,* select an event or time period to research.

Chapters 12–14

Research the historical Owl Child and Malcolm Clark. What was the relationship between the two men? What is the significance of the conversation between Raven and Fools Crow? Compare Raven's persuasive arguments with the arguments of Shakespeare's Macbeth, in his speech to the murderers.

Chapters 15 and 16

Find two descriptive passages that are examples of poetic prose, noting similes, metaphors, or other examples of imagery. Explain a sentence or short passage that demonstrates strong patterns of sound.

Explain the literary devices used and be prepared to discuss their effect on the meaning of the passage.

Chapters 17 and 18

What is the attitude of the Blackfeet attitude toward the Napikwans now? How and why has it changed from the beginning of the novel?

Chapters 19 and 20

Describe one character's internal conflict and resolution.

Chapters 21–24

What statement is the novel making about justice? What does Kipp mean when he thinks, "these people have not changed, but the world they live in has" (252)? List the names of the different chiefs and their philosophical positions on the conflict with the Napikwans. Write a "You are there" dialogue in which you take an active role in the council meeting. What will you advise? Justify your arguments in your dialogue.

Chapters 25–32

Where does Fools Crow journey? What is the symbolism of the turnips? What is honor to the Blackfeet? Where is the hope in this chapter?

Chapters 33–36

Listen to the Big Sky Radio tape of James Welch discussing *Fools Crow.* Research historical names and places from *Fools Crow,* such as Joe Kipp, General Alfred Sully, Marshal Wheeler, Heavy Runner, Colonel Eugene M. Baker, and White Man's Dog, and present results to the class.

Closing Activities

1. Write a case study of Fast Horse.
2. Write a description of the landscape where the Massacre on the Marias occurred.
3. Discussion questions: List events within the major conflict in the novel. Where was the turning point in that conflict? What was the resolution in the novel? Is this romantic fiction or realism? Is it romantic primitivism? How would you describe Welch's style? Identify a theme from this novel and describe how that theme is revealed.
4. Draw a scene, character, or collage of symbols from the novel and be prepared to explain your drawing to the class.

5. Students write questions from three levels of thinking (recall, interpretive, evaluative), which their classmates will answer. Once the questions are written, the class can discuss the questions, helping to revise so the questions represent the three levels of thinking. Then each student draws three questions, one from each level. The students who have written the questions read and evaluate the responses for those questions. The following questions are examples from one class of eight students. As students read the responses to their questions, they discover the possibilities for different interpretations of both the novel and their questions. They also realize that some questions either rely on stereotypes or generate questions about stereotypes, and sometimes these questions elicit responses that also rely on stereotypes.

Recall

a. Describe the role of Medicine Woman. What does she do?

b. Name three important animals from *Fools Crow*. For each animal, describe a situation from the novel that involves the animal.

c. How did White Man's Dog become a man?

d. How did White Man's Dog receive the name Fools Crow?

e. Describe the situation in which Yellow Kidney lost his fingers.

f. What does Fools Crow learn from Feather Woman?

g. Describe the course of Fools Crow's journey following his dream.

h. Describe in detail what happened at the Baker Massacre toward the end of the book.

Interpretive

a. Several characters in *Fools Crow* undergo physical and spiritual changes that transform how they see themselves and interpret their surroundings. Select one character and cite two situations from the text to explain these changes.

b. Why did Yellow Kidney have to die after he had finally found peace with himself and had left the Lone Eaters?

c. What was the function and value of Mik-api to the Lone Eaters?

d. Why do you think Fast Horse decided to leave the Lone Eaters for good?

e. Using Running Fisher's reaction to the eclipse, what does the novel reveal about the belief system of the Blackfeet?

f. In *Fools Crow,* why do men and women receive different presents at their wedding? Cite examples from the wedding of Fools Crow and Red Paint.

g. Explain the effect of James Welch's use of limited third person in *Fools Crow.*

h. What was the reason for Rides-at-the Door's opinion regarding the whites before the conference of chiefs? Was he alone in his position? Why or why not?

Evaluative

a. Select a novel from another culture. Compare four cultural values Welch communicates in *Fools Crow* with values in the other novel. Are the Blackfeet values exhibited in this novel relevant for today? Explain.

b. What was the significance of Fools Crow's visions in the yellow skin of Feather Woman?

c. How do the Pikunis handle situations presented by the seizers in regard to the destruction of their land and culture? Cite one situation and explain. How do you think your father would react if someone more powerful than he were threatening his family's way of life? Which method of handling the situation is more appropriate?

d. Compare the Indian woman's role in *Fools Crow* to that of a stereotypical white woman today. Who has more power? Why?

e. Identify two different Indian leaders and their approaches to the invasion of the white man. Which approach was better? Give reasons for your answer based on the novel and your understanding of human nature.

f. Compare the influence of dreams in the Blackfeet society at the time of the novel and in your world today.

g. Did Fast Horse actually dream about Cold Maker, or did he invent it for attention? Explain your answer.

6. Conduct a trial of Lieutenant Colonel Eugene Baker for the massacre on the Marias River, January 23, 1870.

7. Write a ballad telling the story of *Fools Crow*.

8. Draw a map and plot the places and events that occur in the novel.

9. Tell a story that one of your grandparents has told about a critical moment in your family's history.

10. Draw a map showing the reduction in Blackfeet territory from 1850 to the present.

11. Research a personal story of a settler in Blackfeet territory during the time period of *Fools Crow*.

VIII. 13-Day Unit: Zitkala-Ša's *American Indian Stories*

Themes: Remembering the Old Ways; At Home within Circles; Between Two Worlds; Cultural and Personal Loss and Survival

Scholars believe that Zitkala-Ša (Gertrude Simmons Bonnin) was one of the first Native writers to publish without the gloss of non-Native editors. The developed background that this unit requires demonstrates the complexity of culture, history, language, and biography that informs most contemporary Native American literatures today, especially those in which the authors are bilingual, speaking their Native language and English. Members of an adult Native American literature course, as well as twelfth-grade students enrolled in a Western literature elective, have participated in this unit.

Goals

■ To understand the influence of the author's cultural and personal background on the rhetoric in Zitkala-Ša's three autobiographical essays

■ To develop an appreciation for the importance of landscape in Native American lives

■ To become aware of the impact of Indian boarding schools and Western settlement on Native American people and the ways one person survived

■ To become familiar with the Dakota literary, cultural, and historical tradition and experience

■ To experience the genre of autobiographical essay and Zitkala-Ša's style

■ To reinforce previous knowledge about irony, tone, and the different narrative and editorial voices that may exist in autobiographical essays

Resources

Fisher, Dexter. 1985. "Zitkala-Ša: The Evolution of a Writer." In *American Indian Stories*, by Zitkala-Ša. Lincoln: University of Nebraska Press.

"Gertrude Bonnin (Zitkala-Ša)." 1994. In *Native North American Literature*, ed. Janet Witalec, 169–176. New York: Gale Publishing.

Hoover, Herbert T. 1988. *Indians of North America: The Yankton Sioux.* New York: Chelsea House.

"The People of the Great Plains (Parts One and Two)" and "The People of the Northwest." 1994. *The Native Americans* Series. Atlanta, GA: TBS Productions. Videocassette.

Picotte, Agnes. 1985. Foreword to *Old Indian Legends,* by Zitkala-Ša. Lincoln: University of Nebraska Press.

The Reservations. 1995. The American Indian Series. New York: Time-Life Books.

Susag, Dorothea. 1993. "Zitkala-Ša (Gertrude Simmons Bonnin): A Power(full) Literary Voice." *Studies in American Indian Literatures,* Winter: 3–24.

Walker, James R. 1983. *Lakota Myth.* Lincoln: University of Nebraska Press.

Zitkala-Ša. [1900] 1985. *American Indian Stories.* Lincoln: University of Nebraska Press.

Zitkala-Ša. [1901] 1985. *Old Indian Legends.* Lincoln: University of Nebraska Press.

Background   *The Lakota System of Bands and Alliances: Zitkala-Ša's Linguistic and Cultural Heritage*

Gertrude Simmons was born in 1876 on the Yankton Indian Reservation in what was then Dakota Territory. Throughout her life, she claimed to be "a Dakota woman" and refused definition as a "mixed-blood" (Welch 1985, p. 61). Although biographers and critics of Zitkala-Ša indicate this specific tribal connection, the question remains: Just what is a Dakota or a Lakota or a Sioux? For practical purposes, the entire nation has been and still is called *Sioux* by many writers, historians, and ethnologists. Although Elizabeth Grobsmith does not offer a date, the Chippewas called the whole people Lesser Adders (snake) or *Nadoweisiw-eg* in order to distinguish them from a more feared enemy, the Iroquois, the True Adders. Unable to pronounce the Chippewa word, the French shortened it to *Sioux,* the name by which this Plains people has been known for over two centuries (Grobsmith 1981, p. 11). Yet the name *Lakota* has also represented the larger nation as a whole, as well as a particular alliance and dialect. This double meaning of *Lakota* contributes to the confusion over the appropriate name for these people.

Within this greater Sioux or Lakota nation are three related dialects: Lakota, "a dialect of the 'Dakota Sioux' language within the Siouan linguistic family"; Nakota, spoken by the northern or Yankton Sioux; and Dakota, "the language of eastern or Santee Sioux." These dialects of the Sioux represent three major alliances as well, but "all the Sioux tribes constituted a political unit called the *Oceti Sakowin* or 'Seven Council Fires'" (Grobsmith 1981, pp. 5–6), which traditionally met every summer for the Sun Dance Ceremony.

The largest division, the Tetons or Tetonwan (Prairie Dwellers), was located west from the Missouri River. Seven bands within this Teton division all spoke the Lakota dialect: Oglala (now living on the Pine Ridge Reservation), Sicangu or Brule (living on the Rosebud, Lower Brule, and Crow Creek Reservations), Hunkpapa, Mnikowoju, Sihasapa, Oohnunpa, and Itazipco. (These last four are living on the Rosebud, Lower Brule, and Crow Creek, Cheyenne River, and Standing Rock Reservations.) Four divisions of the Seven Council Fires, speaking the Dakota dialect, were included in the Dakota Alliance: the

Wahpeton, Mdewakanton, Wahpekute, and Sisseton. The two other divisions of the Seven Council Fires, the Yankton (End Dwellers because of their location at the end of the camp circle) and Yanktonais (Little End Dwellers), both formed the Nakota Alliance and spoke the Nakota dialect (Powers 1990, p. 23). Although several sources agree that the Yankton people spoke the Nakota dialect, Raymond DeMaille, in his introduction to *Sioux Indian Religion,* questions it for two important reasons: There is "no historical evidence that these people ever used an initial *n* in their name" and "throughout recorded history, they have called themselves Dakotah" (DeMallie and Parks 1987, p. 7). Other evidence also supports DeMaille's conclusion. They are called Dakotas in the Yankton Reservation Agency reports, and Zitkala-Ša called herself Dakota. Speakers of each dialect could understand speakers from other dialects, yet the complex traditional organization of these tribes demonstrates their heterogeneous nature.

The Yankton Band/Dakota dialect represents a part of the historical, cultural, and linguistic heritage of Zitkala-Ša. Perhaps she was familiar with more than one dialect. Both Dakota and Nakota words appear in her essays and stories (*Iktomi,* a Dakota word, and *Wiyaka-Napbina,* a Nakota word). Despite government efforts to eradicate the languages of indigenous people across the continent, Zitkala-Ša helped to maintain the cultural integrity of her Native heritage.

The Yankton Reservation: 1858–1902

Another aspect of Zitkala-Ša's heritage that informs her writing of *American Indian Stories* was the movement west and the resulting territorial and physical losses for her Yankton people. Before 1800, her ancestors had traveled across half the continent, following the migration of buffalo from the upper Mississippi River valley to the Black Hills. In the early 1800s, because of their location near the Missouri River, many forts and trading posts were established on their land. According to Edwin Thompson Denig, this contact resulted in the loss of "a great many, by diseases caught along" this California route (Denig 1961, p. 38).

The Treaty of Prairie du Chien, 1830, ceded 2.2 million acres to the U.S. government. In 1850 the Yankton band still claimed 13.5 million acres from the upper Des Moines to the upper Missouri River valleys. But when more traders and settlers migrated to this area and "squatted," pressuring the U.S. government to move the Yanktons to a reservation, the Yanktons were forced, on April 19, 1858, to cede all remaining land to the government except 431,000 acres lying 30 miles along the Missouri River. The tribe was to receive $1,600,000—about ten cents an acre—in decreasing annuity payments until 1908.

Within the Yankton Reservation boundaries, and with the annuity funds, federal agents worked toward dismantling the tribal structure and building European American civilization on a farming base. Every year, agents, school superintendents, and physicians filed their reports with the Department of the Interior. However, despite the agents' efforts to demonstrate the success of these programs, the reports proved the devastating effects of farming policies, housing policies, and boarding schools on the lives of all Yankton men, women, and children.

In 1874, an agent recommended that the Yanktons be moved to Indian Territory because the country on the Missouri lacked sufficient resources for farming, and another in 1877 called it a "woodless and desolate prairie." Three out of every four years, fields yielded as little as one bushel to the acre due to hailstorms, grasshoppers, "hot blasting wind," and drought so severe that shade trees died. In 1896, when they did raise a good crop, the Indians were forced to take a "seriously low price" because they had no place to store it and "white neighbors would never pay a fair price." By 1902, no more seed wheat was provided because it cost as much to produce as it would bring in a sale. No doubt agents were reluctant to admit their own failures to build successful farming operations, so they blamed the land, the neighboring whites, and the Indians.

In 1876, the year Gertrude Simmons was born, the agent said that if the rations were removed, there would be "utter destitution and great suffering, and a general breakup of the tribe." Yet eight years later, Agent J. F. Kinney, with paternalistic tone, strongly recommended issuing less flour because "less rations, more farming, more self-reliance, less dependence, more manhood."

In 1874, St. Paul's Episcopal boarding school for girls and boys, three day schools, and two Presbyterian schools served 200 Yankton Reservation children. In contrast with the government schools, St. Paul's was still educating in the Dakota language in 1890. In 1900, Agent John W. Harding recommended ceasing of funding to St. Paul's because "it [was] more sympathetic with Indians in conflict with Government policies." An agent in 1880 offered the most praise for Carlisle, an off-reservation school in Pennsylvania where Zitkala-Ša would teach and write her essays. However, by 1887 and continuing into the next century, agents rejected this same school in favor of the reservation's Industrial Boarding School. Not only did schools like Carlisle take their "brightest" students, but one agent disapproved of the children's extended separation from parents. Children would "lose their health in Eastern schools." Some school officials objected to Eastern schools because they would then have to fill reservation school quotas with "children earlier rejected for ill health."

On May 21, 1895, the government proclaimed, "Lands ceded by Yankton tribe of Sioux Indians are open to settlement. These lands shall be offered for sale to actual and bonafide settlers." In essence, the Allotment Act contributed to the further loss of Indian territorial integrity when much of the "surplus" land was purchased and leased by non-Indians.

By 1902, numerous new lights dotted the reservation landscape, many sod houses had replaced tepees, and parents resisted sending children to reservation schools because they feared they would die. Physician reports prove that the parents' fears were justified. From a population of 2,600 in 1857, the numbers of Yanktons and mixed-bloods on the Yankton Reservation dropped to 1,678 by 1902. Epidemics of sore eyes, sore throats, influenza, consumption, scrofula (tuberculosis), measles, chicken pox, and whooping cough raged through these Yankton people, especially in the schools, where such highly contagious diseases found captive victims. Although one angry agent in 1884 suggested that the prevalence of disease was caused by "stupid indifference to laws of health," a more sympathetic physician in 1901 blamed "poverty and one-room houses devoid of ventilation." In 1894, a physician indicated that few were disease-free; in 1899 21 children died before the end of the school year, and in 1901 95 people died of "consumption and old age." The agency report in 1902 showed a comparison between the death rate among the white population surrounding the reservation of 8 in 1,000 and among the Indians, 24 in 1000. The Yankton people were dying; the Indians themselves knew it, and so did the agents. Mothers kept children home to prevent their contracting a deadly disease, and agents suspected that the deaths of children were kept secret so the families could continue to receive maximum rations (*Annual Reports* 1874–1902). This was the situation for Zitkala-Ša's people, and for the writer herself, at the time she first published her autobiographical essays in the *Atlantic Monthly*, in January, February, and March of 1900.

Classification of Lakota Cosmology

Spirit	Other Lakota Forms	English Gloss
ANOG ITE		Double Face, Double Woman
ANP (contraction of ANPETU)		Day
CAN OTI	CAN OTILA	Tree Dwellers
ETU		Time
EYA (Wiyohpeyata Wicasa)		The West Wind
GNAS	GNASKI	Demon, Crazy Buffalo

Spirit	Other Lakota Forms	English Gloss
HAN		Darkness
HAN-WI (also HANWI)	WI-WIN	Moon
HU NONP (also HUNOMP)	MATO	Bear, Two Legged
IBOM	Another name for IYA	Cyclone
IKTOMI	IKTO, UNKTOMI (Dakota)	Trickster, Spider
INYAN		Rock
ITE		Face
IYA	IYO	Eating Monster
KSA		Wisdom
MAKA	MAKA-AKAN	Earth
OKAGA	from ITOKAGA	The South Wind
PTE-OYATE	OYATE-PTE	Buffalo People
SKAN	TAKU SKANSKAN	The Sky, Something In Movement, Changes Things, That-Which-Moves
TATANKA	TATANKAKAN	The Buffalo
TATE	TATEKAN	The Wind
TOKA	TOKAHE	The First One, First Man, First Woman
UNK	UNKTE	Passion
UNKCEGILA	UNCEGILA	Land Monster
UNKTEHI	UNTEHI	One Who Kills, Water Monster
WAKANKA	KA	The Witch
WAKINYAN		The Thunderbird, The Winged One
WAZIYA	WA	The Wizard
WI	WI-AKAN	The Sun
WI-CAN		Stars
WOHPE		The Beautiful Woman, The Feminine, The Mediator
YANPA		The East Wind
YATA		The North Wind
YUMNI		The Whirlwind, The God of Love

—(Jahner 1983, 30–33)

Prereading Activity

Introduce Zitkala-Ša and *American Indian Stories* with a brief biography of Gertrude Bonnin from the Forewords by Dexter Fisher and Agnes Picotte and locate the Yankton Reservation on a map.

Selection 1: "Impressions of an Indian Childhood" (pp. 7–45)

After their individual reading, each group is assigned two of the following questions, which they will share with the entire class.

1. Looking at the significant figures and names from Lakota cosmology, what evidence of any of these symbols do you see in the text? Pay attention to the name of Gertrude Simmons's mother as given in Agnes Picotte's Foreword to *Old Indian Legends*.

2. What are the characteristics of the child's mother? What is the relationship between child and mother? What are the values and lessons the mother teaches her child?

3. Identify rhetoric that suggests a non-Indian, possibly Puritan writer, and identify rhetoric that suggests Indian or a particular tribal writer. This includes metaphors and vocabulary.

4. What images suggest a reservation landscape?

5. What is the place of traditional story, and Iktomi stories in particular, in this essay and in the child's experience?

6. In this landscape and experience, where does power lie?

7. List evidences of loss (territorial, communal, and personal) in this text.

8. Identify any ironies in the text.

Selection 2: "School Days" (pp. 47–80)

Introduce the second essay, "School Days," with some background information on the history of the Yankton Reservation and on Indian boarding schools.

1. Identify specific European American acculturation practices in this essay.

2. Identify specific evidence (comments and actions) of resistance to European American acculturation.

3. Identify the essay's tone and cite lines from the text that demonstrate tone.

4. Where is the evidence of an ironic voice in the text?

5. List specific aspects of the Eastern experience that might differ from the writer's childhood experiences on the Dakota prairie.

6. How can this essay be read as an Iktomi story or a story featuring the trickster/transformer figure?

7. Look for evidence of the adult voice and the child's voice in the text.

8. How have the child and the child's home changed in the three years since she first left?

9. Explain the conflict the young girl experiences during the speech contest. Does she prevail over the discrimination? If so, how?

10. Does the writer or the child have a consistent support group or system? If so, what is it?

Selection 3: "An Indian Teacher among Indians" (pp. 81–99)

1. Identify evidence in the rhetoric that indicates the writer or child refuses to remain the victim.

2. How does she describe her employer? What inferences might we draw that underlie the surface descriptions?

3. How are the white people in this essay described?

4. Cite evidences of further European American encroachment and personal, communal, or territorial disintegration of the home or Dakota landscape.

5. How are the mother and daughter reconciled?

6. How might we read this essay as an indictment against European Americans?

7. Define the stereotype of European Americans that this essay portrays.

8. Cite evidence in the text that indicates the writer is familiar with Iktomi stories and has used such stories to interpret her experience with European Americans.

9. What do you think was the writer's "new way of solving the problem"?

10. What aspects of this child's life are missing from this story? Sometimes what is missing tells us more about a writer or a story than what is included.

Closing Activities

1. Write your own autobiographical essay or tell a story from your life. What will you include and exclude? Who will be your significant others, both positive and negative?

2. Teachers may supplement Zitkala-Ša's essays with readings that portray similar themes.

IX. 4-Week Unit: Linda Hogan's *Mean Spirit*

Themes: Remembering the Old Ways; Between Two Worlds; Cultural and Personal Loss and Survival

When this unit follows *American Indian Stories,* students can see the further impact on individuals and families as well as the death and territorial loss that resulted from the encroachment of non-Native people in their rush for mineral-rich lands. Some scholars compare Linda Hogan's writing with the magical realist fiction of Gabriel García Márquez, so the novel works well in units with his stories and other similar literatures. *Mean Spirit* may also be combined with novels and stories about the Osage people and the Oklahoma oil boom. Students in an adult Native American Literature class and a high school Western literature elective have studied *Mean Spirit* using the following materials and assignments.

Goals

- To become aware of the impact of boarding schools, allotment, guardianship, and citizenship issues on Native Americans and the ways they survived
- To understand the concept of cultural exchange
- To develop an appreciation for the importance of landscape in Native American lives
- To become aware of the exploitation of natural resources on Indian lands and the genocide that accompanied such exploitation
- To experience the genre of historical fiction with strong female characters
- To become familiar with the narrative style of magical realism and to examine the meaning and effect of symbols in the novel

Resources

Gibson, Arrell Morgan. 1980. *The American Indian, Prehistoric to the Present.* Norman: University of Oklahoma Press.

Hogan, Linda. 1990. *Mean Spirit.* New York: Ivy Books.

"Linda Hogan." 1994. In *Native North American Literature,* ed. Janet Witalec, 333–343. New York: Gale Research.

Mathews, John Joseph (Osage). 1961. *The Osage: Children of the Middle Waters.* Norman: University of Oklahoma Press.

Miller, Arthur. [1952] 1981. *The Crucible.* New York: Penguin.

Mooney, James. 1991. *The Ghost-Dance Religion and the Sioux Outbreak of 1890.* Lincoln: University of Nebraska Press. Originally published in 1896 by the U.S. Bureau of Ethnology.

The Reservations, Tribes of the Southern Plains, and *The Spirit World.* 1995. The American Indians Series. New York: Time-Life Books.

Wilson, Terry. 1985. *The Underground Reservation: Osage Oil.* Lincoln: University of Nebraska Press.

Background: Osage History, 1500–1970

Language System: Siouian

- 1500: The Osage were located in woodland areas of southern Missouri and eastern Kansas: the Mississippi Valley. They had encountered and traded with Spanish and were raiding villages in Arkansas and Canadian settlements to protect their territory.

- 1600s: The French enlisted the Osages to capture Pawnees for slave trade.

- 1700: They moved to their "permanent residence" on grasslands of the Plains.

- 1762: The Spanish felt threatened by the Osages in Louisiana, who were resisting the Spanish invasion.

- 1808: In an attempt to create a pan-Indian confederacy to stand with the British against U.S. expansion, Tecumseh tried to enlist Osages to join the Shawnees.

- 1812: The territories of Arkansas, Missouri, and Iowa were called Indian Country. The federal government planned to make land into reservations for Eastern tribes, but the Osage, Quapaw, Oto, Missouri, and Kansa people lived there.

- 1803–1825: Treaties were enacted to move Osage and other tribes west.

- 1836: Osages were finally moved to the treaty lands, north of 37° in the northern half of Indian Territory.

- Before 1854: Kansas comprised the northern half, and some of the best land, in Indian Territory.

- 1857: The Osages and a federation of Indian nations, the Cherokee, Chickasaw, Choctaw, Creek, and Seminole (also known as the Five Civilized Tribes) were demonstrating assimilationist economic, political, and social lifestyles.

- 1860: Fighting in marginal roles as scouts for other Indian tribes who fought for the Confederacy, the Osages promised 500 warriors to the Confederacy.

- 1865: With the apparent purpose of punishing the Five Civilized Tribes and the Osages for fighting with the Confederacy, "enemies of the United States," these tribes were told they must surrender part of lands to the United States for other tribes and that all tribes must combine to form one government.

- 1870: Precipitating further conflicts between the Osage and white settlers, and the Osage and the Cherokee, Congress passed a law acquiring land for squatters on Osage land and for relocated Cherokees. The Osage were told to move further west, but many full-bloods chose not to move. Other Osage remained behind because they were "assimilated mixed-bloods," and the U.S. government told them they could receive citizenship and allotments, etc. However, the white settlers in Kansas rejected them.

- 1851–1872: 1,500 Osages returned to Indian territory, a rough upland meadow and hill country fit only for grazing, not farming. It was a less desirable reservation than others. They adopted a written constitution.

- By 1880, 67 different tribes occupied Indian Territory. For many it was the fourth relocation in 50 years.

- 1886: The surface land was divided among 2,229 enrollees, but the Osage retained the tribal ownership of minerals.

- 1887: The General Allotment Act, the Dawes Act, resulted in divisions of reservations into small acreages per family head. Those who "cooperated" were promised the possibility of U.S. citizenship. Surplus lands went for as little as three cents an acre. Along with some other tribes, the Osages were exempted because they objected to the allotment, fearing it would result in the destruction of the tribe.

- 1893: Congress decided that the Osages were subject to allotment, but in 1906, after oil was discovered on the reservation, they "won permission from Congress . . . to partition the l.5-million-acre reservation so that each of the tribe's 2,229 members received four plots totaling just over 650 acres. The Osage reserved all subsurface mineral rights for the tribe as a whole, with the proceeds from oil leases and royalties to be divided evenly among tribal members" (*The Reservations* 1995, 154).

- 1906: Burke's Law ended the conferring of citizenship rights, until 25 years of trusteeship had passed, providing the individuals were deemed "competent."

- 1908: To meet their needs for survival, 90 percent of allottees in the entire country had disposed of their lands to non-Indians.

- 1912–1928: Over $157 million in oil-rich lands belonging to the Osage tribe were auctioned off to non-Indian oil men, who paid as much as $1 million for 160 acres. The Osage oil wealth resulted in many attempts to defraud them.

- From 1921–1925 there were 24 unsolved murders, shootings, poisonings, and the burning of a house.

- 1920s: "During the early 1920s, what came to be known as the reign of terror befell the tribe. Unscrupulous whites stopped at nothing, not even murder, in order to gain control of oil-rich Osage land. A wave of murders brought in agents from the Federal Bureau of Investigation (FBI), who discovered that the motives for the killings were elementary. Almost all of the murders involved Osages whose white guardians or white husbands would benefit by taking over the headright. It was common knowledge that a killer could be hired for $500 and a used roadster. The favorite modus operandi was to get the Osage drunk, find a doctor who would attest to this condition, and then later give the victim a lethal injection by morphine. Invariably the cause of death was said to be alcohol poisoning. By some estimates, up to 60 Osages were murdered, nearly three percent of the tribe, before the presence of the FBI and congressional legislation bringing guardians under control of the Indian Bureau helped stop the killing" (*The Reservations* 1995, 155).

- 1934: The Osages were exempt from state descent and distribution of property laws. State law did not determine descent and distribution of individually owned Indian property or as restricted allotments. However, federal officials were designated trustees of tribal funds; the Indians wanted protection but not supervision.

- 1948: Assimilation Crimes Act dictated that specific crimes not covered under state or federal law or statute were to be tried in federal courts.

- By 1952, the total yearly income had decreased to $4,571,644.66 for the entire tribe.

- September 30, 1970: The Justice Department declared a $13.2-million settlement with the Osage Indian Nation of Oklahoma for 28 million acres of lands purchased by the federal government in Arkansas, Kansas, Missouri, and Oklahoma between 1803 and 1819.

Reading Activity

After each reading, students come to class with questions for discussion.

Postreading Activities

1. Supporting answers with references from the text, four workshop groups respond to the following:

   a. Using textual references, define the meaning and significance for each of the following symbols: group 1, corn and redshirt; group 2, bats and oil fires; group 3, parrot and bees; group 4, wind and mean spirit.

   b. Look at each of the following major characters. How do they cope, resist, and survive tragedy, despair, exploitation, and possible extermination? Group 1, Michael Horse, Stace Red Hawk, and John Stink; group 2, Nola, Ruth, Dune-Hog Priest, Joe Billy, and Martha; group 3, Ona Neck, Lettie, Sara, and Belle; group 4, Moses, Benoit, Jess Gold, and Red Shirt.

   c. Explain each of the following conflicts in *Mean Spirit*. How are they manifest? How are they resolved—if they are resolved? Group 1, between those who have the power and those who want the power; group 2, between genders; group 3, between parents and their children; group 4, internal conflicts.

2. Keep a journal and sketchbook with responses to reading.

3. Investigate and report about natural resource issues on local Indian reservations.

4. Write your own Gospel.

5. Compare the subversion and manipulation by wealthy whites in Oklahoma with the 1690 situation in Salem, Massachusetts, as told in Arthur Miller's *Crucible*.

Works Cited

Annual Reports of the Department of the Interior and Indian Affairs, Report of the Commissioner and Appendixes. 1874–1902. Washington, DC: Government Printing Office.

DeMallie, Raymond, and Douglas R. Parks. 1987. *Sioux Indian Religion: Tradition and Innovation.* Norman: University of Oklahoma Press.

Denig, Edwin Thompson. 1961. *Five Indian Tribes of the Upper Missouri.* Norman: University of Oklahoma Press.

Grobsmith, Elizabeth. 1981. *Lakota of the Rosebud.* New York: Holt, Rinehart & Winston.

Jahner, Elaine A. 1983. Introduction to *Lakota Myth,* by James R. Walker. Lincoln: University of Nebraska Press.

Powers, Marilyn Marla Nancy. 1990. *Oglala Women in Myth, Ritual, and Reality.* Dissertation. New Brunswick: Rutgers University—The State University of New Jersey.

The Reservations. 1995. The American Indians Series. New York: Time-Life Books.

Welch, Deborah. 1985. *American Leader: The Story of Gertrude Bonnin.* Dissertation. Laramie: University of Wyoming.

4

Bibliography of Resources for Teachers

Most of the resources listed below provide general information. However, they are especially good for identifying more specific sources for further research. Some of the selections grouped under "Educational Resources" are geared for the primary (designated "P," K–3) and intermediate ("I," 4–6) levels, but the lessons and suggestions can work with students in grades 7–12 ("S") as well.

Historical and Cultural Resources

The American Indians. 1992–1996. Henry Woodhead, series ed. Alexandria, VA: Time-Life Books.

This series is a lengthy and comprehensive historical and cultural resource. Relying on regional consultants for each subject area, as well as historians and anthropologists with extensive backgrounds in tribal history, each book demonstrates the diversity of Indian peoples while it also recognizes and affirms what they have in common. Several of the selections, authors, and resources listed in *Roots and Branches* are referred to in the narratives in this series. Averaging 175 pages each, the books include historical narration, photographs and drawings, bibliography, and index. Some of the consultants are connected with the D'Arcy McNickle Center for the History of the American Indian at the Newberry Library in Chicago.

Champagne, Duane, ed. *The Chronology of Native North American History.* Detroit, MI: Gale Research, 1994. 574 pp.

This is an excellent resource for a comprehensive listing of historical and cultural events about the Native peoples of North America and Canada, and it includes black and white paintings and photos. The *Chronology* includes: Tribal Chronologies; an introductory narrative of Indian history; a Historical Time Line; and Native North American History, separated into three time blocks, with short biographies of many North American Indians, specific dates and descriptions of federal Indian policies and related acts, individual episodes of strong Indian resistance, and contributions by Indians to education, literature, and the general economy; American Indian Orators; Documents of History; Excerpts from Significant Legal Cases; and a General Bibliography.

Fixico, Donald L. *Termination and Relocation: Federal Indian Policy, 1945–1960.* Albuquerque: University of New Mexico Press, 1990. 268 pp.

Operating on the assumption that both Indians and bureaucrats favored a modernized society, with the Indian integrating into the mainstream of modern America, the federal government pursued a policy of "terminating the government's trust relationship over Indian lands and relocating the native residents to new homes in urban areas" (ix). Detailing postwar Indian policies and their devastating effects on Indian peoples, Fixico concludes that the policy failed: "Ironically, the federal government did not learn from its history of relations with Native American peoples that no single policy can be devised that will successfully serve all Indians, who represent many different tribes, languages, and cultures" (197). *Termination and Relocation* includes a Preface that briefly covers federal policy from early 1800s to World War II; nine chapters that conclude with an evaluation of the policies; maps and extensive notes; and an epilogue that looks at policies of the 1960s and 1970s. This is an excellent resource for understanding the devastating social, political, economic, and cultural influences on many of our contemporary writers.

Foreman, Grant. *Indian Removal: The Emigration of the Five Civilized Tribes of Indians.* Norman: University of Oklahoma Press, 1989. 423 pp.

Based on diaries and letters, as well as other primary resources, this book examines in detail the tragic consequences for the Choctaw, Creek, Chickasaw, Cherokee, and Seminole tribes due to their removal from Native lands to the Indian Territory west of the Mississippi, beginning in 1830. All teachers working with nineteenth-century history should read this book. Students can use specific sections for research into the historical experiences of these tribes. At the close of his Preface, Foreman says that "this tragic phase of American history is best understood if one will remember that for the most part the southern

Indians were people of fixed habits and tastes. They were not nomads . . . they were rooted in the soil as the Choctaw chief Pushmataha said, 'where we have grown up as the herbs of the woods.' . . . It is doubtful if white people . . . can understand the sense of grief and desolation that overwhelmed the Indians when they were compelled to leave all these behind forever and begin the long sad journey toward the setting sun which they called the Trail of Tears" (Preface), the death march that took the lives of thousands.

Hoxie, Frederick E. *A Final Promise: The Campaign to Assimilate the Indians, 1880–1920.* Cambridge, MA: Cambridge University Press, 1989. 350 pp.

Frederick Hoxie is director of the D'Arcy McNickle Center for the History of the American Indian at the Newberry Library in Chicago, and he has served as a major consultant to the Time-Life series, *The American Indians.* In his Preface to *Final Promise,* Hoxie makes clear his focus: "My study is a work of history: I discuss individual events, particular ideas, certain pieces of legislation, and important actors. But the point of the discussion is to place the assimilation campaign in the context of a national experience. . . . With this work, we should be able to move away from the accusations of guilt and professions of innocence and begin to understand better both the actions of the inscrutable white man and the responses of Native Americans" (xvi–xvii).

Indians of North America Series. New York: Chelsea House.
    Hoover, Herbert T. *The Yankton Sioux.* 1988. 94–144 pp.
    Hoxie, Frederick E. *The Crow.* 1989. 94–144 pp.
    Porter, Frank W. *The Coast Salish Peoples.* 1989. 94–144 pp.

Chelsea's English catalog includes curriculum programs with literatures traditionally taught in America's English classrooms, as well as works by Black and Hispanic writers and modern men and women writers. As of this publication, it doesn't offer any Native American literatures, but this historical series is one of the best available. Other historical titles from Chelsea House include *The Apache; The American Indians; Archaelogy of North America; The Aztecs; The Cherokee; The Cheyenne; The Chickasaw; The Chumash; The Comanche; The Iroquois; The Lenapes; Literatures of the American Indian; The Maya; The Mohawk; The Navajos; The Nez Perce; The Ojibwa; The Pueblo; The Seminole; The Wampanoag;* and *Women in American Indian Society.*

Jennings, Francis. *The Invasion of America: Indians, Colonialism, and the Cant of Conquest.* New York: Norton, 1976. 369 pp.

This is an essential resource for teachers of American literature because it provides primary source material on William Bradford, John Smith, and other early American figures who have become part of the American myth system. Although students may be shocked by the "new" information they get from this book, they will learn to appreciate the way history textbooks have been reduced to simple conclusions and resultant stereotypes. They can learn to further question whatever they read and hear; they can learn how to conduct research themselves; and they can appreciate the power of language to change the course of history. For example, Jennings suggests that John Smith began to use the word "savage" with respect to Indian peoples when the Indians were of no more use to him and when he desired both military and monetary assistance to remove them.

At the conclusion of his Preface, Jennings says that "The issue is not whether something had to happen, but whether it has to happen again. I have made the assumption that human persons do have some power of choice over their own conduct and that their adherence to moral standards, whatever those standards may be, is a matter of historical concern" (viii).

McNickle, D'Arcy (Salish). *Native American Tribalism: Indian Survivals and Renewals.* London: Oxford University Press, 1973. 190 pp.

Although the events at Wounded Knee, South Dakota, in January of 1973 weren't recorded in this work, McNickle prefaces this publication with references to that anger and violence and the right of Native American people to remain a separate and identifiable people. One way to ensure that right is to use the "word" with all its power to carefully explore the history of tribal relations on this continent since the colonists first arrived. The book begins with a "Generalized View," moves through the last four centuries, and then identifies the surviving peoples and cultures who won't be "lost in anonymity" but will continue to survive as an "integrating tribal people" (170). This is a most important resource for teachers and students who want to know the unromantic Indian experience with America's "manifest destiny."

The Native Americans Series. 1994. Atlanta, GA: TBS Productions. Videocassettes. 48 min. each.

These excellent videos, featuring Native American educators, leaders, poets, and video producers, tell the history and culture of their peoples from precontact up to the present, with Joy Harjo (Creek) providing much of the narration.

Part I. The Tribal People of the Northwest: Living in Harmony with the Land—Lummi, Salish, Chumash, Colville, Yakima.

Part II. The Nations of the Northeast: The Strength and Wisdom of the Confederacies—Iroquois, Mohawk, Seneca, Penobscot, Oneida, Wampanoag.

Part III. The People of the Great Plains (Part One): Buffalo People and Dog Days—Crow, Comanche, Sioux, Kiowa, Arapaho.

Part IV. The People of the Great Plains (Part Two): The Coming of the Horses, the White Man and the Rifle—Crow, Comanche, Sioux, Kiowa, Arapaho.

Part V. The Natives of the Southwest: Artists, Innovators and Rebels—Pueblo Peoples, Hopi, Navajo, Pima, Isleta, Apache.

Part VI. The Tribes of the Southeast: Persistent Cultures of Resilient People—Choctaw, Seminole, Chickasaw, Creek, Cherokee.

Sheehan, Bernard W. *Seeds of Extinction: Jeffersonian Philanthropy and the American Indian.* New York: Norton, 1974. 301 pp.

This is an important book for readers who want a detailed description of the ways in which personal world view and bias both *affect* and *effect* events. *Seeds of Extinction* is a study of the "white man's *ideas* about himself and the Indian" (x). In three sections (Metaphysics; Program; and Illusions), Sheehan explores the roots of Thomas Jefferson's philosophical ideas and surrounding patterns of "humanitarian" thinking. Sheehan does not pass judgment, but he does provide thorough research into the terrible violence and disintegration of Indian peoples that occurred as a result of Jeffersonian policies: "The Indian became a victim of the white man's proclivity for conceptualization and idealization. . . . Typically, Jeffersonian thinking stressed the improving aspects of the human situation" (8). But Sheehan also believes that the major "crime" of philanthropy was its treatment of "the native more like a precious abstraction than a living human being," wanting the best for the Indian and believing that would be "the elimination of the tribal order" (12). *Seeds of Extinction* is an important historical work, but Sheehan's own non-Native bias directs his rhetoric and argument—it appears that he assumes the Indian was not civilized.

Where the Spirit Lives. Anthony-Borgese Communications Presentation. Off Hollywood Video. New York: Studio Entertainment, 1989. 120 min.

An excellent "work of fiction," this two-hour PG-rated film, written by Keith Ross Leckie, directed by Bruce Pittman, and starring Michelle St. John, presents the dark side of North American assimilationist practices. Using school extras from the Blood Tribe and Six Nations Reserves, as well as songs sung by traditional drummers and music written by Buffy Sainte-Marie, *Where the Spirit Lives* makes a remarkable contribution to the list of important resources.

Set in the 1930s in an Alberta Indian Residential School, *Where the Spirit Lives* rings true for tens of thousands of Native peoples and their ancestors. The film opens on a Native village in Northern Alberta where children play and participate in traditional rituals, until an Indian agent arrives and offers them candy and a "ride" in his plane. With this kidnapping they enter an environment where they experience emotional and, sometimes, sexual abuse. Separated from parents and home, the children are taken to an Indian Residential School where the Anglican leaders and teachers will discipline them until their Native language, dress, religion, and all other manners of their "Indianness" have disappeared. The story centers on the oldest girl taken, who resists her name change, resists their forced assimilationist practices, and continues to speak her language and practice her Native traditions. An idealistic young teacher sympathizes with the children and succeeds in teaching "Amelia" how to read and write English. But her apparent collaboration with administrators who lie to Amelia, telling her that her parents have died in a smallpox epidemic, brings about Amelia and her brother's final flight back to her homeland "Where the Spirit Lives."

Where the Spirit Lives can be used in history as well as literature classes to introduce works by a number of authors such as Louise Erdrich, Linda Hogan, Zitkala-Ša, Sherman Alexie, and a number of Canadian Native writers who also portray young people and the emotional, social, and physical consequences of their attending boarding schools distant from their homelands.

Winds of Change: A Matter of Choice. American Indian Collection. PBS Home Video, 1991. 1-800-776-8300. 60 min.

Winds of Change is an excellent video about the Native experience with "living between two worlds." Originally produced by Wisconsin Public Television, this video portrays the contemporary experience of several: those who have remained on the reservation, those who have left, and those who have returned. Hattie Kaufman (Nez Perce/German) narrates, exploring the lives of Hopi women and men as examples of the new opportunities reservation communities can offer while maintaining traditional values and lifeways: "the importance of place, extended family, spirituality, and the connection between homeland, tribal identity, and world view." Speakers share their personal conflicts and the ways they struggle for balance between the old ways and the contemporary world; the ways they work to overcome the consequences of boarding school deculturation, which separated children from parents for many years; and the ways they succeed in the contemporary business world, bringing it into the Hopi community; and finally, the ways they succeed in the economic and social world off the reservation. As they share the possibilities for individual and communal resolutions, they affirm the family as most important to all Indian peoples.

For Further Reading

Adams, David Wallace. *Education for Extinction: American Indians and the Boarding School Experience, 1875–1928.* Lawrence: University of Kansas Press, 1995.

American Indian: A Multimedia Encyclopedia. Version 1.0. Facts on File, 1993. [ISBN: 0-8160-2835-4].

A resource for treaties, land grants, and other rare documents from the National Archives, as well as complete texts of books, audio excerpts from authentic Indian songs, more than 100 legends, maps, time lines, and more 900 photographs which cover 150 tribes from across the continent.

Barreiro, José (Guajiro), ed. *Indian Roots of American Democracy.* Akwe:kon Press, 1992. 209 pp.

The story of the Haudenosaunee, Native people of the Northeast, who introduced colonists to the "Great Law of Peace," which was later incorporated into the U.S. Constitution.

Beck, Peggy V., Anna Lee Walters (Pawnee/Otoe), and Nia Francisco (Navajo). *The Sacred: Ways of Knowledge, Sources of Life.* Tsaile, AZ: Navajo Community College Press, 1988. 368 pp.

A comprehensive examination of the multicultural tradition of Native America, written originally as a textbook for college Native American studies.

Bowker, Ardy (Eastern Cherokee). *Sisters in the Blood: The Education of Women in Native America.* Newton, MA: WEEA Publishing Center, 1993. 354 pp.

A comprehensively researched study of Native Americans in education, and of Native American women in particular, which also draws significant conclusions about the critical position teachers held in the lives of these women.

Bruchac, Joseph (Abenaki). *Roots of Survival: Native American Storytelling and the Sacred.* Golden, CO: Fulcrum, 1996. 206 pp.

A collection of essays detailing the living nature of stories and their purpose and place in Native American lives.

The Civilization of the American Indian Series. Norman: University of Oklahoma Press.

Comprising the most extensive list of resources available, this is a series of 139 separate publications by noted historians and Native American writers. *Roots and Branches* includes several of these publications, listed separately by author.

Clark, William P. *Indian Sign Language.* Lincoln: University of Nebraska Press, 1982. 443 pp.

Cohoe, William. *A Cheyenne Sketchbook.* Norman: University of Oklahoma Press, 1964.

A collection of ledger drawings from a Plains Indian's past and also from his imprisonment in Florida in 1875.

Costo, Rupert. *Indian Treaties: Two Centuries of Dishonor.* San Francisco: Indian Historian Press, 1978. 283 pp.

Danky, James P., ed. *Native American Periodicals and Newspapers, 1828–1982.* New York: Greenwood Press, 1984. 532 pp.

Deloria, Vine (Sioux). *Custer Died for Your Sins: An Indian Manifesto.* Norman: University of Oklahoma Press, 1988. 279 pp.

An Indian point of view of U.S. race relations, federal bureaucracies, Christian churches, and social scientists.

Dixon, Joseph Kossuth. *The Vanishing Race: The Last Great Indian Council.* New York: Popular Library, 1972.

A record in picture and story of the "Last Great Indian Council," with Indian chiefs from nearly every reservation in the United States in attendance—first published in 1913.

Eagle Walking Turtle [Gary McClain] (Choctaw). *Indian America: A Traveler's Companion.* Santa Fe, NM: John Muir Publications, 1995.

> An updated guide that tells the traveler how to find over 300 Indian tribes, where and when visitors are welcome, what ceremonies are performed, what arts and crafts are produced, and where historical sites may be found.

Fedullo, Mick. *Light of the Feather.* New York: Wm. Morrow, 1992. 256 pp.

> A narrative in which Fedullo, an adopted Crow, relates his experiences with the various tribal groups and the way those experiences caused him to drop his own stereotypes for more realistic images of Indian peoples today.

Fowler, Loretta. *Arapahoe Politics, 1851–1978: Symbols in Crises of Authority.* Lincoln: University of Nebraska Press, 1986. 373 pp.

> A demonstration of the way one group of Native American people resisted and accommodated to acculturation pressures.

The Great Law of Peace and the Constitution of the United States of America. Rooseveltown, NY: Akwesasne Notes. 15 pp.

Hertzberg, Hazel W. *The Search for an American Indian Identity: Modern Pan-Indian Movements.* Syracuse, NY: Syracuse University Press, 1981. 362 pp.

> A history of Indian affairs on a national basis covering the years 1889 through 1934.

Hirschfelder, Arlene B. *American Indian and Eskimo Authors.* New York: Association on American Indian Affairs, 1973. 99 pp.

Howard, Joseph Kinsey. *Strange Empire: A Narrative of the Northwest.* New York: Wm. Morrow, 1952. 601 pp.

> A historical narrative that integrates the life and death of Louis Riel with the history of contemporary Canadian and United States military and economic policies and actions, as well as with the history of other related Indian peoples.

Josephy, Alvin M. Jr. *The Nez Perce Indians and the Opening of the Northwest.* Boston: Houghton Mifflin, 1997. 705 pp.

Katz, William Loren. *Black Indians: A Hidden Heritage.* New York: Atheneum, 1986. 196 pp.

> The history of relations between Blacks and American Indians through pioneer days, with black-and-white photographs.

Mihesuah, Devon A. (Choctaw). *American Indians: Stereotypes and Realities*. Atlanta, GA: Clarity Press, 1997. 152 pp.

Morey, Sylvester M., and Olivia Gilliam. *Respect for Life: The Traditional Upbringing of American Indian Children*. New York: Myrin Institute, 1974. 202 pp.

A report of discussions at Harper's Ferry, West Virginia, between Navajo, Mohawk, Crow, Kiowa, Pueblo, and Arapaho people regarding a most critical issue: the lives of their children in today's world.

Native Peoples Magazine. Phoenix, AZ: Media Concepts Group, Inc.

A quarterly publication of culture, history, and art.

Oliver, Eileen Iscoff. *Crossing the Mainstream: Multicultural Perspectives in Teaching Literature*. Urbana, IL: National Council of Teachers of English, 1994. 235 pp.

Resource Reading List. Toronto: CASNIP.

An annotated bibliography of books by and about Native peoples, assembled by the Canadian Alliance in Solidarity with Native People, with topics including: Books for Elementary Schools; Teaching Resources; Books for Youth and Adults; and Back of the Books.

Rutledge, Don (Cree). *Center of the World: Native American Spirituality*. North Hollywood, CA: Newcastle, 1992. 128 pp.

An explanation of the world view of early Native Americans, the basic beliefs and ways of the Native American Tradition, from the perspective of a Plains Cree Pipe Keeper.

Scott, Patricia. *Chippewa and Cree*. Rocky Boy, MT: Rocky Boy School, 1976. 277 pp.

A bibliography of books, newspaper articles, government documents, and other printed and written materials in various libraries of the United States and Canada.

Sneve, Virginia Driving Hawk (Lakota). Native History Series. New York: Holiday House.

Books for intermediate level readers about the culture and history of individual tribes, including *The Apaches* (1997), *The Cheyennes* (1996), *The Cherokees* (1996), *The Hopis* (1995), *The Iroquois* (1995), *The Navajos* (1993), *The Nez Perce* (1994), *The Seminoles* (1994), and *The Sioux* (1995).

Stedman, Raymond W. *Shadows of the Indian: Stereotypes in American Culture.* Norman: University of Oklahoma Press, 1982. 282 pp.

Usner, Daniel H., Jr. *Indians, Settlers, and Slaves in a Frontier Exchange Economy: The Lower Mississippi Valley before 1783.* Chapel Hill: University of North Carolina Press, 1990. 294 pp.

An examination of the economic and cultural interactions among the Indians, Europeans, and African slaves of colonial Lousiana, including the province of West Florida.

Educational Resources

Allen, Paula Gunn, ed. *Studies in American Indian Literature: Critical Essays and Course Designs.* New York: Modern Language Association of America, 1983. 384 pp.
Grade Level: S

This collection begins with Paula Gunn Allen's own essay, "The Sacred Hoop: A Contemporary Perspective," which explicates the oral tradition of non-Western literature for Western readers. The book also includes the following sections:

Section One: Three possible course designs for teaching Oral Literature: an Introduction to American Indian Oral Traditions; Lakota Oral Literature; and Creation and Trickster Narratives.

Section Two: Personal Narratives and Autobiography, with essays about these narratives, and three possible course designs for teaching Indian Personal Narratives.

Section Three: Five essays about American Indian Women's Literature together with three possible course designs.

Section Four: Essays by Ruoff, Jahner, Hogan and others, together with six possible course designs about Contemporary American Indian Literature.

Section Five: The Indian in American Literature and the prevalence of stereotypes throughout that literature.

Studies in American Indian Literature also includes bibliographies of anthologies, texts, research, and periodicals, by A. LaVonne Brown Ruoff, as well as other bibliographies of periodicals, special issues, and presses. This is an invaluable critical resource for all secondary and college-level teachers of American Indian literatures.

Caduto, Michael J., and Joseph Bruchac (Abenaki), eds. *Keepers of the Earth: Native American Stories and Environmental Activities for Children.* Golden, CO: Fulcrum, 1988. 208 pp.
Grade Level: P, I, S

Keepers of the Earth is the flagship book in a series that also includes *Keepers of the Animals, Keepers of Life,* and *Keepers of the Night. Keepers of the Earth* provides stories from various tribal orientations, together with a *Teacher's Guide* and a list of other resources. The stories are organized under the following subjects: Creation; Fire; Earth; Wind and Weather; Water; Sky; Seasons; Plants and Animals; Life-Death-Spirit; and Unity of Earth. Many of the classroom activities inspire environmental awareness. Although the series aims at the primary through intermediate levels, any of the books works well in secondary classes because individuals of any age can identify with the characters in the stories. The stories in *Keepers of the Earth* are also featured in Bruchac's anthology, *Native American Stories.* Because the present volume cannot provide a complete discussion of all texts, and because of the availability of the *Keepers* series, this review includes a more detailed description of individual stories that I hope will serve as examples for ways in which other texts might be used.

The Abenaki story "Gluscabi and the Game Animals" is a favorite of intermediate and secondary students. Featuring Gluscabi, the Abenaki trickster/transformer figure, this story teaches many lessons, but the most obvious is the individual's responsibility to respect nature now and for future generations. Gluscabi goes hunting with a magic bag in which he traps all the animals of the world. After his grandmother expresses her disappointment over his insensitivity to the importance of maintaining a balance and harmony between all things, Gluscabi returns the animals to the forest. Bruchac says that when telling the story, he has had participants share over a dozen different and valid interpretations of the tale.

The Lakota creation story "Tunka-shila, Grandfather Rock" tells about the journey of "all things" to Earth, where "out of the waters, a great burning rock rose up," making dry land appear so life on Earth could begin. The rock is called "Grandfather" because it is the oldest. In Chapter 8, Caduto makes the connection between this story and the action of volcanoes erupting to form "molten rock . . . steam, heat, ash and fire" (57). In essence, science and the Lakota people are telling the same story.

In the traditional Inuit story "Sedna, the Woman Under the Sea," Sedna falls in love with a seabird in the form of a man, who lures her to his impoverished home far away. There she realizes her mistake and sings a song to her father: "The birds do not look kindly / on me, for I am a stranger. / Cold winds blow about my bed / and I have little food" (96). Her father finally comes to rescue her, and in their escape across the sea, her father cuts off the ends of her fingers, which fall and become whales and seals. According to Caduto, the story teaches the "importance of the whales and seals as food, and how the angakok or shaman can influence Sedna to assure successful hunting of these animals" (97). Demonstrating the value of communal survival and the foolishness of an individual's pursuit of singular happiness, this story may help students to discover how its values contrast with the predominant individualism of the novel *Julie of the Wolves* by Jeanne Craighead George.

"White Buffalo Calf Woman and the Sacred Pipe" is a Lakota story in which the White Buffalo Calf Woman gives the people the Sacred Pipe, which represents animals, plants, and breath. She also gives them the lessons and rituals that will help them continue to live with respect and in harmony with all things.

"How Coyote Was the Moon" is the Kalispel story of how Coyote became the moon and used his position to spy on the people of the Earth below. Consequently, the people who "wished to do things in secret" took Coyote out of the sky. The story shows how individuals can improve their situations through action.

The Siksika (Blackfeet) story "The Origin of Death" teaches the importance of living with the consequences of our decisions. In the beginning, when the "world was new," Old Man and Old Woman decided how humans should look and how long they should live.

"How Turtle Flew South for the Winter," a Dakota story, tells of why only birds fly south for the winter and also why turtles sleep all winter. The story also communicates the importance of "keeping your mouth shut."

Teachers who are looking for available and authentic materials will find the books in the *Keepers* series invaluable.

Fedullo, Mick. *It's Like My Heart Pounding: Imaginative Writing for American Indian Students.* Ogden, UT: Weber State College, Mountain West Educational Equity Center, 1990.
Grade Level: P, I, S

Mick Fedullo now lives on the Crow Reservation in Pryor, Montana. He has taught writing to Indian students throughout the United States, and this excellent publication presents his educational philosophy, his approaches for the teaching of imaginative writing, and eighteen specific assignments.

Fedullo's first chapter, "Copyright; Plagiarism; Words Not to Use; Titles; Stanzas; When and How to End a Poem; Rhythm; The Matter of Rhythm; Revision," provides a curriculum he recommends for grades four through nine, but any of the lessons may be adapted for either lower or higher grades. Even teachers who have little experience with writing poetry will find this resource easy to use.

Fedullo's second chapter is entitled "Setting the Mood; Technical Terms; Focusing; Writing Time; Creative Silence; Positive Criticism." The eighteen lessons in Chapter Two "follow a sequence which advances from an emphasis on learning new expressive language techniques to exploring both personal and tribal values, while always involving the students in writing their own experiences" (vii). But Fedullo has found that older students are more interested in the values, and so he suggests teachers might want to "work backwards, or mix up the value-oriented lessons with the technique-oriented lessons" (vii).

Fedullo suggests that his "Formula for Success" is the following "four-step" pattern:

1. Model poems

2. Discussions

3. Writing time

4. Oral reading of work

Fedullo doesn't intend to create a multitude of "Indian poets"; instead he wants to "take the fear out of writing" and "build the self-confidence so necessary in completing an education and facing the future" (vii). Evidence of his program's success exists in the enthusiastic communities of poets he leaves behind, and in the increasing number of publications which feature his students' poetry.

No other "imaginative writing" resource for teaching Indian children, or for teaching non-Indian children who are living in a community with Indian peoples, can equal this one.

Francis, Lee (Laguna Pueblo), and James Bruchac (Abenaki), eds. *Reclaiming the Vision, Past, Present, and Future: Native Voices for the Eighth Generation.* Greenfield Center, NY: Greenfield Review Press, 1996. 153 pp.
Grade Level: S

This volume is the result of the work of many of the Native writers who had been a part of "Returning the Gift" (the July

1992 conference of more than 200 North American Native writers) and the Native mentoring organization Wordcraft Circle (an outgrowth of the 1992 festival). It includes transcripts from the plenary sessions of "Returning the Gift," including Leslie Silko's comments about Native writing and Native identity; Eleanor Sioui's comments about poetry writing; and Carter Revard's comments about the way he developed a Native American literature course: "I didn't think of the literature as just 'here are these words on the page that I'm teaching in class.' I thought of it as coming from the People all over the country who are trying to say 'we're here'" (25) *Reclaiming the Vision* also includes an anthology of poetry and prose by "Emerging Native Voices," sections on storytelling, the writing of poetry, fiction and autobiography, and lessons and exercises in "Writer's Workshops" that use Native American writing to generate work from student writers. This section is especially useful for teachers because the workshops were written by published Native writers. Each one focuses on one or two short poems or memoirs, with background discussion about the poet and culture, followed by discussion questions and writing exercises. Joseph Bruchac believes that "*Reclaiming the Vision* is a book to be treasured by anyone interested in Native American literature or the teaching of Native American students." I agree.

Indian Reading Series. Portland, OR: Northwest Regional Educational Laboratories, 1977–82.
Grade Level: P, I

Intended as a supplemental reading program to help children improve reading comprehension and enhance verbal and written communication, this series also aims to develop and reinforce students' positive self-image and pride. All of the story content has been researched, written, and illustrated by American Indians. The National Institute of Education, participating tribes, and the Pacific Northwest Indian Program of the Northwest Regional Educational Laboratory, a group of more than 250 "reservation-based planners, writers, and artists" cooperated to produce this series, which was tested for more than five years and has been used in the following programs: Language Arts; Indian Language and Culture; Special Education; Multicultural Awareness; Gifted and Talented; Head Start; Adult Basic Education; and Libraries.

According to the *Northwest Report*, Northwest Regional Educational Laboratory: "The pages are alive with the animals and birds that shared the Indian's domain—coyotes and buffalo, eagles and ravens, bears, whales, and wild horses. Told with grace, wit, and wisdom, the stories have been handed down over many generations from a time when storytelling was the vehicle for transmitting culture, for teaching values and survival skills, and for explaining natural phenomena."

Although each of the four teacher's manuals suggest activities to accompany the stories, almost sixty pages in the *Levels I, II, and III Teacher's Manual* explain and illustrate the following teaching activities: Dramatization; Talking About; Retelling the Story; Writing Down; In Other Words (Making Books): and Word Study. The *Level IV Teacher's Manual* provides historical information about the participating reservation communities, including Flathead, Blackfeet, Fort Belknap, Fort Peck, and Northern Cheyenne. "Teacher Guided Activities" accompany each story for this level. The *Level V Teacher's Manual* provides vocabulary studies and science and social studies activities. The series also includes a *Parent/Teacher Guide.* Elementary as well as secondary schools will find this an invaluable resource for the teaching of Native American literatures.

The series includes ninety-nine student booklets, one book, four teacher's manuals and a parent/teacher guide. The series is currently out of print, but it is available online through the Educational Resources Information Center's ERIC Document Reproduction Service at www.edrs.com, under ERIC Document Numbers ED258757–258766.

Plains Native American Literature. Multicultural Literature Collection. Virginia Seeley, series ed. Englewood Cliffs, NJ: Globe, 1993. 151 pp.
Grade Level: I, S

Compiled for the middle school level, this anthology is organized according to the following Western European and Native genres: Oral Tradition; Nonfiction; Fiction; Poetry; and Drama, although most are excerpts from larger works. Taken from widely published and more popular works, the selections represent a balance in gender and tribes from the area east of the Rocky Mountains to just west of the Mississippi River, from Southern Alberta and Saskatchewan to Southern Texas. Also, introductions to selections provide tribal, geographical, and historical information about each culture. The compilers hope to inspire students to appreciate the values and beliefs of these cultures. Questions and activities for thinking, writing, and speaking follow each selection, and the *Teacher's Resource Manual* provides more background, vocabulary exercises, questions for class discussion, suggestions for further reading, and assessment worksheets. This is a useful resource for teachers who want to introduce students to a variety of Native cultures and literatures and who want accessible tools for teaching. To "fill in the gaps about Indian boarding schools" in American history studies, middle school teachers have used readings such as Zitkala-Ša's "School Days of an Indian Girl."

Reyhner, Jon, ed. *Teaching American Indian Students.* Norman: University of Oklahoma Press, 1992. 328 pp.
Grade Level: All levels

Teaching American Indian Students, together with Ardy Bowker's *Sisters in the Blood,* should be required reading for all teachers of Native students. Originating at the Indian Bilingual Teacher Training Program at Eastern Montana College in Billings, Montana, it includes work done at many Indian schools, colleges, and universities. Essays, formal and informal studies, and personal experiences of educators who know Indian children, are organized into five sections: Multicultural Education; Instruction, Curriculum, and Community; Language Development; Reading and Literature; and Teaching in the Content Areas. Although the text reflects the work of twenty contributers, they all operate on the following assumptions: that new teachers on reservations know very little about the students they teach; that "American Indians can learn to participate successfully in white society while, at the same time, retaining their language and traditional Indian values" (77); that Indian students deserve to learn through strategies that meet their individual needs; and that Indian students will respond best when the classrooms are stimulating and when educators involve parents and communities in the process.

Slapin, Beverly, and Doris Seale (Santee/Cree), eds. *Through Indian Eyes: The Native Experience in Books for Children.* Philadelphia: New Society, 1992. 312 pp.
Grade Level: P, I, S

The purpose of *Through Indian Eyes* is to enlighten teachers of all children so that they might nurture their students "to grow up to create a more equitable, bias-free society" (2). For teachers at all levels, this is an invaluable resource for essays, poems, reviews, and bibliographies of literature by and about Indian peoples. Beverly Slapin's Introduction provides a background to American Indians' historical and cultural experiences that justifies such a publication. From Indian perspectives, six essays view Columbus Day, Thanksgiving, and popular literature taught in many K–12 schools. Thirty-three poems by Native writers provide a good way "to know the heart of a

People." Essays by Joseph Bruchac, Mary Gloyne Byler, Ceni Myles, Beth Brant, and Lenore Keeshig-Tobias express their Native insights into experiences with traditional Indian education and with education in America's schools. Slapin and Seale's eighty-four reviews of books currently used in the primary and intermediate grades are an important resource for teachers who are truly concerned about the ways literature can communicate both positive and dangerously negative stereotypes to young children. Examples and twenty-five criteria for evaluating books for racial bias and stereotypes follow the reviews. The book closes with an annotated list of resources, publication centers, and "A Selected Bibliography" of recommended works and authors. Teachers may use *Through Indian Eyes* as a resource, but many of the selections can be told or read aloud to students of all ages.

For Further Reading

Antell, Lee. *Indian Education: Guidelines for Evaluating Textbooks from an American Indian Perspective.* Denver, CO: Education Commission of the States, 1981. 19 pp.
Grade Level: P

Brewer, Linda Skinner (Choctaw). *'O Wakaga': Activities for Learning about the Plains Indians.* Seattle: Daybreak Star, 1984. 40 pp.
Grade Level: P, I

Caduto, Michael J. *All One Earth—Songs for the Generations.* Cedar House Sound and Mastering, 1994.
Grade Level: I, S

A musical companion to the *Keepers of the Earth* books on cassette and CD.

Caduto, Michael J., and Joseph Bruchac (Abenaki), eds. The Keepers Series. Golden, CO: Fulcrum.
Keepers of the Animals: Native American Stories and Wildlife Activities for Children. 1991. 286 pp.
Keepers of the Earth: Native American Stories and Environmental Activities for Children. 1988. 208 pp.
Keepers of Life: Discovering Plants through Native American Stories and Earth Activities for Children. 1994. 265 pp.
Keepers of the Night: Native American Stories and Nocturnal Activities for Children. 1994. 160 pp.
Grade Level: P, I, S

This series of books presents an excellent interdisciplinary approach to Indian culture and stories, with detailed explanations of storytelling methods, numerous activities regarding the specific cultures, as well as related areas of science and social studies, and explicit procedures for creative projects and activities.

Daybreak Star Indian Reader. Seattle, WA: Daybreak Star Press. 24 pp.
Grade Level: P, I

A monthly publication with cultural information, geographical locations, legends, word games and puzzles, and a nature science section.

"Finding Your Roots." No. 2364. Carson, CA 90746: Educational Insights, 1978.
Grade Level: I, S

An approach to research into heritage, using old newspapers, marriage and death certificates, inscriptions on books, family Bibles, etc.

Kovacs, Edna. *Writing across Cultures: A Handbook on Writing Poetry and Lyrical Prose.* Hillsboro, OR: Blue Heron, 1994. 165 pp.
Grade Level: I, S

Patacsil, Sharon (Blackfeet) and Colleen Neal (Squamish). *Daybreak Star Preschool Activities Book.* Seattle, WA: Daybreak Star Press, 1979.
Grade Level: P

Project Learning Tree. Olympia, WA: Western Regional Environmental Education Council, 1988.
Grade Level: P, I

A collection of written science and social studies activities in Native American cultural contexts.

Stott, Jon C. *Native Americans in Children's Literature.* Phoenix, AZ: Oryx Press, 1995. 238 pp.
Grade Level: P, I

Szumski, Bonnie. *Christopher Columbus: Recognizing Stereotypes.* Opposing Viewpoints Juniors. San Diego, CA: Greenhaven Press, 1992. 36 pp.
Grade Level: I, S

Verall, Catherine, and Lenore Keeship-Tobias, comp. *All My Relations: Sharing Native Values through the Arts.* Toronto: Canadian Alliance in Solidarity with Native Peoples, 1988. 120 pp.
Grade Level: P, I

Lessons featuring ways to express the values learned through creative drama, words, songs, art, and action.

Windy Boy, Sam, and Ruth Weasle (Chippewa/Cree). *Sign Language.* Rocky Boy, MT.

Grade Level: P, I, S

A video portraying the differences between Indian sign language and sign language as used by deaf people today. The video may be obtained by contacting the library at Stonechild College, Rocky Boy Reservation, Box Elder, MT.

Literary Criticism Resources

Owens, Louis (Choctaw/Cherokee). *Other Destinies: Understanding the American Indian Novel.* Norman: University of Oklahoma Press, 1992. 285 pp.

A professor of literature in the University of California–Santa Cruz, Louis Owens admits that "to begin to write about something called 'the American Indian novel' is to enter a slippery and uncertain terrain. Take one step into this region and we are confronted with difficult questions of authority and ethnicity" (3). But Owens uses Bakhtin's critical approach (and others) and places the texts within their cultural, historical, and geographical contexts, thereby establishing the studied texts as important literary representatives of literature in general as well as what he calls "the Native American Indian novel." The book is "for mixedbloods, the next generation," and the texts he has selected serve well to represent the multidimensional mixed-blood experience in the postcontact era. His Introduction (3–31) provides a valuable analysis of genre in the Native American novel:

1. Identity is the central issue and theme.
2. World views of "Indian" ways are almost always in direct conflict with the dominant *ideologemes* of Euramerica.
3. Authors are challenged to make themselves understood in a prose form, and a language, quite foreign to traditional Native American discourse.
4. Trickster tales, the crucial role of play and humor, are integral to many contemporary Indian novels and stories.
5. Many works do not reinforce traditional cultural values embodied in [European American] canonical texts.
6. Protagonists frequently resemble the typically displaced, modernist figure.
7. The authors seek to transcend fragmentation, placing humanity within a carefully, cyclically ordered cosmos, giving humankind

irreducible responsibility for the maintenance of that delicate equilibrium.

8. Many include an intense didacticism and insistence upon certain immutable values.

9. The word has very real power.

10. Indian writers today have come to expect, even demand, that readers learn something about the mythology and literary (oral) history of Native Americans, and about crucial moments in Native American history of the past two centuries.

In this collection of criticism, Owens examines the works of John Rollin Ridge, Mourning Dove, John Joseph Mathews, D'Arcy McNickle, N. Scott Momaday, James Welch, Leslie Silko, Louise Erdrich, Michael Dorris, and Gerald Vizenor. Secondary school teachers will find this an important resource.

Ruoff, A. LaVonne Brown, ed. *Literatures of the American Indian.* Indians of North America Series. New York: Chelsea House, 1991. 109 pp.

Probably the best and most thorough narrative resource for teachers and students of American Indian literatures, *Literatures of the American Indian* briefly looks at American tribal history, defines "literature" and its relevance to American Indian peoples, explains the meaning of *ceremony* and *song* to American Indians, and shares their traditions in story and in painting. Ruoff also examines the time of contact and "As-Told-To" oratory and autobiography first written in English. She summarizes Native writing in English from 1772–1967, and then describes the Native American "Literary Renaissance," beginning with N. Scott Momaday's book *House Made of Dawn,* which won the Pulitzer Prize in 1969. Illustrated with photographs and samples of Indian art, the text weaves bibliographic information and excerpts from many works into a very readable narrative. In absolute denial of the the notion that "Indian is Artifact," the book closes with a poem by Simon Ortiz: "It Doesn't End, Of Course . . . in all soothing / the aches of all years, / it doesn't end" (101).

Witalec, Janet, ed. *Native North American Literature: Biographical and Critical Information on Native Writers and Orators from the United States and Canada from Historical Times to the Present.* Detroit, MI: Gale Research, 1994. 706 pp.

For teachers who want a single resource about American Indian literature and authors, *Native North American Literature* is invaluable. Like the yearly publication *Contemporary Literary*

Criticism, also by Gale, *Native North American Literature* provides a comprehensive collection of biography and published criticism about seventy-eight Native North American writers, storytellers, and orators. Lists of "Major Native Nations" according to regions, and maps of reservations and culture groups follow the Preface. Three separate indexes help readers locate specific authors and texts—Tribal Index; Genre Index; and Title Index. Students who want to know more about Native authors they are reading will find *NNAL* interesting and helpful. *Native North American Literature* is a resource for all school and public libraries, but it should also be available in classrooms where students are regularly reading Native literatures.

For Further Reading

Bataille, Gretchen M., and Kathleen Mullen Sands. *American Indian Women: Telling Their Lives.* Lincoln: University of Nebraska Press, 1984. 209 pp.

Bevis, William W. *Ten Tough Trips: Montana Writers and the West.* Seattle: University of Washington Press, 1990. 233 pp.

Lincoln, Kenneth. "Introduction: Sending a Voice." In *Native American Renaissance.* Berkeley: University of California Press, 1983, pp. 1–14.

Ruoff, A. LaVonne Brown. *American Indian Literatures: An Introduction, Bibliographic Review, and Selected Bibliography.* New York: Modern Language Association of America, 1990. 200 pp.

Studies in American Indian Literatures. A Journal of the Association for the Study of American Indian Literatures. University of Richmond VA 23173

The only scholarly journal that focuses exclusively on American Indian literatures (published quarterly).

Swann, Brian, and Arnold Krupat, eds. *Recovering the Word: Essays on Native American Literature.* Berkeley: University of California Press, 1987. 644 pp.

5

Bibliography of Anthologies

Some of the following collections represent Native voices from across the continent, while others are more specific to the North Central and North Western regions. For some collections, themes and genres are not designated because they are specific to individual selections in the text. Although this list is in no way exhaustive, most of these collections are available, and they represent works that can create a high level of student interest.

Achimoona. Introduction by Maria Campbell (Métis). Saskatoon, Saskatchewan: Fifth House, 1992. 98 pp.

Genre: Traditional/Contemporary Story

Themes: Remembering the Old Ways; At Home Within Circles; Change and Growth; Between Two Worlds

Grade Level: I, S

With an available teacher's guide, this is an excellent collection of Cree stories by Native writers who met at Gabriel's Crossing, Batoche, Saskatchewan, in March 1985. In her Introduction, Maria Campbell explains the meaning of *achimoona,* or stories, and the sacred craft of storytelling: "Storytelling was only done during the winter months and it had to stop when the frogs started to sing in the spring. . . . *Achimoona* are for everyone. Each person, young or old, finds the things in the story that are meant for him or her. That is one of the special gifts of the oral storyteller—to be able to weave all the lessons, messages or jokes into a story and not leave anyone out." The book includes eleven stories, biographical information on each storyteller, and full-color reproductions of artwork by Native artists such as Ruth Cuthand, Gerald McMaster, Raymond McCallum, and Lorne Fineday, which are accompanied by the artists' commentaries about their world views and their work. The Native protagonists interact with the voices from their surrounding natural and supernatural worlds, experience conflicts and resolutions with the neighboring white people and cultures, travel through traditional stories arising out of their contemporary situations, and learn the important value, "you must respect everything."

Allen, Paula Gunn (Laguna Sioux), ed. *Voice of the Turtle: American Indian Literature 1900–1970*. New York: Ballantine, 1994. 321 pp.
Grade Level: S

In the Introduction, Paula Gunn Allen provides a rationale and background for each writer and selection, beginning with E. Pauline Johnson and ending with Simon J. Ortiz: "The stories are an aggregate of U.S. history, national and international Native American history, spirituality, and personal narrative. Their structures, especially as the formative period of Native fiction drew to a close in 1970, came to resemble traditional Native narrative more and more while the voice, tone, and style ever more closely replicated a communal voice: multiple, integral, and accretive" (6). She goes on to say that "Native American fiction in the twentieth century has two sides: the Oral Tradition of the Native Nations, and Western fiction and its antecedents . . . [ceremonial texts and Western traditions] interact, as wings of a bird in flight interact" (7).

Voice of the Turtle offers readers moving and enlightening short stories and excerpts from longer works of the following writers, most of whom are rooted—and torn—in the Plains landscape and traditions: E. Pauline Johnson, Charles A. Eastman, Arthur C. Parker, Mourning Dove, Pretty-shield, Luther Standing Bear, Estelle Armstrong, John Oskison, Black Elk and John G. Neihardt, Zitkala-Ša, John Joseph Mathews, D'Arcy McNickle, Don C. Talayesva, N. Scott Momaday, Ronald Rogers, Grey Cohoe, and Simon Ortiz.

This is excellent reading for secondary students, especially, and teachers can use these essays to teach the themes suggested in *Roots and Branches,* especially "Between Two Worlds," and "Cultural and Personal Loss and Survival."

Bruchac, Joseph (Abenaki), ed. *Songs from this Earth on Turtle's Back.* New York: Greenfield Review Press, 1983. 294 pp.
Grade Level: I, S

Fifty-two contemporary poets, with brief biographies and pictures, are presented in this excellent and very readable anthology. In his Introduction, Bruchac says, "[These writers] share traditions of respect for the Earth and the natural world . . . they share strong folk cultures which have either been transmitted to them by family or learned through a continuing personal seeking. They share respect for the awesome power of the Word—power which can make or destroy, break or heal . . . they share English as a different language for them . . . the language brought by those who dispossessed them . . . they share the experience of being viewed as outsiders in their own land . . . and they share a high level of accomplishment, for they are among the best American poets . . . " (xi).

The poems described below reinforce the values of the Old Ways for Native peoples: the values of grandparents, land, and eternal relationships within the universe.

Duane Big Eagle (Osage). "My Grandfather was a Quantum Physicist." The speaker's grandfather always knew what scientists are just discovering today: "that the intimate details / of our lives / are influenced by things / beyond the stars / and beyond time." The poem teaches the value of Respect for Elders and Respect for Nature (22).

N. Scott Momaday (Kiowa). "The Delight Song of Tsoai-Talee" is Momaday's "Name" poem—his celebration of himself who stands in "good relation to the earth . . . to the gods . . . to all that is beautiful . . . to the daughter of Tsen-tainte / You see, I am alive, I am alive" (158). And the poem ends without a period. This poem is recorded in *N. Scott Momaday, Storyteller.* Narrated and read by the author, music and ambient effects by Rusty Crutcher. Native American Audio Library, Lotus Press. Sante Fe, NM: Sunset Productions Inc.

Ted D. Palmanteer (Colville). "Granma's Words." The poet offers his grandmother's remembrance of the Old Ways, her words of wisdom—a solution—for the bad times: "Be strong / in the heart, / nothing lasts / forever" (196).

Intermediate- and secondary-level students respond very positively to oral reading, and they especially enjoy drawing freely while they listen because the poems carry such strong concrete images and because the students say they "don't have to work." With any novels, stories, or essays involving family or environmental themes, these poems work to further the students' experience with literature.

Hirschfelder, Arlene B., and Beverly R. Singer, eds. *Rising Voices: Writings of Young Native Americans.* New York: Scribner, 1992. 107 pp.
Grade Level: P, I, S

These poems and short essays have been previously published in school publications and creative writing journals. Organized in six sections—Identity; Family; Homelands; Ritual and Ceremony; Education; and Harsh Realities—the poems represent the writing of children and young adults nationwide. In the Foreword, Hirschfelder says, "Young people speak to these issues with intelligence, dignity, wit, and remarkable insight. Their words bear vivid, often eloquent witness to the realities of their lives over the past hundred years" (1).

Kittredge, William, and Annick Smith, eds. *The Last Best Place: A Montana Anthology.* Helena: The Montana Historical Society Press, 1990. 1,158 pp.
Grade Level: S

Many selections throughout this anthology represent Native voices from Montana. An essay by James Welch prefaces the first section, "Native American Stories and Myths," and the twenty-eight selections represent eight Montana tribes. Although the section "Journals of Exploration" represents the non-Indian voice, it is useful to study for its early European American bias toward Montana Indian peoples.

The section "Stories of Early Pioneers and Indians" includes memoirs of tragic conflict and loss during the nineteenth century. For example, "Iron Teeth, a Cheyenne Old Woman," told to Thomas B. Marquis, begins with Iron Teeth's memories of her childhood in the Black Hills, the food they planted, and vegetable foods that grew wild. She tells about the traditional ways of Cheyenne women and the effect on her, and on her people, of the encroachment of whites into their lands. One of the Northern Cheyennes who were taken to Oklahoma, where they "all got sick with chills and fever," Iron Teeth was also one of those who followed Little Wolf in his escape to the Dakota country. After surrendering, they were taken to Fort Robinson, where they continued to experience persecution, freezing temperatures, and terrible hunger. Still, she and her party refused to return to Oklahoma. This memoir portrays the strength and bravery of just one woman who never failed to fight for her people and their right to live by the old ways. Speaking through an interpreter, she said, "I think the government ought to do better in keeping its promise to take care of the old Indians" (248). Teachers may use parts of this memoir (233–49), depending on the age of students and intended theme.

Contemporary Indian writers represented in this anthology include Minerva Allen (Assiniboine), Linda Weasel Head (Salish), James Welch (Blackfeet), D'Arcy McNickle (Salish), Debra Earling (Salish), John Tatsey (Blackfeet), and Roberta Hill Whiteman (Oneida).

One story that addresses the problems of being a young adult and living "Between Two Worlds" is Debra Earling's "Perma Red." With "faded" hair and "last night's liquor a cotton-dry whisper on her thick tongue," Louise hitchhikes back to Dixon, where her mother lies dying from what "Aunt Suzy says is bad medicine." There Louise finds her grandmother burning sweetgrass and listening for the night owl to signal Annie's death. Even though Louise has been running away, "wishing she had made it to Missoula, or Wallace, anywhere, off this reservation," her "heart [becomes] her drumbeat home." Sitting in the pickup and watching her mother's burial, Louise sees in the truck mirror that "the red color of her hair [doesn't] match her dark skin." And so she looks for "something to cover her [peroxided] head" as she slowly approaches the grave. Beside the grave, Grandma lifts "her palms to the sky" and chants a "slow, meandering song [in Salish] that [makes] Louise very sad." Although "Perma Red" is a story of loss and disconnection, a story about being caught between two worlds, the conclusion affirms the Native tradition that will always hold Louise: her grandmother "sang to a part of Louise that was lonesome" (1025). Set in the 1940s, "Perma Red" sensitively portrays the conflicts and resolutions many young people experience even today (1019 –1025). This story may be combined with James Welch's contemporary novels *Winter in the Blood* and *The Death of Jim Loney,* or with D'Arcy McNickle's novel *The Surrounded* and Louis Owens's *Wolfsong.*

Lerner, Andrea, ed. *Dancing on the Rim of the World: Anthology of Northwest Native American Writing.* Tucson: University of Arizona Press, 1990. 266 pp.

Grade Level: I, S

This excellent anthology, alphabetically organized according to author, includes contemporary Northern Plains and Northwest area writers, including the following:

Janet Campbell Hale (Coeur D'Alene). "Ancestress." With images of continuity, circles, and drums, and flying eagles, the speaker affirms her relationship to her grandmother, who tells her she "lived here once" and who will "endure" through her granddaughter (87).

Victor Charlo (Bitterroot Salish). "Flathead River Creation," "Dixon Direction," "Frog Creek Circle," and "The Milltown." Victor Charlo's poetry affirms life with the possibility and power in personal (re)creation repeated again and again: "You are the creation of the universe one more time"; "We are remembered today in circles / of family, of red pine, of old time chiefs, / of forgotten horses that thunder dark stars"; "We are the stories now / . . . And now / we burn yes, we sing yes to world we find / in us" (27–30). Identifying himself as a "Bitterroot Salish parent, poet, philosopher, theologian and teacher," and working as a counselor at the Kicking Horse Job Corps, Charlo knows the needs of young people. His poetry speaks to all levels.

Jo Whitehorse Cochran (Lakota). "Halfbreed Girl in the City School." This poem demonstrates the social and personal conflicts for contemporary Indian young people who attend multiracial schools. It specifically addresses the issues of cultural and racial stereotypes and their influence on the Indian's personal identity and voice (41–42).

Debra Earling (Salish). "Winter Keeps," "Summer Humming 1946," "Montana Burial Wind," and "Summer of Bees." In Earling's poetry, we hear voices alive in dust and wind and bees; we share in the living presence of those who have gone before, and we hear and live "the stories of other times." In her poetry, voices are "always calling, / The creak of a summer screen door, / A car turns off the highway lighting / A pale dust road going / Home. Your mother waving, / The drowned girl laughing, / The high buzzing wires, / The dry-dust soil, / Then wind." Just as in Momaday's *The Way to Rainy Mountain,* Earling's poetry expresses the powerful way memory and imagination re-create sounds and images into each new experience. Working well to demonstrate a cyclical and communal world view, the poem "Summer of Bees" can easily be included in a unit on contemporary American poetry (54–62).

Several of the introductory biographical sketches represent the voices of the writers themselves. Andrea Lerner compiled this collection to dispel the stereotype of the Vanishing Indian and to celebrate "the creativity, enthusiasm, and craft that marks [contemporary and alive] literary efforts" (xvii) in the Northwest Region. The voices in this collection, which secondary students can appreciate, are tribal voices addressing disturbing issues such as suppression, disease, political repression, and dispossession.

Lesley, Craig, ed. *Talking Leaves: Contemporary Native American Short Stories.* New York: Dell, 1991. 385 pp.
Grade Level: S

An exceptional collection of contemporary Native American short fiction, *Talking Leaves* includes the works of thirty-five established writers, lesser-known writers, and new writers, including Paula Gunn Allen, Joseph Bruchac, Elizabeth Cook-Lynn, Anita Endrezze, Rayna Green, Joy Harjo, Linda Hogan, N. Scott Momaday, Gerald Vizenor, James Welch, and Elizabeth Woody. In the Introduction, Craig Lesley says: "The stories here in no way reflect a 'romantic' view of nature or contemporary Native American life. Change is the rule rather than the exception, and enormous stresses operate on the culture and the individual. Frequently, the characters are torn between two worlds. Families are wrenched by displacement, alcoholism, spouse or child abuse. Remarkably, the characters manage to survive in spite of overwhelming odds. And as these voices attest, they survive with courage, and dignity, and humor" (xviii).

Most of the protagonists in *Talking Leaves* are Native American young adults, making this an excellent anthology of Native American literature for a secondary classroom. One of the best stories is also the most controversial, but a high school student commented that it was his "favorite story because it tells it like it is—these are the truths of puberty!" In Debra Earling's "The Old Marriage," Louise recalls her experience with Clarence Yellow Knife, who "used to follow her around, a beaver-dark boy with a stinking mouth full of rotting teeth." The son of the "rattlesnake woman," Clarence carries the power of the rattlesnake, but Louise's grandmother helps her bury the rattles under "three red-colored rocks" so she can avoid their power. Still Clarence Yellow Knife pursues Louise and asks her to marry him. She runs away to the security of her grandmother's house, where she remembers "her grandma talking about the choices of men, of bad medicine and the power of the old marriage." The story "The Old Marriage" is grounded in a traditional Salish belief system as well as in Earling's understanding and honest communication regarding the sexual conflicts young teens experience. Because of the sexual imagery, this story is best saved for the more mature readers (61–69).

A non-Indian, eleventh-grade reader responded by writing about the number of stories featuring the "respect for elders, the importance of the past, the whole family as captained by the Grandmother, and the family's reliance on the Grandmother's wisdom." Another twelfth-grade reader concluded her reading of *Talking Leaves* by writing: "When storytellers tell about their experiences and hardships, they accept them as reality and, perhaps, will have a greater chance for change."

Nabokov, Peter, ed. *Native American Testimony: A Chronology of Indian-White Relations from Prophecy to Present.* New York: Harper & Row, 1978. 232 pp.
Grade Level: I, S

Organized according to theme and subject matter—Premoni-
tions and Prophecies; Face to Face; Exchange Between Worlds;
Bearers of the Cross; Living Beside Each Other; The Long
Resistance; The Treaty Trail; Exiles in Their Own Land; and The
Nation's Hoop Is Broken and Scattered—this collection represents over fifty first-person accounts of Native experiences
with the white man. In his Foreword, Vine Deloria, Jr. suggests
this volume provides the other side of American history, the
"informality of human experience, which colors all our decisions and plays an intimate and influential role in the historical
experiences of our species." He concludes with the recommen-
dation that readers "discard presumptions and preconceptions
and immerse the soul in the richness of the human condition"
(xvii–xix). This collection is especially useful as a contrast to
many contemporary non-Indian works that carry romantic or
negative stereotypes of Indian peoples.

Niatum, Duane (Klallam). *Harper's Anthology of 20th Century Native
American Poetry.* San Francisco: Harper & Row, 1988. 395 pp.
Grade Level: I, S

Niatum has brought together thirty-six contemporary poets
who "attest to the health of both the Native American spirit
and American literature," and he has provided biographical
sketches of all included authors (ix). In his Preface he suggests
these writers generate a sense of "coming from the land and
not to it," and Niatum recognizes commonalities in style,
theme, and subject matter (xi). Brian Swann, in his excellent
and comprehensive Introduction, surveys the history of Native
American literature, looks at what distinguishes Native American Poetry while trying to avoid calling "Indian literature" a
"genre" (xviii). He looks at the changes in Native American
poetry, the themes, the ways ancient voices present themselves
in these contemporary voices, their reverence for tradition, and
he applauds their "courage to continue" in spite of "loss, in
spite of living divided in two worlds, and in spite of alienation" (xxxi). This collection is an excellent resource for intermediate and secondary libraries

Riley, Patricia (Cherokee), ed. *Growing Up Native American: An Anthology.* New York: Wm. Morrow, 1993. 333 pp.
Grade Level: S

Growing Up Native American would be an excellent classroom
text for high school students, especially those of Native American heritage. Excerpts from larger works, essays and short sto-

ries are included in four sections: Going Forward, Looking Back; The Nineteenth Century; Schooldays; and Twentieth Century.

In the Introduction, Patricia Riley recalls her own growing up, suggests that she never read authentic American Indian literature because "it was shelved in the anthropology section of the downtown library," and regrets the books she did read with characters who "bore no resemblance to the lives of [her] neighbors or friends." Riley says she has put together this anthology "as a chance to rectify, in some small way, the situation of my childhood, not only for myself and my own children, but for anyone, Indian or non-Indian, interested in the real-life experiences of Native American people" (23). She has included many of these particular authors and stories because they have strongly influenced the way she views herself and the world around her, and because many of the stories "resonate" for her on a "deeply personal level":

> The truth is, we have not vanished, though we have often "disappeared" from the minds and hearts of America, even as we continue to be romanticized and exploited by various "New Age" philosophers who appropriate and distort Native American spiritual traditions, but never look for nourishment in their own ancient European tribal traditions. (23)

An introduction prefaces each section, briefly suggesting the historical, geographic, and cultural context for the readings, and a short biographical introduction prefaces each reading. This collection is neither escape literature nor adventure or fantasy literature, and none of the readings may be labeled as romantic. This is literature that disturbs, that confronts the reader with realities only participants in the experience are qualified to share. Although adults may appreciate all the selections in this anthology, the protagonists, for the most part, are young adults, in the middle of their growing, who confront and survive even the most devastating circumstances. Riley hopes her audience will not only be non-Indians who wish to learn the truths about being Native American, but also "many Native American readers who will see the text as a respectful opening into the multilayered and intricate worlds from which they (we) come" (8). Each reading may be completed in one sitting. Students will find this anthology a beginning to their reading of contemporary Indian literatures, and they will want to read the entire works of authors such as Black Elk, Joseph Bruchac, Ella Deloria, Michael Dorris, Louise Erdrich, Linda Hogan, Sara Winnemucca Hopkins, N. Scott Momaday, Leslie Marmon Silko, Anna Lee Walters, and others.

Rosen, Kenneth, ed. *The Man to Send Rain Clouds: Contemporary Stories by American Indians.* New York: Penguin, 1992. 178 pp.

Grade Level: S

Understanding this collection was first published in 1974 helps to explain Rosen's opening comments that these stories represent "a small but important and growing body of literature that has until now been virtually ignored" (ix). The numbers of anthologies listed in the bibliography here written definitely contradict Rosen's statement. Most of the stories feature male protagonists; several demonstrate the important connections between the old and the young, between humans and their environment; and several depict the fragmented lives so many contemporary Native and non-Native young people live today.

The title story is "The Man to Send Rain Clouds," by Leslie Marmon Silko (Laguna Pueblo), one of the most widely anthologized Native short stories today. When an old Indian grandfather dies, two boys put his body in the back of a pickup so the old man's daughter might perform a traditional burial ritual. The daughter finally asks the local priest to come, not to perform a Christian burial but to sprinkle holy water over the body so the people might receive rain. They succeed in pulling him into participation in their Native ritual. Still, the priest remains an outsider, but he has achieved more insight into the values of the traditional Indian ways. The story demonstrates the cyclical nature of all life and experience, and it shows the ways Indian people can make use of the dominant culture while still holding to the "Old Ways." This story may be compared and contrasted with Margaret Craven's novel, *I Heard the Owl Call My Name,* in which a Catholic priest experiences the strengths of the Kwakiutl Indian culture and ritual.

In "Humaweepi, the Warrior Priest," also by Silko, nineteen-year-old Humaweepi travels into the hills with an old man. There Humaweepi learns to trust his survival to nature in the ways of animals; he sees a bear, "magic creature of the mountains, powerful ally to men" (166), and Humaweepi sings the song of the "warrior priest."

"Saves a Leader," by Larry Littlebird and the members of Circle Film, tells a story that can be used for all levels. It is a communal story about an old woman (Grandmother), and "Lazy Coyote. He slept by the river" (155). Grandmother tells the children a story about "Saves a Leader," who had "gained the respect of all" because he was brave. When she finishes her story, the best swimmer among the children tries to swim across the river and is caught in the fast water. Lazy Coyote wakes and saves him, earning the new name, "He Too Saves a

Leader." This story communicates the importance of each person's responsibility to work for the welfare of each other: "Together, the power of the people was strong. / The people were very happy together" (160).

At the end of his Introduction, Rosen writes about contemporary American Indian writers: "Poetry and traditional tales still seem to be the dominant genres . . . but fiction is attracting the efforts of more and more young people . . . who are faced with the monumental task of somehow reconciling an inherent concept of tradition with a contemporary non-Indian world in which the exploitation of the individual talent is forever being encouraged" (xiv).

Vanderwerth, W. C., comp. *Indian Oratory: Famous Speeches by Noted Indian Chieftains.* Norman: University of Oklahoma Press, 1989. 291 pp.
Grade Level: I, S

Using transcriptions of early white men who had heard Indian tribal council meetings and speeches, and using the Indian oral tradition, Vanderwerth suggests in his Preface that "every effort was made to trace the speeches as far back as possible, so that little would be added or subtracted in the telling and retelling" (ix). In the Foreword, William R. Carmack recognizes the way the "wit and sarcasm" in these speeches "destroys the stereotype of the stoic, silent, humorless red man" (viii). A picture, a short biographical sketch, and a description of the situation and date preface each of the twenty-six speeches, and students will recognize the names of familiar chieftains from across the continent.

Although probably recorded and translated by non-Native people, the speeches by Tecumseh and Pushmataha, both delivered to the Chickasaws just five years before their removal to the Indian Territory west of the Mississippi, are fine examples of oratory which may be compared with Patrick Henry's speech to the Virginia House before the Revolutionary War. Also, in light of the bias of many history textbooks toward Andrew Jackson and his "removal policy," these speeches present an opportunity for students to question the implications of serious political decisions for all involved people, not just for the winners.

Also included in this book of oratory are the last words attributed to Crazy Horse (Sioux): "At ten o'clock [September 5, 1877], he called Indian Agent Jesse M. Lee to his side and spoke to him, shortly after which he died" (215). Although we have no other record of these words by Crazy Horse, they may serve as a primary source (214–217). Teachers can use this "speech" in conjunction with Benchley's story, *Only Earth and Sky Last Forever.*

Vizenor, Gerald (Chippewa), ed. *Native American Literature: A Brief Introduction and Anthology.* HarperCollins Literary Mosaic Series. Berkeley: HarperCollins, 1995. 372 pp.
Grade Level: S

Native American Literature is part of a series for college-level classes, which includes *Hispanic American Literature, African American Literature,* and *Asian American Literature,* but secondary-level students appreciate reading this independently. With a Foreword and Introduction by the general editor, Ishmael Reed, the book is organized according to genre—Autobiography; Fiction; Poetry; and Drama—and each is prefaced with a short biography, a list of the writer's complete works, and a paragraph that establishes a focus for the reader. There is also an "Alternate Table of Contents by Theme": Identity; Place; Family; Struggle; Tricksters and Transformations; and Language.

In Reed's description of Gerald Vizenor, he says: "Vizenor insists that the story of Native Americans in the United States should be told by Native Americans and not by intermediaries or translators" (ix). *Native American Literature* does just that. There are no as-told-to stories here, no separate and isolated traditional tribal stories which Vizenor would probably say are meant to be spoken, not printed in "Dead Voices," and none by storytellers whose voices may have been twisted in translation or editing. Although the collection includes works by nineteenth-century writers William Apes, Luther Standing Bear, and John Rogers, most of the writers are mixed-bloods born after World War II.

Ishmael Reed also refers to N. Scott Momaday's comment about Gerald Vizenor: "He has the richest sense of humor of anyone I know, and in addition he's the most articulate person—he's a man to be reckoned with" (ix). Vizenor's own contributions demonstrate his sense of humor. His stories have the power to convince readers that Indians are survivors who understand trickery, who will themselves play tricks, and who will not be victimized again. One of the two plays included is Vizenor's *Ishi and the Wood Ducks: Postindian Trickster Comedies.* Since many young people have read Alfred Kroeber's *Ishi, the Last of His Tribe,* they will be interested in Vizenor's approach, which portrays Ishi as a character in the story of his life after his death. *Native American Literature* selections prove the truth in Momaday's observation. They tell some terrible stories, but they lack the overtly negative tone that appears in other contemporary collections—as well as works by some of the included writers. Vizenor's own wordplay, his use of complex symbols, his vivid imagination, and his profound sense of the ironies and paradoxes in the lives of Native Americans have definitely influenced his choice of the works included in this anthology. It is an excellent collection of contemporary Native American literatures.

Walker, Deward E., Jr. *Myths of Idaho Indians.* Moscow: University of Idaho Press, 1980. 197 pp.

Grade Level: S

In his Introduction, Walker, an anthropologist, defines myths: They "impart the basic values and beliefs of a society and give moral instruction to its members . . . they serve as mechanisms for educating children, stimulating social interaction, and amusement" (7). He also includes an explanation of the Trickster (Coyote), who he says "acts out man's socially disruptive drives, thereby revealing the disastrous results of violating conventional mores" (8–9). The Introduction concludes with suggestions about the most reliable and least biased ethnological works. Six tribes are represented in this collection: Kutenai, Kalispel, Coeur d'Alene, Nez Perce, Shoshone, and Northern Paiute.

For Further Reading

Ahenakew, Freda (Cree), and H. C. Wolfart. *Our Grandmothers' Lives as Told in Their Own Words.* Saskatoon, Saskatchewan: Fifth House, 1992.

Grade Level: I, S

Reminiscences and personal stories telling about the daily lives of Cree women.

Allen, Paula Gunn (Laguna Sioux). *Grandmothers of the Light: A Medicine Woman's Sourcebook.* Boston: Beacon, 1991. 245 pp.

Grade Level: S

A collection of twenty-one "goddess" stories from a wide variety of nations across the entire continent.

———, ed. *Spider Woman's Granddaughters: Traditional Tales and Contemporary Writing by Native American Women.* New York: Fawcett Columbine, 1989. 277 pp.

Grade Level: S

Twenty-four stories by Native women writers from various tribal traditions, beginning with an Introduction that includes a brief historical outline of the literary tradition of American Indian women.

Anderson, Gary Clayton, and Alan R. Woolworth, eds. *Through Dakota Eyes: Narrative Accounts of the Minnesota Indian War of 1862.* St. Paul: Minnesota Historical Press. 316 pp.
Grade Level: I, S

Eyewitness accounts of the war and its aftermath.

Brafford, C. J. (Oglala Sioux), and Laine Thom (Shoshone/Goshiute/Paiute). *Dancing Colors: Paths of Native American Women.* San Francisco: Chronicle Books, 1992. 120 pp.
Grade Level: I, S

Glossy color and black-and-white photographs of Indian women, their landscapes and the clothing, tipis, jewelry, and household implements, interwoven with stories, all demonstrating the power and respect which Native women have traditionally been afforded.

Braided Lives: An Anthology of Multicultural American Writing. St. Paul: Minnesota Humanities Commission, 1991. 287 pp.
Grade Level: I, S

A multicultural collection, including selections from the following Native American writers: Paula Gunn Allen, Diane Burns, Louise Erdrich, Diane Glancy, Linda Hogan, Maurice Kenny, Barry Milliken, N. Scott Momaday, Leslie Marmon Silko, Mary TallMountain, Laura Tohe, and Roberta Hill Whiteman.

Brant, Beth (Mohawk), ed. *A Gathering of Spirit: A Collection by North American Indian Women.* Ithaca, NY: Firebrand Books, 1988. 239 pp.
Grade Level: S

Bruchac, Joseph (Abenaki). *Flying with the Eagle, Racing the Great Bear.* Mahwah, NJ: BridgeWater Books, 1993. 128 pp.
Grade Level: I, S

Sixteen transition or "rites of passage" stories with male protagonists, where young people benefit from the wisdom of elders.

————, ed. *Returning the Gift: Poetry and Prose from the First North American Native Writer's Festival.* Tucson: University of Arizona Press, 1994. 369 pp.
Grade Level: S

A collection of emerging Native writers.

Bruchac, Joseph (Abenaki), and Gayle Ross (Cherokee). *The Girl Who Married the Moon: Tales from Native North America.* Troll Medallion, 1994. 127 pp.
Grade Level: I, S

Stories with female protagonists that demonstrate the important balance that existed between the sexes in Native American cultures.

Clark, Ella E. *Indian Legends from the Northern Rockies.* Norman: University of Oklahoma Press, 1966. 350 pp.
Grade Level: I, S

A collection of myths, legends, and historical traditions from the tribes of Montana, Wyoming, and Idaho, with brief historical backgrounds of the tribes.

Erdoes, Richard, and Alfonso Ortiz (San Juan Pueblo). *American Indian Myths and Legends.* New York: Pantheon Books, 1984. 526 pp.
Grade Level: S

Over 150 stories plus a brief history and geographical location of the tribes represented. All the stories are essentially authors' "retellings" and so may differ from the same stories told by local tribal people. Since the collection has not been compiled for children, teachers of intermediate students should be selective about which stories they use.

Erdoes, Richard, ed. *The Sound of Flutes.* Pantheon, 1976. 129 pp.
Grade Level: I, S

A collection of twenty-nine traditional tales told by Lame Deer, Jenny Leading Cloud, Leonard Crow Dog, and others from Pine Ridge and Rosebud, South Dakota, illustrated by Paul Goble.

Farley, Ronnie, ed. *Women of the Native Struggle: Portraits and Testimony of Native American Women.* New York: Orion, 1993. 158 pp.
Grade Level: I, S

One of the most powerful books published today, which strongly contradicts the negative stereotypes of Indian women, providing evidence of the positive ways in which Native American women have confronted and survived change.

Gattuso, John, ed. *A Circle of Nations: Voices and Visions of American Indians: North American Native Writers and Photographers.* Portland, OR: Beyond Words. 128 pp.
Grade Level: I, S

Hamilton, Charles. *Cry of the Thunderbird: The American Indian's Own Story.* Norman: University of Oklahoma Press, 1972. 284 pp.
Grade Level: I, S

Over fifty Native Americans who describe events in their own words.

Legends of Our Nations. North American Indian Traveling College. Cornwall Island, Ontario: NAITC Press, 1984.
Grade Level: I

Swann, Brian, and Arnold Krupat, eds. *I Tell You Now: Autobiographical Essays by Native American Writers.* Lincoln: University of Nebraska Press, 1987. 283 pp.
Grade Level: S

A good resource for teachers as well as students, offering insight into the philosophies and experiences of published writers.

Velie, Alan R., ed. *American Indian Literature: An Anthology.* Norman: University of Oklahoma Press, 1991. 373 pp.
Grade Level: I, S

A collection of "literature by Indians on Indian subjects" that is organized according to genre and collected on the basis of "literary quality" and for gender balance, rather than according to region or tribal orientation.

Vizenor, Gerald (Chippewa), ed. *Touchwood: A Collection of Ojibway Prose.* Minneapolis: New Rivers Press, 1987. 177 pp.
Grade Level: S

6
Bibliography of Native Literatures

Although the following annotations and reviews cannot include an extensive list of recommended uses for the selections, most include suggestions for use with other literatures and with themes normally covered in language arts programs. Each annotation includes the genre, themes, and grade level for each work, as well as the tribal affiliation of the author(s). For additional biographical notes and excerpts of critical reviews, teachers and students may consult the 1994 Gale Research publication, *Native North American Literature,* edited by Janet Witalec. Within the following annotations, *NNAL* designates the authors who are included in the Gale resource.

Regrettably, by the time *Roots and Branches* is published, some of the books listed here, especially those from smaller publishing houses, may no longer be in print. However, they may be obtained through public, college, and tribal libraries, and I hope that an increasing demand may encourage publishers to reprint.

Ahenakew, Freda, trans. and ed. *How the Birch Tree Got Its Stripes.* Saskatoon, Saskatchewan: Fifth House, 1988.
> **Genre:** Traditional Story
> **Theme:** Remembering the Old Ways
> **Grade Level:** I

Illustrated by George Littlechild, this traditional Cree story was written by Cree-speaking students. It is the story of the Cree trickster/transformer Wisahkecahk, who wants to test his endurance beyond common sense. Among other lessons, the story communicates the dangers of too much pride. However, third-grade Sioux and Assiniboine children were saddened and disturbed by the violent ending, asking their teacher what "whipping" meant. This situation demonstrates the difficulties of using traditional stories in other cultural contexts without adequate preparation for the listeners.

Alexie, Sherman (Spokane/Coeur d'Alene). *The Lone Ranger and Tonto Fistfight in Heaven*. New York: The Atlantic Monthly Press, 1993. 223 pp.

Genre: Short Story

Themes: Cultural and Personal Loss and Survival; Between Two Worlds; Remembering the Old Ways

Grade Level: S   *NNAL* (119–124) Alexie

Sherman Alexie was born in 1966 on the Spokane Reservation in Wellpinit, Washington, where he still lives. His poetry, novels, and short stories depict the Spokane Reservation landscape and some of the harshest realities of Native American lives today. In particular, the stories in *The Lone Ranger and Tonto Fistfight in Heaven* reveal the vast distance between illusion and reality and the resulting loss. The narrator of many of these stories is Victor, a Spokane Indian who suffers from poverty, despair, and alcoholism. Still, the stories construct and connect figures like Victor, Jimmie, and Thomas with each other, with their past heroes, and with those they have fought and loved. Beginning with fierce "hurricanes" raging in fistfights, in broken promises and treaties, and in mud-puddle drownings across the reservation, the stories multiply into metaphor. Here, past heroes sing and dance again in a Crazy Horse basketball warrior and through a storyteller who may never "answer a question straight" (39).

In *The Lone Ranger and Tonto Fistfight in Heaven,* Alexie the storyteller provides answers through a creative landscape of ironies and juxtapositions. The parents of two "warriors" shine with pride for their "very brave" car-stealing sons. Traditional tribal ties split and splice into community surrounding "a bottle and broken dreams." Anorexic and bulimic teens throw up their lunch while "back on the reservation [mothers stand] in line" for commodities. And the aunt holds "her baby close to her chest" while the doctor ties her tubes, "with the permission slip [she] signed because the hospital administrator lied and said it proved her Indian status for the BIA" (81). After reading this section aloud to a group of educators on one of our reservations, a middle-aged woman told about a doctor who drowned two newborns in a bucket of water.

Within the stories, Alexie's characters, like Coyote, are transformed from horses to warriors to contemporary storytellers: "His eyes are looking past the people who are looking past us for the coyote of our soul and the wolverine of our heart and the crazy man that touches every Indian who spends too much time alone" (116). And Samuel tells the story of Coyote himself, the creator of all, whose toenail clippings accidentally drop and fall to the earth, burrow into the ground, and grow "up to be the white man" (135).

More than anything, though, this collection of stories is about the power of stories, and laughter, and imagination to ensure survival. "Survival = Anger × Imagination. Imagination is the only weapon on the reservation" (150). In "This is What it Means to Say, Phoenix, Arizona," Thomas Builds-the-Fire has a dream, telling him to go to Spokane and "stand by the Falls." When Victor's father appears and asks what Thomas is doing, he says, "Waiting for a vision." Later, after Victor's father drives Thomas back to the reservation, Thomas says to Victor: "Your dad was my vision. *Take care of each other* is what my dreams were saying. *Take care of each other*" (69). In "A Good Story," the narrator's mother tells him to "write a story about something good" (140). And so he tells a story of the friendship between "the best basketball player in the reservation grade school" and Uncle Moses, an old teller of a "good story," who knows "we are all given something to compensate for what we have lost" (143).

No one who reads these stories can escape the heartbreak or the laughter—or the possibility of hope through imagination and community: "Imagine an escape. Imagine that your own shadow on the wall is a perfect door. Imagine a song stronger than penicillin. Imagine a spring with water that mends broken homes. Imagine a drum which wraps itself around your heart. Imagine a story that puts wood in the fireplace" (152).

The publishers appropriately suggest that Sherman Alexie "evokes the complex density of life in and around the Spokane Indian Reservation, an existence filled with pain, anger, and bitterness but also, more importantly, with forgiveness and resilient hope. What is explored here is the distance between people: between Indians and whites, reservation Indians and urban Indians, men and women, and, most poetically, between modern Indians and the traditional figures from their past" (back cover).

The Lone Ranger and Tonto Fistfight in Heaven pulls readers in and demands understanding and empathy, making it very popular with adult as well as secondary readers. Reservation students know this world well, and teachers will find that they can easily use it as a class novel. Several story selections may be used with intermediate-level students. This book can work to break down racial and cultural barriers between Indian and non-Indian students in surrounding communities, especially when they first explore the oral tradition of the Coeur d'Alene and the history of federal Indian policy. Alexie is an artist, and teachers can use his work well to achieve current NCTE/IRA language arts standards for literature, writing, and oral communication.

Teachers and students who enjoy Alexie's work might also appreciate *Smoke Signals,* a motion picture released in 1998 that is based on stories in *The Lone Ranger and Tonto Fistfight in Heaven.* The film, which Alexie wrote and coproduced, won the Audience Award and the Filmmaker's Trophy at the 1998 Sundance Film Festival.

Big Crow, Moses Nelson (Lakota). *A Legend from Crazy Horse Clan.* Chamberlain, SD: Tipi Press, 1987. 28 pp.
Genre: Traditional, Historical Story
Themes: Remembering the Old Ways; At Home within Circles; Between Two Worlds
Grade Level: I

Legendary Tashia Gnupa (Meadowlark) and her baby raccoon are left behind after a buffalo stampede scatters their camp. Befriended by a buffalo calf, Tashia becomes a member of the Buffalo Nation. Years later, warriors find and take her with them. After marrying one of the warriors, she bears sons, one of whom was Crazy Horse, the "pride of all Lakota." Although Paul Goble has published a story that resembles this legend, Big Crow's story is more believable because the characters display human weaknesses as well as strengths. When the girl finds herself alone, she cries and wanders, is unable to build a fire because the "stones won't work," and speaks Lakota like a five-year-old when she is finally found years later. Lakota phrases, names, and some dialogue are integral to the story, as are the traditional Lakota behavior patterns of men and women, and Big Crow has included a "Lakota Word Glossary" at the end. Children today who enjoy intimate relationships with their horses or dogs, or with deer, like the boy in Rawling's *The Yearling,* can identify with the girl who travels with a buffalo herd because she made friends with a buffalo calf who wanted to play. Illustrated by Daniel Long Soldier, *A Legend from Crazy Horse Clan* is an excellent resource for teachers who want to read or tell the story to primary level children, or for children from third grade up who will read it themselves. The story communicates the Lakota tradition of accepting strangers into a clan or community, the problems for individuals who must live between two cultures or life ways, and it shows how even the youngest children are taught to respect and express gratitude to Wakan-Tanka, the "Great Mystery," who brings every new day.

Young Sioux children, hearing this story read, ask if it is all true. In response, one teacher focused on the true interdependent relationship between humans and animals and the way history becomes legend when distanced by time.

Black Hawk (Sauk). *Black Hawk: An Autobiography.* Donald Jackson, ed. Champaign: University of Illinois Press, 1990. 164 pp.

Genre: As-Told-To Autobiography

Themes: Cultural and Personal Loss and Survival; Between Two Worlds

Grade Level: S   *NNAL* (59–67) Black Hawk

First dictated to a U.S. interpreter, Antoine LeClair, and published in 1833, this autobiography represents the story of a man who fought Andrew Jackson's "removal policy" to preserve his village, surrounding corn fields, and a way of life. Deceived by chiefs and medicine men, and pressured by fearful squatters and a relentless U.S. military, he was unable to prevent the starvation and final slaughter of his band, even as they intended to surrender. Prefaced by an Introduction based on information from the military's historic records, this edition poses interesting contrasts in points of view. No doubt, Meridel Le Sueur used *Black Hawk: An Autobiography* as a source for her young-adult novel *Sparrow Hawk,* and so students of American and Indian history can benefit from reading both accounts.

Brass, Eleanor (Cree). *Medicine Boy and Other Cree Tales.* Illustrated by Henry Nanooch. Saskatoon, Saskatchewan: Fifth House, 1979.

Genre: Traditional and Contemporary Story

Theme: Remembering the Old Ways

Grade Level: I

In this collection of twenty-six stories, Eleanor Brass explains the legendary trickster/transformer figure, Wesuketchuk: "He originated every act, both good and bad, that humanity has ever done since the beginning of creation. He was also a friend to animals and nature. He spoke to them and addressed them all as his little brothers. He played many tricks on them and so they were wary when he approached but he nearly always outwitted them." This excellent collection includes creation stories, stories which reflect the influence of the French language and culture, a few contemporary stories, and stories featuring Wesuketchuk. In the story "Abandoned," a contemporary young Cree woman learns she was the abandoned child of a "frightened white girl." Having been raised in a Cree family, she regards such abandonment as "unpardonable according to tribal laws." Maintaining her commitment and relationship to the family that raised her, she says, "you are my real mother and my family will never be abandoned by me." This story teaches the solidarity of families and the commitment required by all members to maintain that solidarity, but it also teaches that relatives are defined by behavior rather than blood. Although all the stories communicate traditional values, some close with the essential teaching of the story: to always listen to warnings, to remember to think of others, to never be greedy and neglect responsibilities, and to be grateful for all gifts on earth. Students from all grade levels can appreciate these stories.

Bruchac, Joseph (Abenaki). *Children of the Longhouse.* New York: Dial, 1996. 150 pp.
Genre: Young Adult Novel
Themes: Remembering the Old Ways; Change and Growth; At Home within Circles
Grade Level: I, S   *NNAL* (184–198) Bruchac

This is a story of the Mohawk, The Flint Nation, one of the Six Iroquois Nations that were organized under The Great Law of Peace, the forerunner of the United States Constitution. Ohkwa'ri and Otsi:stia are eleven-year-old twins, at home in a Flint Nation village in the late 1400s. The children learn the ways of their people through historical and sacred stories, while they work and play beside their elders. But they also come into conflict with an older group of boys after Ohkwa'ri overhears their plans of war against a people who had once made slaves of the Mohawk. The elders commend Ohkwa'ri for telling them of the plan and publicly chastise the group and refuse to sanction the attack because the consequences could be devastating for the entire community. But the leader of the group wishes revenge, and this provides motivation for succeeding events that climax when the boys fight during Tekwaarathon, a sport that centuries later would be known as lacrosse. As Ohkwa'ri and Otsi:stia change and grow, they learn about the importance of peace and the obligation of all people to give thanks for all gifts. They learn to respect the elders and the powerful role women and men hold in maintaining peace, and they learn about the ways to avoid conflicts.

Like Michael Dorris' *Morning Girl,* the voices and story of a brother and sister in *Children of the Longhouse* are carried throughout the novel in alternating chapters. Joseph Bruchac demonstrates a sensitivity to the feminine experience that creates a believable balance throughout the novel, while he tells the archetypal story of males battling for power. Students will want to discuss and possibly argue about the way the elders intervene to avoid hazardous conflicts between young people. Since so many students today would never "tell on" their peers, even when they are in great danger, they might disapprove of Ohkwa'ri's actions after he overhears the plan of war.

Kanatsiohareke, the village which provides the setting for this novel, has been restored after the people raised funds to purchase a five-hundred-acre piece of land at auction. Today it is a place where "Mohawk children climb Ohkwa'ri's hill, and the sound of the water drum Otsi:stia loved so well is heard on moonlit summer nights as the old social dance songs are sung" (150). *Children of the Longhouse* is an excellent novel, and teachers can easily combine it with science, history, geography, and storytelling activities.

————. *Turtle Meat and Other Stories.* Duluth, MN: Holy Cow! Press, 1992. 115 pp.

Genre: Short Story

Themes: Remembering the Old Ways; At Home within Circles; Cultural and Personal Loss and Survival

Grade Level: I, S   *NNAL* (184–198) Bruchac

Rendering laughter, insight, tears, and the absolute certainty that dreams are real, all of the stories in *Turtle Meat* are short enough to be read aloud—or told—and teachers may easily use them in combination with science, social studies, and other literature and writing activities. Some of the seventeen stories are traditional, and a few occur in historical settings and situations such as eighteenth century New England and World War II.

One story, "Code Talkers," is patterned after the historical World War II story of a group of Navajos that the United States Army recruited to create a code using the Navajo language as a base. In "Code Talkers," Bruchac tells his own World War II trickster story where two Indians from different cultures confuse German intelligence: "Wayne was an Apache and I wasn't. I didn't know his language for beans and aside from that year I spent in the mountains with my grandfather when he kidnaped me from the Indian school, my native Indian language had been English." They conspire to frustrate "German intelligence officers who listened in on [their] conversations" by speaking "basic German so badly that no one else could understand a word [they] were saying." This story humorously demonstrates the way the "powerless" can outwit those "in power" (33–38).

Other stories portray the way foxes, bears, fish, and wolves can prevail over entrapment and exploitation with the assistance of their human brothers. "The Fox Den" demonstrates the interdependent relationship between animals and humans and the importance of respect for all living things, even for the foxes who kill chickens. When Grandfather and his collie catch and kill a fox, they rescue her only living cub and bring it back to Grandmother, who will care for it even though she knows it will grow up to kill her chickens. Many years later, although years before that fox had been "shot as he was chasing chickens," the narrator meets another fox in the field who "for that one moment and forever after" was as close to him as the one his mother and "grandparents kept as a pet . . . two decades" before he was born (27–32).

The trickster appears throughout these stories, but clever people outwit him and foil his plans. Through Bruchac's story-teller's voice, we can hear the wisdom of Abenaki "old people," especially in the story, "Jed's Grandfather." When Jed visits his grandfather, who is dying of cancer, old Joseph Sabael teaches the boy that "cancer smells" and that "it's as natural as anything else" (21–26). As Jed learns to overcome his fear of his grandfather's pending death, the old man and Jed tear apart the bread Jed's mother has sent for the grandfather, and they toss it to the gulls flying over the "waveless lake," demonstrating the cyclical, and natural, patterns of life and death. The story "How Mink Stole Time," about cultural differences with respect to time, offers lessons to all people: "Because Mink stole Time, it now owned him and the People. It has been that way ever since then. Time owns us the way we used to own the Sun" (69–70).

Bullchild, Percy (Blackfeet). *The Sun Came Down: The History of the World as My Blackfeet Elders Told It*. New York: Harper & Row, 1985. 390 pp.
> **Genre:** Traditional Story
> **Themes:** Remembering the Old Ways; Change and Growth; At Home within Circles
> **Grade Level:** I, S

Divided into four parts—creation stories; Napi tales; "Kut-Toe-Yis, Bloodclot Tales"; and "Honoring Creator Sun"—this book is an excellent resource of traditional Blackfeet literature and could be used in part or whole for teaching units. In the section "Earth's Beginnings," Bullchild tells the story of the Blackfeet world from its inception to the preservation of the future, and he tells how Creator Sun created the earth, the universe, humans, and all that is necessary for human survival. Percy Bullchild indicates these stories have been handed down from generation to generation, but they also represent cultural change as they reflect the influence of Christianity on the Blackfeet culture. In the story "Earth's Beginning," Bullchild tells about Creator Sun who took space dust and spit on it to make a ball out of the clay. Then he created snakes, which increased so many times that he tried to destroy them. Still one survived to continue to populate the earth. Then Creator Sun made grass to grow so the earth would be more beautiful. At the end of the story, Creator Sun wishes for something that "will look like [his] image." "Moon and Big Dipper Come into Being" is about the way Creator Sun made the Moon for his mate and how their seven children became the Big Dipper, but still the snakes are reproducing to make trouble for Creator Sun. These stories communicate the dependent relationship between the creatures on earth and the Sun and Moon.

The Napi tales are humorous and enlightening, teaching traditional lessons and values that the Blackfeet needed to survive in their society. "A Disciple of Creator Sun" tells of the creation of Napi, Creator Sun's idea to "send a small part of himself to watch over his children and to teach them to come out of the bad ways they had been doing." But Napi, Old Man, takes the power given him by Creator Sun and does mischief, coming to "admire himself for his doings, even if they were crazy doings." Not all people followed him; many knew of his foolishness.

The third section includes stories about Kut-Toe-Yis, who was created by Creator Sun and Mother Earth to undo the wickedness that Napi had brought to the earth. The fourth part tells about the Native religion, rituals, and ceremonies.

Campbell, Maria (Métis). *Halfbreed.* Lincoln: University of Nebraska Press, 1973. 154 pp.

Genre: Memoir

Themes: Remembering the Old Ways; Change and Growth; At Home within Circles; Cultural and Personal Loss and Survival; Between Two Worlds

Grade Level: I, S   *NNAL* (199–209) Campbell

A best-seller in Canada, *Halfbreed* is a very popular book with female readers. Growing up as one of the thousands of landless "Road Allowance" Métis in Northern Saskatchewan and Alberta, Maria Campbell struggled to prevent starvation, poverty, and the disintegration of the bonds between herself and her six brothers and sisters after her mother's death. This memoir provides insight into the lives of Indian mixed-bloods who grew up with strong grandmothers, their *Cheechum,* who constantly reinforced family and community pride. However, this quickly turns to shame and self-abasement once the Cheechum leaves. At the age of fifteen, Maria marries a "wealthy" white man she doesn't love, believing he will provide a comfortable life for her brothers and sisters. And so begins her lonely battle with alcohol and drugs. Yet the strength of the grandmother's voice prevails even at the end of the memoir when Maria recalls Cheechum's promise: "You'll find yourself, and you'll find brothers and sisters." She finally conquers her addictions and begins to work with the Native movement in Canada for the thousands of other women and men like herself who must set aside their differences in order to survive as individuals and as a community. *Halfbreed* is the story of loss and survival, of cultural integrity and of hopelessness conquered. Students who read *Halfbreed* recognize the value of the ways the family struggled for years to keep together. Although the strong language may prove to be a sensitive issue for some students, the insight into the life of one survivor makes this a valuable book for older high school students, both Indian and non-Indian alike. Teachers may also use excerpts to demonstrate the powerful, negative impact of racial stereotypes on the self-esteem and spirit of Indian people.

Charbonneau, Eileen (Cherokee). *In the Time of the Wolves.* New York: Tom Doherty, 1994. 180 pp.
Genre: Young Adult Historical Novel
Themes: Change and Growth; Between Two Worlds; Remembering the Old Ways
Grade Level: I, S

Beginning her writing career in print journalism, Charbonneau has relied on her mixed heritage to write mysteries featuring Cherokee themes and historical novels that address multicultural and mixed-blood issues for American young people. In a presentation to teachers at an NCTE convention in Chicago, she said that she writes in the mystery genre because it "appeals to young people's sense of justice—when young adults solve the problems through reading, they can experience a sense of empowerment." Also interested in film and the media, she was co-writer of an award-winning educational film narrated by Christopher Reeve, *Endowment for the Planet.* *In the Time of the Wolves,* nominated as a 1995 Library Association "Best Book for Young Adults," is the second in a trilogy which Kirkus calls "Good, appealing historical fiction."

Set in the Catskill Mountains of the northeastern United States, *In the Time of the Wolves* begins with the narrator's violent reaction to verbal assaults, "Heathen!" and "Ugly savage," directed at his sister. Living between the worlds of "heathen" and Catholic, Native, French, and Dutch ancestry, fourteen-year-old Joshua and his family face discrimination and conflicts throughout the summer of 1824, when they trust the prediction of Quinn Delaney: "It will be a year without summer . . . there will be frosts in every month, little sun and too much rain. You must plant carefully, you must protect your animals, for the wild creatures of the mountains will become crazed with hunger. It will be a year . . . [of the wolves]" (29–30). "Struggling with his heritage," and with the community's rejection of his father's belief, Joshua follows an older woman, whom he has befriended, into a trap where he is expected to betray his family for the sake of his desired Harvard education. Joshua changes and grows when he recognizes and asserts the values of both his parents: "My father is not evil. He does not even recognize evil, his heart is so good. It is my mother's wisdom that surrounds us. . . . We are of the mountains, and of wilder stock than yours, but we are created equal Americans . . . we are like the balsam trees: we know how to live and we will not be uprooted" (145).

Although the story is fiction, Charbonneau explains in the "Author's Notes" that in 1816 a killing frost occurred in every month of the year, with snowstorms in July and August. Scientists believe it was caused by the eruption of Mount Tambora on the Indonesian island of Sumbawa, when "dust circled the earth, reducing the amount reaching the ground. The event led to strange weather, massive crop failures, soaring prices, and perhaps even a pandemic of cholera" (181). The narrator's voice at times appears too sophisticated for his age and experience, especially when he refers to his father as "Daddy." But having grown up in a "house without books," Charbonneau demonstrates her skills in dialogue and intrigue, as well as her sensitivity to the desires and conflicts young adults experience. *In the Time of the Wolves* would work well with Arthur Miller's *The Crucible*, which also features the theme of an individual's responsibility to think for himself or herself no matter what the emotional cost.

Cook-Lynn, Elizabeth (Crow Creek Sioux). *From the River's Edge.* New York: Arcade, 1991. 147 pp.

Genre: Historical Novel

Themes: Cultural and Personal Loss and Survival; Between Two Worlds

Grade Level: I, S   *NNAL* (216–221) Cook-Lynn

This book is based on the true story of John Tatekeya, "a Dakotah and a cattleman," who lost his land to flood and his cattle to thieves, and who suffers under the "justice" of the "white man's court of law." Although he lives traditionally, John has bought into the white man's concept of ownership, and so his loss is all the greater. In the end, his identification with the "antiquities of the universe" is affirmed, "his eyes, wide open in the total darkness," and he adjusts "by degrees, to his own triviality" (147). In the final image of the novel, young Philip puts sage into the hands of "his venerable grandfather, Harvey Big Pipe." One eleventh-grade student responded with this realistic insight: "Even though he won his case, his battle was not nearly won." Students from farming and ranching backgrounds especially appreciate John Tatekeya's conflicts and frustration with a system he can't control.

Crow Dog, Mary (Lakota), and Richard Erdoes. *Lakota Woman.* New York: Harper, 1990. 263 pp.
Genre: As-Told-To Autobiography
Themes: Between Two Worlds; Personal and Cultural Loss and Survival
Grade Level: S   *NNAL* (180–183) Crow Dog

With Richard Erdoes, Mary Crow Dog tells her story, which won the American Book Award in 1991. The memoir opens with "I am Mary Brave Bird. After I had my baby during the siege of Wounded Knee they gave me a special name—*Ohitika Win,* Brave Woman, and fastened an eagle plume in my hair, singing brave-heart songs for me. I am a woman of the Red Nation, a Sioux woman. That is not easy" (3). Much of her story concerns Leonard Crow Dog, her husband. But it is her voice we hear, telling her story of personal and cultural conflict and survival: "My Voice you shall hear: I will live!" A high-school freshman girl called *Lakota Woman* "tragically sad and shockingly real . . . a book about growing up," and valuable for ages fifteen and older. There is a video by the same title that is based on this story.

Culleton, Beatrice (Métis). *In Search of April Raintree.* Winnipeg: Peguis Publishers, 1995. 228 pp.
Genre: Contemporary Novel
Themes: Between Two Worlds; Personal and Cultural Loss and Survival
Grade Level: S   *NNAL* (232–239) Culleton

In response to questions about her reasons for writing *April Raintree,* Culleton said, "[There] had been two suicides in my family, the rest of my family members were alcoholics, and we had to be raised in foster homes. I wanted to know why: Was it because we were natives?" A novel of two sisters, victimized by an uncaring social service system as they search for lost identities, *April Raintree* represents what critics call "Native counterdiscourse"; like Armstrong's *Slash,* discourse that subverts the dominant European-American discourse to fight against injustice of any kind. When the book was reissued in 1984 as *April Raintree,* the graphic rape scene had been cut for high-school use. In an interview with Hartmut Lutz, in *Contemporary Challenges: Conversations with Canadian Native Authors,* Culleton said: "But I'm not angry at white people. If it were, say, the Indians and they were oppressing the white people, I would be angry with the Indians, of course. It's the injustice that people do to each other! There's just no reason for it!"

Deloria, Ella Cara (Yankton Sioux). *Dakota Texts.* Vermillion, SD: Dakota Press, 1992. 142 pp.
   Genre: Traditional Story
   Themes: Remembering the Old Ways; At Home within Circles
   Grade Level: I, S   *NNAL* (240–245) Deloria

First published in 1932, this is the most extensive collection of Dakota oral literature available. Ella Deloria, as a native speaker herself, recorded and translated sixty-four traditional stories. Born in White Swan, South Dakota, in 1889, Ampetu Waste wi (Beautiful Day) lived most of her young life on the Standing Rock Reservation, where her father was an Episcopalian minister. Later she attended All Saints' School in Sioux Falls, Oberlin College in Ohio, and Columbia University in New York. She taught at Haskell Indian School, as well as schools she had herself attended, but she spent much of her life collecting ethnological and linguistic materials for the anthropologist Franz Boas. *Dakota Texts* represents her work with traditional Dakota storytellers. The current collection includes her Introduction, her synopses of tales, her free translations, and her notes to the English version. The first eight stories feature Iktomi, the Dakota trickster, and thirty-one stories feature characters such as Double-Face, Iya, Stone-Boy, the Rolling Skull, and the European characters, Orpheus and Eurydice. The next fourteen stories include "tales of bewitchment and magical transformations" such as "the story of the girl who changes into a rock, giving the name to Standing Rock Agency." Most of the other stories take place in the Pine Ridge Area, dealing "with the clash between the Dakota and the Crow during the not-too-distant past" (vii). Students enjoy comparing this literature with other collections of Dakota stories, but they also find value in examining the stories within twentieth-century contexts. In a unit featuring works from a single tribal culture, this collection can preface the reading of Deloria's *Waterlily* and Zitkala-Ša's *American Indian Stories.*

————. *Waterlily.* Lincoln: University of Nebraska Press, 1988. 244 pp.
Genre: Historical Novel
Themes: Remembering the Old Ways; At Home within Circles, Change and Growth; Cultural and Personal Loss and Survival
Grade Level: I, S   *NNAL* (240–245) Deloria

First written in 1944, this mid-nineteenth-century novel provides insight into the traditional Dakota customs, rituals, and values of the Old Ways while it tells the story of Waterlily, a Dakota girl. In the "Afterword," Raymond DeMallie suggests *Waterlily* uniquely portrays "nineteenth-century Sioux Indian life, unequaled for its interpretation of Plains Indian culture from the perspectives of women" (233). For Ella Deloria and other traditional Lakota people, responsibility to relatives and community was a most important value. Not only does *Waterlily* demonstrate that value, but so does Deloria's lifelong work with the Sioux people. *Waterlily,* with a female protagonist, may be taught in conjunction with James Welch's *Fools Crow,* with a male protagonist, especially since both represent the cultural and personal loss and survival of mid-to-late nineteenth-century Plains Indians.

Dorris, Michael (Modoc). *Morning Girl.* New York: Hyperion, 1994. 74 pp.
Genre: Historical Novel
Themes: Remembering the Old Ways; Change and Growth; At Home within Circles
Grade Level: I   *NNAL* (258–268) Dorris

In alternating chapters—and in separate voices—Michael Dorris creates the lives of two Taino children on a Bahamian island in 1492. Twelve-year-old Morning Girl is "always doing things in her dreams, swimming or searching on the beach for unbroken shells or figuring out a good place to fish." Star Boy, her brother, sees "everything so upside down from [her]." At the end, they welcome "the strangers [Columbus and his men] . . . who had decorated their faces with fur and wore shiny rocks on their heads" (69). With dramatic irony, Dorris closes his story of Morning Girl and Star Boy with an excerpt from one of Christopher Columbus's letters to the King and Queen of Spain, dated October 11, 1492: "They should be good and intelligent servants, for I see that they say very quickly everything that is said to them . . . at the time of my departure I will take six of them from here to Your Highnesses in order that they may learn to speak" (74). Although lacking the action that many young readers demand, the strong sensory images, flowing language, and realistic characterizations make *Morning Girl* appealing to all ages.

————. *A Yellow Raft in Blue Water.* New York: Henry Holt, 1987. 342 pp.
Genre: Contemporary Novel
Themes: Between Two Worlds; Cultural and Personal Loss and Survival; At Home within Circles
Grade Level: S   *NNAL* (258–268) Dorris

Set on a Montana reservation, somewhere east of Havre on Highway 2, *A Yellow Raft in Blue Water* is a three-generational account of Rayona, the estranged fifteen-year-old daughter, Christine, her strong-willed mother who is dying, and Ida, the matriarch of their clan. Each tells her story as the novel moves from contemporary reservation life to the past. The novel addresses the cultural aspects of the women's lives, but it has universal themes and is especially useful for teaching structure and point of view. Episodic in time and sequence, *A Yellow Raft in Blue Water* also shifts points of view and comes full circle where whole pictures are connected. The painful realism in the novel might be objectionable to some, and female readers have questioned the author's ability to accurately write about the feminine experience, although some critics suggest that Louise Erdrich edited the text.

Eastman, Charles A. (Santee Sioux). *Indian Boyhood* (190 pp.) and *Old Indian Days* (279 pp.). Greenwich, CT: Fawcett, 1972 (originally published in 1902 and 1907, respectively).
Genre: Memoir
Themes: Remembering the Old Ways; At Home within Circles; Between Two Worlds; Personal and Cultural Loss and Survival
Grade Level: I,S   *NNAL* (269–275) Eastman

Born a Santee Sioux in Minnesota, in 1858, Ohiyesa was later named Charles Eastman because his father, who had been imprisoned at Davenport, Iowa, in 1862, with those who took part in the uprising or in the battles following, was converted in prison by the pioneer missionaries (*Indian Boyhood*, 189). After Lincoln pardoned Many Lightnings for lack of evidence, he searched for his son, Ohiyesa, until he found his camp in Canada. The boy, baptized Charles A. Eastman, was educated in eastern boarding schools, attended Dartmouth, and became a government physician at the Pine Ridge Agency in South Dakota.

Indian Boyhood is a text that illustrates the conflict for Eastman of living "Between Two Worlds." The language usage in this book indicates Eastman wrote it for a non-Indian audience, which had defined Indian belief systems as "superstitious" and Indian stories as "legends or fairy stories." Eastman also provides explanations for names and cultural practices unfamiliar to a non-Indian audience, and he defines the Indian as "savage" and the white culture as "civilized." Nevertheless, the entire work demonstrates his affection for his Native culture. Whenever he introduces an "alien" practice to his audience, he appears to apologize for it by using non-Indian terminology, but each episode concludes with an affirmation of its truth and value to the people (including Eastman).

Written in both the first and third persons, this memoir includes Ohiyesa's recollections of his grandmother, his playmates and their games, his pet grizzly and other animals, family and tribal traditions, storytellers and their legends, encounters with Cree, Chippewa, and Blackfeet, harvests of rice, sugar, and hunting buffalo, and his early impressions of the white man and his technology. In one of the last chapters, Eastman contradicts the "stern-faced" stereotype of Indian peoples when he tells about "The Laughing Philosopher" who could keep "the community in a convulsive state (179)."

Teachers may use individual chapters with units regarding various aspects of the Native experience as lived in the North central Plains west of the Mississippi and north of the Missouri into Canada. But the entire text may be paired with Ella Deloria's *Waterlily,* with collections by Luther Standing Bear and Zitkala-Ša, or it may be contrasted with Conrad Richter's *Light in the Forest* or with the romantic and counterfeit voice of Forrest Carter in the *Education of Little Tree.*

———. *Indian Heroes and Great Chieftains.* Lincoln: University of Nebraska Press, 1991. 241 pp.

Genre: Biography

Themes: Between Two Worlds; Cultural and Personal Loss and Survival; Remembering the Old Ways

Grade Level: I, S   *NNAL* (269–275) Eastman

An important alternative to many popular biographies of Native American warriors and leaders, this collection from the Native perspective provides sensitive, and sometimes firsthand, stories of fifteen Plains leaders. The first ten chapters tell the stories of famous Sioux heroes who lived and fought during the transition period: Red Cloud, Spotted Tail, Little Crow, Tamahay, Gall, Crazy Horse, Sitting Bull, Rain-in-the-Face, Two Strike, and American Horse.

At the beginning of "Crazy Horse" (Sioux), Eastman acknowledges the stereotypes that have dominated the public's image of Crazy Horse: "Notwithstanding all that biased historians have said of him, it is only fair to judge a man by the estimate of his own people rather than that of his enemies. Big-heartedness, generosity, courage, and self-denial are the qualifications of a public servant, and the average Indian was keen to follow this ideal" (84–85). Telling several stories of Crazy Horse's boyhood, Eastman closes with a contradiction of the "savage" stereotype: "He was never involved in any of the numerous massacres on the trail, but was a leader in practically every open fight. Such characters as those of Crazy Horse and Chief Joseph are not easily found among so-called civilized people" (83–106). This work may be compared with *Only Earth and Sky Last Forever* by non-Indian author Benchley.

Eastman himself spoke with Chief Joseph (Nez Perce) about his flight and how he and his people resisted leaving his homeland in the Grande Ronde Valley in Oregon: "I call him great because he was simple and honest. Without education or special training he demonstrated his ability to lead and to fight when justice demanded. He outgeneraled the best and most experienced commanders in the army of the United States. . . . He was great finally, because he never boasted of his remarkable feat" (194–212).

The biography of Dull Knife shows a Cheyenne hero who was "devoid of selfish aims, or love of gain . . . a pattern for heroes of any race." Dull Knife, called the "panther of the Cheyennes" by whites, led his people to escape imprisonment in Indian Territory where they were dying. Although most died in the effort, Eastman suggests that at least they died together with their "dauntless leader," as "fighting Cheyennes." Of Roman Nose, a contemporary of Dull Knife, Eastman says, "No other chief attacked more emigrants going west on the Oregon Trail between 1860 and 1868." Roman Nose died in a battle with General Forsythe: "In order to inspire [his men] to desperate deeds he had led them in person, and with him that meant victory or death" (179–93).

Hole-In-The-Day (Ojibway) lived when many people believed this continent could easily hold both the Indian people and the white people. The stories in this chapter reflect Hole-In-The-Day's belief that Indian people must accustom themselves to the white ways. However, the chief opposed the removal of the Mississippi River Ojibways in 1867 to the White Earth reservation. Eastman says he was " one of the most brilliant chiefs of the Northwest, who never defended his birthright by force of arms" (225–41).

When Eastman served as a government physician sent to the Sioux and Northern Cheyenne, he knew Little Wolf. Although much is heard about Chief Joseph and his march toward freedom, little is told about Little Wolf's flight from imprisonment in "Indian Territory" to Montana. He and his followers went to "Montana and then to Pine Ridge, where he and his people remained in peace until they were removed to Lame Deer, and there he spent the remainder of his days" (213–24).

Students enjoy reading these stories and comparing and contrasting them with their previous views of these figures.

Endrezze, Anita (Yaqui). *at the helm of twilight*. Seattle: Broken Moon Press, 1992. 120 pp.
Genre: Poetry
Themes: Change and Growth; Cultural and Personal Loss and Survival; At Home within Circles
Grade Level: S

With a sensual and lyric voice, and with insight into the ways we can die or survive, Anita Endrezze writes about the feminine in relationship to others, about the way human beings need and give to each other, and about the way these relationships weave into our individual identities. The poem "One Thing, Too Much" may be used with the study of *Macbeth, Death of a Salesman,* or other selections featuring themes of obsession, but it also provides one of the important reasons for multicultural education: "We all love one thing too much. / Chocolate. Coffee. Liquor. / . . . We all fear one thing too much. / Being alone. Dying. / The stranger at the door. / . . . But we don't know / what our own backs / look like / unless we're willing to see / from a different perspective . . . We don't know that too much / of one thing / is like a burning woman / calling for more wood" (86–87).

Erdrich, Louise (Chippewa). *Love Medicine.* New York: Holt, Rinehart, & Winston, 1984. 275 pp.
Genre: Contemporary Novel
Themes: Remembering the Old Ways; Between Two Worlds; Cultural and Personal Loss and Survival
Grade Level: S   *NNAL* (276–289) Erdrich

Love Medicine is a saga of two Native American families, the Kashpaws and the Lamartines, and of those who left the Indian land and those who stayed. Set in North Dakota and Minnesota, the narration of *Love Medicine* works the way stories are told, retold, and reinterpreted by those who hear them and tell them again. The point of view changes from chapter to chapter, and by the end of the novel readers are enmeshed in a community through the stories they have shared. June Kashpaw is the Deer-Woman, haunting the lives of the people she knew and changing even before her husband's eyes. The novel is a kind of trickster-transformer story, with stories of characters changing the way those characters appear to others within the story and to those who read the story. Not a simple tale of the healing power of love, Erdrich's novel is instead about June and her Love Medicine—a power or curse—appearing throughout the stories to draw in the elements of her universe, beyond their own will or control. Within the stories, Louise Erdrich spins metaphors into meaning upon meaning just as she spins the tales of her characters. After reading *Love Medicine*, an eleventh-grade girl wrote: "Many traditional values are presented in this book . . . the value of nature (an example of the transformation of a deer into June in the back seat of the car; also humans are metaphorically compared to animals), the value of remembering the dead (in every instance of a death, a person close to the deceased had an experience of meeting or feeling the spirit of the dead, reassuring them that they would always be with them), and the most important value of family." Another non-Indian senior student wrote: "After reading *Love Medicine*, I became aware of the amount of understanding we need to use when reading literature that comes from a different culture than our own. We also can feel the confusion and frustration of Indian children who are forced to read non-Indian literature." *Love Medicine* is an excellent novel for the more sophisticated readers who want to explore the contemporary world of mixed-bloods and Indians relocated to the cities, a world where change is inevitable and survival is definitely possible.

———. *Tracks.* New York: Henry Holt, 1988. 226 pp.
Genre: Contemporary Novel
Themes: Remembering the Old Ways; At Home within Circles; Cultural and Personal Loss and Survival; Between Two Worlds
Grade Level: S   *NNAL* (276–289) Erdrich

Tracks is the third in a series of related novels that also includes *Love Medicine*. Beginning with the devastating Anishinabe losses from smallpox or the "spotted sickness" in 1912, the novel tells old man Nanapush's story to his granddaughter, Lulu. (Nanabush is the Ojibway trickster/transformer figure.) The other storyteller in the novel, Pauline, causes trouble throughout and finally becomes an insanely fanatical nun. One senior reader, who "wanted to turn the pages until the very end," identified Pauline as the trickster, holding "loyalty to no one and causing mischief to Fleur and anyone else who tried to help her. . . . It is ironic that Pauline later became a nun because she had caused so much harm, and people usually view the Catholic Church as good." It is the story of Nanapush's fight against "bureaucrats [who sank] their barbed pens into the lives of Indians" to survive with land and family and dignity.

Fraser, Frances. *The Bear Who Stole the Chinook.* Vancouver, BC: Douglas and McIntyre, 1990. 129 pp.
Genre: Traditional Story
Theme: Remembering the Old Ways
Grade Level: I, S

Growing up in Alberta, Canada, just south of the Blackfoot Reserve, Frances Fraser learned the Blackfoot language, listened to songs and stories, and developed a deep respect for the Blackfoot culture and people who visited her father's farm. Hugh Dempsey, associate director of the Glenbow Museum, suggests that the Blackfoot Indians supported her writing and publishing. Included in this collection of thirty-one stories are tales about Napi (Old Man), the Blackfoot trickster/transformer figure, who exhibits contradictory and very human characteristics such as courage and cowardice, wisdom and foolishness, kindness and cruelty. Heroic adventures, general legends, and religious tales are also represented in this collection. While some stories portray individuals who lived in the nineteenth century, others explain the origin of certain ceremonial practices. Fraser intended the stories to be read aloud to all levels, but middle school and high school students will especially appreciate reading the entire collection. This book works well as an introduction to Blackfeet/Blackfoot culture before reading novels such as *Fools Crow* and *Winter in the Blood.*

Geiogamah, Hanay (Kiowa). *New Native American Drama: Three Plays.* Norman: University of Oklahoma Press, 1980. 113 pp.
Genre: Contemporary Play
Themes: Between Two Worlds; Cultural and Personal Loss and Survival
Grade Level: S   *NNAL* (290–297) Geiogamah

Regarded as America's best-known Native playwright, Hanay Geiogamah "employs humor, realism, and idiomatic language to subvert negative stereotypes about Native Americans and to address the alienation felt by the Indian in contemporary American society" (*NNAL* 290). *The Body Indian* features Bobby Lee, a crippled alcoholic, as the main character. Of *Foghorn*, Geiogamah says, "Almost all the characters in this play are stereotypes pushed to the point of absurdity." The central character in the third play, *49,* is Night Walker, a holy man who is the voice of the past, present, and future. Geiogamah's plays are about survival and resurrection, and "they are considered optimistic in outlook because of their focus on the importance of developing pride, unity, and self-respect among Native Americans."

Grayson, Chief W. G. (Creek). *A Creek Warrior for the Confederacy.* W. David Baird, ed. Norman: University of Oklahoma Press, 1988. 164 pp.
Genre: Memoir
Themes: Between Two Worlds; Cultural and Personal Loss and Survival
Grade Level: S

Born in 1843 near present day Eufaulag, Oklahoma, Grayson served as a Confederate army officer during the Civil War and in various offices of the Creek Nation from 1870 until his death in 1920. This is an important work for two major reasons: It reveals the participation of Native Americans in America's military and war efforts, involvements which go unrecognized in many history textbooks; and it affirms the way Native Americans resisted annihilation and survived as a people. Any serious study of the Civil War should include this book. Grayson's memoir is part of the "Civilization of the American Indian" series.

Hale, Janet Campbell (Coeur d'Alene). *Jailing of Cecelia Capture.* New York: Random House, 1985. 198 pp.
Genre: Contemporary Novel
Themes: Between Two Worlds; Cultural and Personal Loss and Survival
Grade Level: S   *NNAL* (304–307) Hale

An urban Indian with roots to her tribe in Northern Idaho, Cecelia Capture experiences an identity conflict. She grows up in a home with a mixed-blood mother who denies her own Indian identity, and with an Indian father who expects Cecelia to succeed but who fails to follow through with those expectations because of his own alcoholism. At nineteen, she becomes an unwed mother and then later marries a white graduate student. Living in the midst of many conflicts, she begins to drink and considers suicide. While achieving success in law school, she is jailed for drunken driving, but Cecelia's memories sustain her. At the end, she decides to let go of what she has lost, "feeling more like herself than she had felt in a long time. . . . She was not able to return to the beginning, of course, and remake her life more to her liking, but now she was free to go on with the life she did have" (201). Some independent readers find the format difficult to follow because "it moves from one time in her life to a totally different time." But they also recognize this as a powerful book about loss and survival. Although some readers find the language too rough and the sexual imagery too explicit, it is no more so than in many contemporary films.

————. *The Owl's Song*. New York: Bantam Books, 1991. 153 pp.
Genre: Young Adult Novel
Themes: Between Two Worlds; Cultural and Personal Loss and Survival; Remembering the Old Ways
Grade Level: I, S   *NNAL* (304–307) Hale

As a child on the reservation in Idaho, Billy White Hawk would listen to the aged Waluwetsu tell stories about the times before the Suyappi (white men) came, and before the Jesuit missionaries, when "the land had been wild and free, without roads and houses of any kind, places where trees were chopped down, not torn, plowed, and cultivated fields." But Waluwetsu also told of the coming time when the owl, who brings messages of coming death, will sing "for our race." By the time the boy is fourteen years old, the old man and Billy's mother have died, his father, Joe, gets drunk many evenings, and Billy witnesses the suicide of his closest friend. After a dream where Waluwetsu calls Billy to come across a river, Billy decides to travel to San Francisco, where he believes he will find a new life. There he finds himself utterly alone, experiencing racism from both classmates and counselors. But he survives through memories that take him "far, far away," and he claims his identity in those memories. The novel closes after Billy has returned home to be with his dying father: "It was all right, though. Billy knew it was good that it happened this way, [after Joe has vigorously chopped down a tree] with his last day being one spent in hard work 'like the old days.' It was all right" (152). In spite of the theme of alienation and loss,

Janet Campbell Hale's novel affirms the values of tradition, ancestors, dreams, and "manhood" visions brought by the Manitous: "He loved these Benewah hills, this place where the people of his tribe first came into being when the earth was very young. It was, as Waluwetsu had said, that there was very little of what had been. It seemed there was no way of staying and living any more. Still, all this would remain with him when he went away and would not change. . . . It was all right, now . . . Manitous, spirits of earth, wind, rain, sun. Father and grandfather and unknown ancestors" (153). Billy knew he could carry them with him wherever he went. This book works especially well as a preparation for reading McNickle's stories and novels.

Harjo, Joy (Muskogee Creek). *In Mad Love and War.* Middletown, CT: Wesleyan University Press, 1990. 74 pp.
Genre: Poetry
Theme: Personal and Cultural Loss and Survival
Grade Level: I, S   *NNAL* (308–318) Harjo

Joy Harjo, poet, scriptwriter, musician, and activist, narrated much of the TBS video series *The Native Americans.* In *In Mad Love and War,* through the passions of "Love and War"—personal, communal, and racial—Harjo's mythic poetic voice transforms the dead and cold into blooming, living stories. Coyote, Rabbit, and Crow, all tricksters, laugh and live again and again, and in tribute to Jacqueline Peters, an activist who was lynched in Lafayette, California, in 1986, dance "anyway from this killing tree." One poem, dedicated to "Anna Mae Pictou Aquash, Whose spirit is Present Here and in the Dappled Stars (for we remember the story and must tell it again so we may all live)," may be used in conjunction with Johanna Brand's *The Life and Death of Anna Mae Aquash.* Although critics describe Harjo's poetry as dark, "feminist poetry of personal/political resistance," her prose poems represent survival. *In Mad Love and War* is a collection of poems that all secondary students can easily read, learn from, and appreciate.

Hogan, Linda (Chickasaw). *Mean Spirit.* New York: Ivy, 1990. 377 pp.
Genre: Historical Novel
Themes: Cultural and Personal Loss and Survival; Between Two Worlds; At Home Within Circles
Grade Level: S   *NNAL* (333–343) Hogan

This historical novel begins with the 1922 murder of an Oklahoma woman after she becomes the richest Osage in the

Oklahoma Territory. Learning to respect his people and their past, a Native American government official, Stace Red Hawk, uncovers the mystery of her murder. At issue are the federal Indian policies that non-Indians used to obtain treatied lands: the Dawes Act, which left unallotted lands open property for white settlers; competency rulings, which prevented the Indian people from privately owning and controlling their own allotted lands; the noncitizen status of all Indians at this time, which prevented Indians from inheriting or obtaining lands belonging to family members outside their immediate family; and federal mandates, which forced Indian children to leave their families to attend distant boarding schools. *Mean Spirit* retells the story of twenty-four Osage full-bloods and mixed-bloods who were murdered or died mysteriously, their homes sabotaged and burned. The characters in *Mean Spirit* increasingly fear and distrust non-Indian businessmen, lawyers, and doctors, and relatives. Although John Hale, the wealthy and "friendly" oilman, is eventually found guilty of murder and fraud, the novel closes without complete resolution. Other "John Hales" will appear to manipulate and circumvent laws, and more Indians will die as they continue to be victimized and as they enact their own justice whenever the federal system fails to adequately defend them. At the novel's end, Linda Hogan quotes an Osage woman, Diane Fraher:

We know we are all only visitors in this world, and that no matter what has happened, we have refused to let the strength of spirit be taken from us. Out of love for my family, I wanted to share this love and spirit and let it find its way into this story. (377)

The characters who still survive at the end watch the burning of their "house, the barn, the broken string of lights"—all symbols of the white man's way. Nevertheless, despite all their losses, they retain the Osage values of community and tradition.

Written from a woman's perspective, *Mean Spirit* vividly demonstrates the terrible impact women experience when they, and their husbands and children, suffer and die. The *Los Angeles Times Book Review* has compared Hogan's writing with the magical realism of Gabriel García Márquez and Isabel Allende, as she wraps "wonder and magic around some brutal American truths." The reading of this novel might be combined with the 1992 film *Thunderheart*, which examines the exploitation of Oglala Sioux Indians and their resources; a reading of Arthur Miller's *The Crucible*, which reveals the subversive actions of individuals who used Salem's fear of witchery to increase their wealth; a novel such as *Fools Crow* by James Welch, which features the loss and survival of the Pikuni people during the later nineteenth century; Louis Owens's *Wolfsong,* about a young man who fights to protect ancestral lands in the Cascade mountains from the intrusion of roads and mines; or with a historical study of federal Indian policy and its consequential impact on the lives and lands of all Indian peoples. After reading *Fools Crow,* by James Welch, and *Mean Spirit,* a senior girl wrote, "I always resented the Indians I knew who seemed to get money without working, spending it on cars and alcohol. But after reading these novels, I know I wouldn't take a million dollars for what they have lost. A class that teaches you not to hate is the most important kind of success."

King, Thomas (Cherokee). *Green Grass, Running Water.* Boston: Houghton Mifflin, 1993. 469 pp.
Genre: Contemporary Novel
Themes: Remembering the Old Ways; Cultural and Personal Loss and Survival; Between Two Worlds; At Home within Circles
Grade Level: S   *NNAL* (373–382) King

Thomas King's novel begins and ends with Coyote, the archetypal trickster, and his self-proposed mission to "fix the world," with a dream, with "all that water," and with a combination of unique yet familiar characters who meet and (re)meet for the annual Sun Dance celebration in a Blackfoot reservation town called Blossom. Of central concern for each character, and his or her story, is the dam, which the "Government built to help Indians," to make them "millionaires," but which surely will kill the water and the lake. King's characters "talk" on every page. And mythologies are mixed with "floating imagery," cultures, histories, provoking shocking irony as well as laughter for the reader. Four "old Indians," Lone Ranger, Hawkeye, Ishmael, and Robinson Crusoe, have again disappeared from a mental institution just as they have before, whenever significant "natural" environmental "disasters" have occurred: the summer "Yellowstone was in flames," the spring Mount Saint Helens erupted, and on several other occasions as long ago as 1883. There is an "attractive university professor" who is pregnant, with the paternity uncertain, the conception somehow "immaculate." There are three "stolen" cars, "A Nissan, a Pinto, and a Karmann-Ghia," which the builders see "sailing" toward the dam. And when an earthquake, or possibly Coyote, ultimately destroys the dam, the waters recede after "just over a month."

Green Grass, Running Water is a powerful novel that with wit, trickery, and a deep sense of tragedy similar to Gerald Vizenor's, offers a different view of American culture, of history, and of the most "sacred" Western and Biblical historical and mythological beliefs. In the end, Hawkeye urges Coyote to apologize, "in case we hurt anyone's feelings"; and chaos resolves into harmony where nature is once again in balance. Still, we know that as history repeats itself, the possibility for more trouble exists. With the very last line of the novel, Coyote begins again: "And here's how it happened." Nevertheless, the reader, who has been smart enough not to be tricked on every page, can honestly say that "that was a good true story" because it represents the universal experience of being human.

Secondary students who know North American history, tribal and treaty history, literature, and Judeo-Christian literature, and who know enough of Coyote and other trickster/transformers, will especially appreciate this novel. Teachers might use it with D'Arcy McNickle's *Wind from an Enemy Sky,* Linda Hogan's *Mean Spirit,* or Louis Owens's *Wolfsong* in a unit about the tribal/federal government conflict over the use of lands and natural resources.

Linderman, Frank B. *Plenty Coups: Chief of the Crows.* Lincoln: University of Nebraska Press, 1962. 324 pp.
  Genre: As-Told-To Autobiography
  Themes: Remembering the Old Ways; Between Two Worlds; At Home within Circles
  Grade Level: I, S

Not a speaker of Native languages, Frank B. Linderman relied on interpreters and sign language to communicate with Plenty Coups for this "as-told-to" autobiography. Also, writing primarily for a non-Native or nontraditional Native audience, Linderman included definitions and explications of Native words and cultural practices in his narrative text. Linderman's rhetoric suggests a European-American or Judeo-Christian world view through which Plenty Coups's own story and personal philosophy is filtered. For example, Indians are "red men"; those who die go to "The Father," and Linderman is astonished that Plenty Coups's memory of an event so closely resembles the "written account." Included in the text are the names of many dead warriors, names he obtained from others after his interview with Plenty Coups because Plenty Coups would not speak the names of the dead. Nevertheless, we can trust Frank B. Linderman as an honest collaborator. Included in the text are Plenty Coups's criticisms of the "white man" for his stupidity in battle, for his confusion over religion, and for his inability to practice what he preaches. Furthermore, in his Foreword, Linderman himself qualifies his authority when he admits that he doesn't know much about "the Indian," even after studying him "for more than forty years." But he also places himself and his authority above those who know much less, who write "all there is to learn" about Indians after spending "a week's vacation . . . alternately fishing and talking to an English-speaking tribesman."

Originally published in 1930, *Plenty Coups: Chief of the Crows* portrays the traditional life of a Crow boy and his early manhood, but it also provides insight into the Crow's relationship with the "white man" and with the Crow's traditional enemies, the Sioux, Cheyenne, Blackfeet (Pikuni), and Flatheads. As a young man, Plenty Coups experienced a dream in which he saw the disappearance of the buffalo and their replacement with domestic cattle. Believing that the best way to safeguard the land and culture of his people, Plenty Coups fought with the white man, providing scouts, warriors, and supplies to the military. Among many other war stories, Plenty Coups tells the stories of the men who fought with Generals Crook and Custer in the Battles of the Rosebud and the Little Bighorn in the summer of 1876, battles they may have survived had they listened to the wisdom of seasoned Crow warriors such as Plenty Coups. Although Plenty Coups did not wish to talk with Linderman about the time after the buffalo had gone, he interjects observations and his grief over the ways their young men and women have changed since the white man took over: they lost their knowledge of medicine and ceremony, and they lost the strength gained from physical and mental challenges.

———. *Pretty-shield: Medicine Woman of the Crows.* Lincoln: University of Nebraska Press, 1972. 256 pp.

Genre: As-Told-To Autobiography

Themes: Remembering the Old Ways; Between Two Worlds; At Home within Circles; Cultural and Personal Loss and Survival

Grade Level: I, S

Pretty-shield, whose husband was a Crow scout for General Custer, tells Frank B. Linderman about her life before reservation days and before the disappearance of the buffalo. One of the earliest accounts of Indian women, the text communicates the importance of tribal cooperation. Students appreciate the feminine perspective, and critical readers recognize, through the interactions between Linderman and Pretty-shield, some of the problems in communicating between cultures and genders. Although Linderman interprets her comments, readers can recognize the places where Linderman definitely does not understand Pretty-shield. On one occasion, Pretty-shield expresses her resentment of Linderman's stereotyping when he offers her a cigarette. She responds with "No . . . my mother did not smoke, and I have never smoked." And then she goes on to say, "and I do not know if whisky is sweet or sour (16)." During a later session, Pretty-shield asks "Sign-talker" (Linderman) if any of the animal-people talk to him. But when he responds that he understood what "[his] horse or [his] dog wished [him] to know," she appears dissatisfied because her experience with animals is much more intimate and real. Linderman and Pretty-shield tell a good story that captures the attention until the end, but it also provides invaluable insight into the personality of a woman who lived at a time of tremendous change and who was trying her very best to be both useful and happy during a difficult time.

Marquis, Thomas, interpreter. *Wooden Leg: A Warrior Who Fought Custer.* Lincoln: University of Nebraska Press, 1931. 384 pp.

Genre: Interpreted Memoir

Themes: Remembering the Old Ways; Cultural and Personal Loss and Survival

Grade Level: I, S

Through sign language and the corroboration of Wooden Leg's contemporaries, Thomas Marquis has interpreted this compelling story of an individual Cheyenne's experiences. Wooden Leg's boyhood and the traditional Northern Cheyenne cultural beliefs and practices are compared and contrasted with neighboring cultures such as the Crow, Sioux, Pawnee, and Blackfeet: "As I now think back upon those days, it seems that no people in the world ever were any richer than we were." Wooden Leg describes the rituals of war, the buffalo hunts, and visions, and he discusses the importance of "The Great Medicine" to his people along with the Cheyenne means of discipline and punishment for the breaking of rules. Wooden Leg also describes the age-old conflict between the Crow and Cheyenne and the way it manifested itself in the conflict between the Cheyenne and the U.S. military, which culminated in the "Battle of the Little Bighorn." Throughout the memoir, contemporary names and places accompany references to historical events. In careful detail, Wooden Leg remembers the gathering of approximately 16,000 people on the Little Big Horn in 1876, the surprise attack and ensuing battle from his particular point of view, and the experiences and events of the next year, which culminated in the Cheyenne people's removal to Oklahoma. After reading this independently, an eleventh-grade student wrote: "I learned about the government of the tribe, and the different warriors' classes . . . and how each person functions to work with another in the tribe." He also was surprised by several "facts" about the Battle of the Little Big Horn: "The attack surprised the Indians . . . the soldiers lasted longer . . . most of the soldiers were new recruits . . . and the total Indian casualties were 32." Students might compare this account with Two Moons' story in *The Last Best Place*, with U.S. military accounts, with Crow accounts of the same battle, and with stories of Dull Knife's flight.

McNickle, D'Arcy (Salish). *The Hawk is Hungry and Other Stories.* Birgit Hans, ed. Tucson: University of Arizona Press, 1992. 179 pp.
  Genre: Short Story
  Themes: Between Two Worlds; Cultural and Personal Loss and Survival
  Grade Level: I, S   *NNAL* (417–428) McNickle

D'Arcy McNickle, Cree-born, probably Métis, was raised on the Flathead Reservation, the home of the Salish and Kootenai people. Organized under subject matters—The Reservation; Montana; and The City—all the stories in this book depict polarized outsiders and insiders: reservation superintendents and tribal elders, mixed-bloods and full-bloods, newcomers and old-time homesteaders, women and men, and the young and the old. Resembling the naturalistic writings of Hemingway and Steinbeck, McNickle incorporates the traditional trickster/transformer figure in the "Reservation" and "Montana" stories. When prefacing these with a telling of a Coyote story, such as in Mourning Dove's *Coyote Stories* collection, students can learn to watch for Coyote at work in McNickle's stories. They can also appreciate the writer's use of irony and the mental agility of those who outsmart the trickster. The following stories will particularly interest secondary students: "Hard Riding," about an Indian superintendent who is outsmarted by tribal elders; "En roulant ma boule, roulant . . ." about a group of "mentally tattered and physically ragged half-bloods" who attempt to try an eighteen-year-old full-blood for rape; "Meat for God," an unusual hunting story about an old man and his nine-year-old grandson; "Snowfall," about an old man's death; "Train Time," about Major Miles and his boarding-school train; "The Hawk is Hungry," about the contrast between romantic expectations and harsh realities on the Montana prairie; and

"Man's Work," about the gender and generationally different definitions of work.

In response to a favorite story, "Meat for God," ninth-grade students have written: "It shows how a kid wasn't taken seriously—just like most kids today . . . it shows how when people today do something wrong, they try to hide it so they won't get into trouble . . . it is a story that inspires sympathy for the old man who no longer has control over his life—his killing the deer symbolizes his effort to regain that control."

———. *Runner in the Sun: A Story of Indian Maize.* Albuquerque: University of New Mexico Press, 1987. 249 pp.
Genre: Young Adult Novel
Themes: Change and Growth; At Home within Circles; Cultural and Personal Loss and Survival
Grade Level: I, S   *NNAL* (417–428) McNickle

Salt, a young Indian boy, is sent on a long journey southward in search of some "unknown" that will save his people, who are threatened by poverty, drought, and discord from within. When Salt returns, his community acquires a new, higher-yielding breed of corn and a new member, Quail. With these gifts, Salt brings needed change to his people in a way they can accept. He learns to trust the dreams of the elders, his own instincts about his new and different wife, his desire to act for the welfare of his people, and to value peace on earth. *Runner in the Sun* can be used with the poetry of Luci Tapahonso.

———. *The Surrounded.* Albuquerque: University of New Mexico Press, 1936. 296 pp.
Genre: Contemporary Novel
Themes: Between Two Worlds; Remembering the Old Ways; At Home within Circles; Cultural and Personal Loss and Survival
Grade Level: S   *NNAL* (417–428) McNickle

In *The Surrounded*, McNickle's first novel, Archilde, a young man of Salish/Spanish descent, returns to the Flathead Reservation after attending an Indian boarding school. There on the reservation, in the early twentieth century, he experiences the intense conflicts of living "Between Two Worlds," an outsider to both. After reading this novel, an eleventh-grade student wrote: "I believe the closeness Archilde feels toward his fellow people is something that he could not experience in the white world. Despite the internal closeness to his people, Archilde is disrespectful of many views and actions. He wants the best of both worlds . . . and is hopelessly caught. . . . At the end, these conflicts remain unresolved." Too many on the reservations are still living Archilde's experience, and high school students can identify with the turmoil of a young man who is looking for a place to belong.

————. *Wind from an Enemy Sky.* San Francisco: Harper & Row, 1978. 256 pp.
Genre: Historical Novel
Themes: Between Two Worlds, Personal and Cultural Loss and Survival; Lifeways and Stereotypes; At Home within Circles
Grade Level: S   *NNAL* (417–428) McNickle

When the federal government builds a dam on an Indian Reservation in the sacred Northwest mountains, culture and personal conflicts grow within Indian families and between the Indians and government representatives. *Wind from an Enemy Sky* is the tragic story of a people's struggle to regain their sacred and communal power while well-intentioned, yet ignorant, whites bring destruction on both Indians and themselves when they fail to understand the culture and strength of the Little Elk people. Woven throughout this narrative are explications and consequences of federal Indian policies from the nineteenth to the mid-twentieth centuries: John Marshall's Supreme Court decision; the kidnaping and transfer of Indian children from their homes to distant boarding schools; forced farming practices on unrelenting lands; federal government fraud over land deals with Indians; and the allotment of tribal lands. Yet the power of their Indian values—cooperation, respect for the sacred, generosity, commitment to relatives and to justice—survives beyond the tragedy, proving this following truth: "Above all else, a man learned to be strong in support of his kinsmen. A man by himself was nothing, a shout in the wind. But men together, each acting for each other and as one—even a strong wind from an enemy sky had to respect their power" (197). In response to reading this book, an eleventh-grade student wrote: "The book will be valued as a story of the general injustice of white people toward Indians while it also illustrates the white people's inability to right their wrongs, leaving Indians perpetually repressed." Non-Indian students will require some background on Indian cultural values and tribal history before they read this book. Teachers who want to further explore the way the Native writers employ the trickster, Coyote, in contemporary works will find Thomas King's novel *Green Grass, Running Water* an excellent selection to follow *Wind from an Enemy Sky.* Just as the very traditional Bull of the Little Elk people views the dam as a "killer of the water," so too do Coyote, four "old Indians," and Eli, from *Green Grass* view the government's dam as a river killer.

Medicine Crow, Joseph (Crow). *From the Heart of the Crow Country: The Crow Indians' Own Stories.* New York: Orion, 1992. 138 pp.
Genre: Memoir, History
Themes: Between Two Worlds; At Home within Circles, Lifeways and Stereotypes
Grade Level: I, S

Born in Lodge Grass in 1913 and raised by his traditional grandparents, Joe Medicine Crow is "the acknowledged historian of the Crow tribe—and a teacher and lecturer with a M.A. in anthropology from USC in Los Angeles." As a child, Joseph Medicine Crow would listen to stories from elders, as well as to war stories from one of Custer's scouts. *From the Heart of the Crow Country* provides information about ancient and recent history, tribal/U.S. Government relations, culture and language, and a list of important events in the history of the Crow tribe from 1500 onward, as well as personal stories. *From the Heart of Crow Country* offers a realistic contrast to the mid-nineteenth-century romantic writings of George Catlin.

Momaday, N. Scott (Kiowa). *House Made of Dawn.* New York: New American Library, 1968. 191 pp.
Genre: Contemporary Novel
Themes: Remembering the Old Ways; Between Two Worlds
Grade Level: S   *NNAL* (432–448) Momaday

Momaday was awarded the 1969 Pulitzer Prize for this novel, which centers on the contemporary problems of Indian people who live "Between Two Worlds," both psychologically and physically displaced. The protagonist, Abel, becomes separated from the Jemez Pueblo and traditions, travels to Europe as a soldier during World War II, and returns to Los Angeles. *House Made of Dawn* celebrates the survival and value of oral and ritual tradition as it provides the foundation for Abel's sense of self, tribe, and place. In the end, Abel experiences himself at the center, from where he could see "the canyon and the mountains and the sky. He could see the rain and the river and the fields beyond. He could see the dark hills at dawn." And he sings the Jemez prayer of restoration and healing: "House made of pollen, house made of dawn." *House Made of Dawn* is the only Native-authored book for which Cliffs Notes are available.

———. *The Way to Rainy Mountain.* Albuquerque: University of New Mexico Press, 1969. 89 pp.

Genre: Traditional Story, History, Contemporary Story
Themes: Remembering the Old Ways; Cultural and Personal Loss and Survival
Grade Level: I, S   *NNAL* (432–448) Momaday

Momaday's journey to Rainy Mountain spans "many generations and many hundreds of miles" to define the culture of the Kiowa people. This journey is an "evocation of three things in particular: a landscape that is incomparable, a time that is gone forever, and the human spirit which endures" (4). While the storyteller suggests that "the young Plains culture of the Kiowas withered and died like grass that is burned in the prairie wind," (3) the entire novel affirms his belief in cultural continuity and contemporary relevance. The Kiowa culture, defined in a "remarkably rich and living verbal tradition" lies "within reach of memory still" (86). In each of the twenty-four, two-page chapters, the storyteller shares three stories—a traditional story, a historical story, and a contemporary experience—which are connected to each other as well as to the preceding and following chapters. But unlike the more predictable, abstract thematic connections Western Europeans may make, each story merges and diverges on concrete images such as fire, antelope, buffalo, arrows, horses, and words. For example, Chapter 8 tells the story of Grandmother Spider, whose grandsons are saved from smoke and suffocation when they repeat the powerful words she told them to say: *thain-mom,* "above my eyes." The second story discusses the way the "word has power in and of itself, [giving] origin to all things." And the third story features Momaday's grandmother Aho who, confronted with some kind of evil, would repeat the word *zei-dl-bei,* or "frightful." "It was not an exclamation so much, I think, as a warding off, an exertion of language upon ignorance and disorder" (33).

The Way to Rainy Mountain addresses the issues of death through disease and starvation, loneliness, the importance of dogs and horses to the Kiowa people, and the loss of "summer's freedom"—when the Comanches and Kiowas could ride across "the long sweep of the earth itself" (61). As readers imagine, reflect, and reread the stories, they will discover surprising connections and a multiplicity of possible meanings. For just as the traditional stories imbue the historical and contemporary stories with particular meaning, so do the contemporary stories further enrich the traditional stories. *The Way to Rainy Mountain* is an excellent introduction to Native literature.

Mourning Dove (Okanagan/Colville). *Cogewea, The Half-Blood.* Lincoln: University of Nebraska Press, [1927] 1981. 301 pp.

Genre: Novel

Themes: Remembering the Old Ways; Lifeways and Stereotypes; Between Two Worlds

Grade Level: S   *NNAL* (463–471) Mourning Dove

Considered the first novel written by an Indian woman, *Cogewea* represents the collaboration of both Lucullus McWhorter (the editor), and Hum-ishu-ma, or "Mourning Dove." At least three distinct voices exist in the text: the stilted and formal narrator, the strong "Western" dialect of the cowhands, and the lyric voice of Stemteema, the grandmother. Cogewea is caught "Between Two Worlds," in love with an unscrupulous white man and loved by a mixed-blood, and pulled by both the Anglo culture and the traditional tribal culture of her grandmother. The story is fashioned after the popular romance novel, but it also incorporates much of Mourning Dove's Salish background. In response to her reading, an eleventh-grade student wrote: "[Cogewea] learns to respect and follow the traditions of her Native culture. If we today would treat elders the way Mourning Dove's people did, then the elders would be treated as they deserve, instead of being abused and neglected." Teachers could use this novel in combination with traditional Salish stories, with other collaborative works such as *Plenty Coups,* and with contemporary poetry and stories by Salish writers such as Janet Campbell Hale, Debra Earling, and D'Arcy McNickle. With some preparation regarding the different voices in the text, students can enjoy reading *Cogewea* independently.

———. *Coyote Stories.* Lincoln: University of Nebraska Press, [1933] 1990. 246 pp.

Genre: Traditional Story

Themes: Remembering the Old Ways; At Home within Circles

Grade Level: I, S   *NNAL* (463–471) Mourning Dove

Collaborators for this edition include Mourning Dove (Hum-ishu-ma); the original editor and illustrator, Heister Dean Guie; L. V. McWhorter; Jay Miller; and Chief Standing Bear, who wrote the Foreword. In her Preface, Mourning Dove explains the paradoxical nature of Coyote: "He did more than any of the others to make the world a good place in which to live . . . he amused himself by getting into mischief and stirring up trouble" (7). For students reading other works by Mourning Dove or by other contemporary Salish writers, reading this collection first is beneficial since traditional cultural beliefs, plot lines, and characters appear throughout contemporary writers' works.

Of all the short stories read and/or told in a single ninth-grade unit, "Coyote and Wood Tick" was the favorite. One Native boy wrote what he learned from the story: "If I don't give anyone respect, I'm going to starve." When "Coyote and Wood Tick" is told before McNickle's "Meat for God," students can look for the way the Game Warden (trickster) is at work, and how the old man, also like Coyote, desires more than he deserves. However, they can see how the old man outsmarts the trickster, refusing to play the fool, and maintains his pride when he burns the deer at the end. These stories are beneficial for the important ethical, environmental, and social lessons each one teaches. We can all learn from Coyote who, according to student readers, "doesn't think about the consequences of his actions."

Neihardt, John G. *Black Elk Speaks.* Lincoln: University of Nebraska Press, [1932] 1988. 298 pp.

Genre: As-Told-To Autobiography

Themes: Remembering the Old Ways; Cultural and Personal Loss and Survival

Grade Level: S

The is the story of an Oglala Sioux medicine man who lived during the later half of the nineteenth century and the beginning of the twentieth, when the Sioux were forced to live on reservations. Written through the voice of Neihardt, with Black Elk's son acting as interpreter, Black Elk tells about his visions and his tribe's world view, as well as his own life experiences. Included in the book are eyewitness accounts of major conflicts between the Sioux and the U.S. military, such as the Battle of the Little Bighorn and the Wounded Knee Massacre. According to Vine Deloria, Jr., in his Introduction, "The most important aspect of the book . . . is in its effect upon the contemporary generation of young Indians who have been aggressively searching for roots of their own in the structure of universal reality." Because *Black Elk Speaks* was one of the first works of its kind, it has become the "criterion by which other books and interpretive essays are to be judged," according to Deloria. Its most important value for students of Indian culture and history, though, is in the way it represents the personal and tribal experience of one Oglala man who believed that he must share the "Great Vision" given to him.

Owens, Louis (Choctaw/Cherokee). *The Sharpest Sight.* Norman: University of Oklahoma Press, 1992. 264 pp.
Genre: Novel
Themes: Cultural and Personal Loss and Survival; Remembering the Old Ways
Grade Level: S   *NNAL* (508–513) Owens

Novelist, educator, nonfiction writer, and Steinbeck scholar, Louis Owens has received several grants and awards including one from the National Endowment for the Humanities and an Outstanding Teacher of the Year award. He currently teaches at the University of California–Santa Cruz. A perceptive and articulate critic of contemporary Native American writing, he is praised for his own fiction. *The Sharpest Sight* is a mystery about a mixed-blood Vietnam veteran, part Native American, Mexican American, and Catholic, who has been murdered by his ex-lover's family, and whose bones are somehow missing. At issue is the Choctaw tradition that bones must be properly treated or the world will be disturbed. With a tone that ranges from serious to very funny, *The Sharpest Sight* is an engaging story that pulls readers into the conflict between good and evil and the individual's search for identity.

———. *Wolfsong.* Albuquerque, NM: West End Press, 1991. 249 pp.
Genre: Contemporary Novel
Themes: Remembering the Old Ways; Between Two Worlds; Cultural and Personal Loss and Survival; Lifeways and Stereotypes
Grade Level: S   *NNAL* (508–513) Owens

Set in the Cascade mountains of Washington, *Wolfsong* is the story of Tom Joseph, who leaves a California university when he learns that his uncle, Jim Joseph, has died. At home in Stehemish country, thinking "a hundred years ago I would have known who I was," Tom Joseph searches for a meaningful identity as he confronts serious contemporary environmental issues such as clear-cutting, preservation of old-growth cedars, road building in wilderness areas, and open-pit mining. "Between Two Worlds," Tom Joseph must choose to work for the mining or road-building company, to work for the Forest Service as a ranger with little power to protect the sacred wilderness, to work as a logger, to return to college, or to remain and fight the relentless intrusion of technology and waste into their ancestral landscape, just as his uncle had as a traditional Stehemish. In the end, after dynamiting the Hill Company's ten-thousand-gallon water tank, Tom Joseph listens and follows the "rising howl of the wolf." Pursued by old friends and enemies, Tom Joseph still follows the call of the wolf, "growing louder and louder and spinning in everwidening circles through the thin air until it was deafening and seemed a part of the air he breathed" (249), to the feet of "Dakobed, the great mother mountain," and then to the glaciated rocky ridges of the Stehemish mountains. In spite of the devastating losses depicted in *Wolfsong,* the lyrical narrative voice reveals a world view where all things living—word, spirit, and landscape, all creation—can exist together in harmonious balance. *Wolfsong* also challenges many persistent stereotypes of Indians:

An image of a plains warrior padding silently through the forest came to him and he smiled. Books and movies seldom showed Indians who looked like the Salish people of these mountains. Short, dark people dressed in woven cedar bark weren't as exciting as Sioux warriors in eagle-feather headdresses on horseback, the sun always setting behind them. (83)

He thought of the way his uncle liked to describe Columbus's discovery of America. "That's like when you need a new radio, so you go in the back window of your neighbor's house when he ain't home and discover his radio. Then you say, 'Oh, look at this wonderful radio I have discovered.'" (81)

Although for some students the language in *Wolfsong* might prove controversial, this is an excellent novel for older secondary students. It would work well with *Mean Spirit* by Linda Hogan; *Green Grass, Running Water* by Thomas King; and *Wind from an Enemy Sky* by D'Arcy McNickle, novels that also deal with conflicts over the use of natural resources in sacred Indian lands.

Power, Susan (Sioux). *The Grass Dancer.* New York: Berkeley Books, 1997. 333 pages.

Genre: Contemporary Novel

Themes: Remembering the Old Ways; Between Two Worlds; Change and Growth; Cultural and Personal Loss and Survival; Lifeways and Stereotypes

Grade Level: S

An enrolled member of the Standing Rock Sioux tribe and a native Chicagoan, Susan Power's mixed heritage and personal landscape is reflected in her characters' lives. Set primarily on a North Dakota Sioux Reservation along the "sluggish Missouri," with chapters featuring a variety of narrators, protagonists, and time periods, *The Grass Dancer* resembles the works of Louise Erdrich, who calls this "a wild river of a book."

Integral to the text are the Dakota words and phrases, with the controlling metaphors of grass and dancer that magically dance beyond the literal and sweep into dreams.

This is a saga of two families and their "living" ancestors, who act and react within the conflicts between cultures, between themselves, and within themselves. Beginning with an annual powwow in 1981, and the death of a champion grass dancer from Chicago, the novel depicts the ways these ancestors and relatives search out truths about their own heritage, and the ways they impact and direct one year in the lives of two teenagers, Harley Wind Soldier and Charlene Thunder. Theirs is the continuing story of Ghost Horse and Red Dress, who "died so long ago," but is "all wrapped up in her descendants and still looking for her lover." *Grass Dancer* is the story of both white and Indian "ghosts," of trickery and transformation, and of good and bad "medicine" and the women who possess and use it. But most important, it is a human story, encompassing both humor and tragedy as they exist in all of our lives.

Although *The Grass Dancer* is a novel about growing up and finding a personal identity that is linked to heritage, it is also a political work. Within the various plots and story lines, Power addresses a variety of critical issues. The influence of the church is visible in the lives of all the characters, but most of them are capable of using it as a tool to resist or to manipulate those who would overpower them. The novel also addresses the issues of German prisoners of war and Japanese internment during World War II.

According to Heidi Juel, AP English teacher at Roosevelt High School in Sioux Falls, South Dakota, *Grass Dancer* "clearly deals with adolescents' search for identity and place. It is difficult sometimes to sell them on the history or even the culture of a particular people, but that search for identity within peer and familial relationships, and, in the case of the book, ancestral relationships, is a classic theme that all adolescents seem able to grasp, discuss, and respond to. That 'hook' is pretty important. Then they are more willing to discuss other issues the book presents because they can already identify a reality which they understand."

Silko, Leslie Marmon (Laguna Pueblo). *Ceremony.* New York: Signet, 1977. 275 pp.
Genre: Contemporary Novel
Themes: Between Two Worlds; Cultural and Personal Loss and Survival
Grade Level: S   *NNAL* (575–586) Silko

Silko, a writer who emerged in the 1970s Native American literary renaissance, is one of the most widely anthologized Native writers today, and *Ceremony* is a classic American novel. In *Ceremony*, Tayo, the son of an Indian mother and a white man, has grown up a displaced mixed-blood, neither white nor traditionally Indian. His return to the Laguna Pueblo from World War II action in the Philippine jungle precipitates an identity search that culminates in his shifting from a confused individual identity toward a healthy communal identity. According to Louis Owens in *Other Destinies*, everything in the Pueblo cosmology, "whether animate or inanimate—is significant and has its ordered place and is knowable and therefore controllable" through "formula, ritual, and ceremony" (172). By the end of the novel, Tayo learns his personal responsibility toward this Laguna world when he "tells his own story" and locates himself within a context of myth, history, and ceremony. The text of *Ceremony* represents what Owens calls a "web" of interrelated "story, ceremony, and cure while also pointing toward the male-female balance that is the desired state in Pueblo ritual." Traditional story, especially the Corn Mother myth, provides the foundation of Tayo's story which "Silko [remakes, reforms, and molds] to fit new situations and times" (170). Mature secondary readers will find *Ceremony* a strong novel that exemplifies the contemporary Indian experience of "Living Between Two Worlds."

———. *Storyteller.* New York: Seaver, 1981. 281 pp.

Genre: Traditional Story, Memoir, Poetry

Themes: Between Two Worlds; Cultural and Personal Loss and Survival

Grade Level: S   *NNAL* (575–586) Silko

The stories of Silko's Laguna tradition wind through her own personal and family stories. Through poetry, prose, and photographs, Leslie Marmon Silko communicates the historical realities of place, connections between generations and peoples, and the dark realities of "hunger, poverty, and injustice." There is the story of Aunt Susie, "the last generation here at Laguna that passed down an entire culture by word of mouth" (5–6), and then there is one story Aunt Susie used to tell, about "the little girl who ran away." There is the story of her great-grandmother Marie Anaya, and her great-grandfather, who wouldn't stay in a hotel that refused to house his Indian sons, and the "one thing he had to remember [at Laguna]: No matter what is said to you by anyone, you must take care of those most dear to you" (256).

This collection of stories, and their connections in photographs and place, works well to stimulate students' own personal storytelling or story writing, and encourages them to use whatever format works best for them.

Slapin, Beverly. *Basic Skills Caucasian Americans Workbook.* Berkeley: Oyate, 1990. 32 pp.
Genre: Culture
Themes: Between Two Worlds; Lifeways and Stereotypes
Grade Level: I, S

This entire book takes a satirical look at the "mysterious world of the Caucasian," after the manner of workbooks about Indians. *Basic Skills* describes "Caucasian American Homes" and the "couch potato (kowch'-po-ta-to)"; "Caucasian American Clothing and Fashion," and her conclusion that "Men dictated (dik'-ta-tid) the customs, and women obeyed (o-bayd') them"; as well as the topics Language, Food Production, Education, Family Life, Government, Religion, Ceremonies, and Beliefs, and Leaders such as Leona Helmsley, Ivan Boesky, Lee Iaccoca, and George Bush.

While they enjoy laughing at themselves, students begin to understand the way stereotype denies individuality. After reading sections aloud, students can also discuss the impact such stereotypes might have on young people with low self-esteem, and they can discuss ways young people of all cultures and races can separate themselves from personal definitions that others (from outside their group) create. *Basic Skills,* an invaluable resource for teaching about bias and stereotype and for counteracting racism, is a joint project of Oyate and the Teaching Peace with Justice Task Force.

Sneve, Virginia Driving Hawk (Lakota). *The Chichi Hoohoo Bogeyman.* Lincoln: University of Nebraska Press, 1975. 63 pp.
Genre: Contemporary Story
Themes: Remembering the Old Ways; Change and Growth; At Home within Circles; Between Two Worlds; Lifeways and Stereotypes
Grade Level: I

This is the story of adventure, of loyalty to peers, of responsibilities to parents and to grandparents, of the effects of stereotypes on children, and of the strength of traditional cultural values and beliefs. When three cousins meet a strange man in the woods, they playfully name him the Chichi Hoohoo Bogeyman, after hearing Uncle George tell a story about his car honking in the middle of the night. Just as many parents have used the "bogeyman" to discipline their children, the Crow have used the *chedah*, the Sioux people have used the *chichi* spirit, which represents the enemy, and the Hopi have used the *hoohoo* to inspire children to behave appropriately. This novel easily contrasts with literature that exhibits traditional stereotypes of Indians. If Virginia Driving Hawk Sneve were to write more novels such as this one, we might see a dramatic turn away from romantic—and stereo-typical—stories about Indians, and toward Native-written works that depict young people in contemporary, more real-istic situations.

Standing Bear, Luther (Sioux). *Stories of the Sioux.* Lincoln: University of Nebraska Press, 1934. 79 pp.
   Genre: Historical and Traditional Story
   Themes: Remembering the Old Ways; Change and Growth; At Home within Circles
   Grade Level: I, S   *NNAL* (598–606) Standing Bear

Primarily for pleasure, Grandfathers and Grandmothers told and retold these stories of important events and historical hap-penings to children of the Sioux. Only a few stories in this col-lection provide explanations for natural and unnatural phenomena. Within each story are lessons for living the good Sioux life: to practice generosity and hospitality, especially to strangers; to welcome as relatives those who want and need a home; to trust in the power and truth of visions; to value highly the welfare of the entire community; to trust in the wis-dom of elders; to value bravery and endurance; to always face and respect the enemy; to value personal sacrifice, coopera-tion, and the practice of ritual for the welfare of all; to value self-reliance and resourcefulness in solving problems; to see the important way stories are linked to the landscape; to appreciate animals as relatives and for their value to humans; and to always value the giver as much as the gift. Students of all ages can enjoy these stories while they consider the ways the lessons may be applied to their present lives. Luther Standing Bear's stories suggest that, with utmost respect, the lives of animals must be sacrificed if the people are to live. They also demonstrate the ways stories are rooted in the sur-rounding landscape.

Stands in Timber, John (Cheyenne), and Margot Liberty. *Cheyenne Memories*. Lincoln: University of Nebraska Press, 1972. 330 pp.

Genre: As-Told-To Autobiography

Themes: Remembering the Old Ways; At Home within Circles; Between Two Worlds; Personal and Cultural Loss and Survival

Grade Level: S

Margot Liberty first met John Stands in Timber when she was teaching in a government school in eastern Montana in 1956. With a background in anthropology, and assistance from historians and other collaborators such as Alvin Josephy, Jr. and Liberty's mother, Helena Huntington Smith, Margot Liberty recorded and edited John Stands in Timber's memories. *Cheyenne Memories* includes stories of chiefs, tribal societies, medicine and ceremony, intertribal wars, the Custer fight, Dull Knife's flight from Oklahoma, and the reservation years from 1890. Belle Highwalking, John Stands in Timber's sister, also has a written memoir. Students who want to concentrate on this time period and this tribe can also read the novel *Cheyenne Autumn* by Mari Sandoz and other nineteenth- and early twentieth-century Cheyenne stories.

Sterling, Shirley (Interior Salish). *My Name is Seepeetza*. Vancouver, BC: Groundwood Press, 1992. 126 pp.

Genre: Novel

Themes: Between Two Worlds; Cultural and Personal Loss and Survival; At Home within Circles

Grade Level: I, S

Written in diary form, Sterling has created a novel based on her own experiences. As a ten-year-old Seepeetza attends an Indian residential school, she is forced to deny all that being Indian means to her. The novel covers one school year in which Seepeetza experiences conflicts with teachers, nuns, priests, and other students. The novel concludes with her return to the Joyaska Ranch, her "home," and her experiences with a loving father who drinks, with berry picking, and with her brothers and sisters. This is a story of living "Between Two Worlds," two cultures, two religions, and two ages. The narrative voice is neither an adult nor a child, as written. Instead, it is a combination of both, which can result in the reader's distrust and confusion over the narrator's identity. Still, it is a valuable voice that articulates the experience of thousands of young Indians.

Tapahonso, Luci (Navajo). *A Breeze Swept Through.* Albuquerque: West End Press, 1987. 51 pp.

Genre: Poetry

Themes: Remembering the Old Ways; Between Two Worlds; At Home within Circles; Cultural and Personal Loss and Survival

Grade Level: P, I, S   *NNAL* (628–634) Tapahonso

These lyrical poems, dedicated and written for family, friends, and neighbors, reflect cultural and personal survival. Tapahonso uses concrete images of "white silver" moons, "hair tied securely in the wind and dust," and sighs, cries, and prevailing and enduring laughter. In "Yes, It Was My Grandmother," the speaker celebrates her connection with her grandmother. In others, she celebrates her children's births, her brother's death, "old stories," and a ritual performed "For Misty Starting School," when the speaker sprinkles "cornmeal here / by the door of your classroom" to "[bless] us and / [strengthen] us" so Misty may remember [she is] no different" from the earth "where the cornmeal is from" (20–21). No matter what the family tradition, all young people can identify with this experience of carrying their values of home into the public school. Realistic, yet optimistic, these poems can lift the spirit and communal pride of even the youngest readers.

————. *Sáanii Dahataal: The Women Are Singing.* Tucson: The University of Arizona Press, 1993. 94 pp.

Genre: Poetry, Story

Themes: Remembering the Old Ways; At Home within Circles

Grade Level: P, I, S   *NNAL* (628–634) Tapahonso

Again, Luci Tapahonso shares her poems and stories, which have provided "a means for returning, for rejuvenation, and for restoring [her] spirits to the state of *hohzo,* or beauty, which is the basis of Navajo philosophy" (xii). In her Preface she says, "To know stories, remember stories, and to retell them well is to have been 'raised right'; the family of such an individual is also held in high esteem . . . I was taught that the way one talks and conducts oneself is a direct reflection of the people who raised her or him. People are known then by their use of language" (xi).

Taylor, Drew Hayden (Ojibway). *Toronto at Dreamer's Rock/Education Is Our Right.* Saskatoon, Saskatchewan, 1990. 139 pp.

Genre: Drama

Themes: Between Two Worlds; Remembering the Old Ways; Cultural and Personal Loss and Survival

Grade Level: I, S

Obliquely echoing Charles Dickens' *Christmas Carol,* the first play, *Toronto at Dreamer's Rock,* dramatizes the story of three boys who hold a surprise "Toronto," a word for "where people gather to trade . . . a place where important things happen" (37). When Rusty goes to an age-old dreaming place on the Birch Island Reserve to drink his beer and listen to his walkman, he is suddenly joined by Keesic, a precontact Odawa boy, and later by Michael from the year 2095, an intellectual, who applies his knowledge of history and his analytical abilities to understand the other two boys. Keesic challenges Rusty to learn and practice "The Old Ways," to know the language, the rituals, the sacred ceremonies, and Michael shows both boys how very much will be lost before the people begin to recover. But when Michael takes out a newspaper clipping from 2023, Rusty learns that he will one day be the "first Grand Chief of the Aboriginal Government." When the play ends, Rusty is alone, and he holds a feather up to the Four Directions. The audience is left with the hope that Rusty will find a way to live up to the prophecy printed in the newspaper, and a way to apply "The Old Ways" to the problems in the future. Although Taylor is Canadian, *Toronto at Dreamer's Rock* will appeal to young adult readers who can identify with a young boy trying to escape reality while he remains separated from the traditions of his ancestors.

Education Is Our Right also borrows from Charles Dickens, but in this version, the Spirits of Education Past, Present, and Future attempt to show the minister of Indian Affairs the error of his ways. The play was produced less than a year after Pierre Cadieux, then the Federal Minister of Indian and Northern Affairs in Quebec, announced a cap on post-secondary education for Native students. The walk to the nation's capital, a hunger strike in Ottawa, residential schools, and the Elders' storytelling in the play are all based on real incidents.

Two Leggings (Crow). *Two Leggings: The Making of a Crow Warrior.* Ed. Peter Nabokov. New York: Crowell, 1967. 226 pp.

Genre: Memoir

Themes: Remembering the Old Ways; Growth and Change; At Home within Circles; Between Two Worlds

Grade Level: S

This work is the result of a collaboration between: Two Leggings (1847–1923) who communicated in Crow and sign language; Jasper Long and possibly Thomas H. Leforge, and Mrs. Taylor who would take Long's translation in shorthand; William Wildschut, the interviewer who wrote down Two Leggings' reminiscences between 1919–1923; and Peter Nabokov, who edited Wildschut's manuscript.

Through the memory of an old man, Nabokov sees the idealized "coming-of-age struggle" Two Leggings experienced, regretting the loss of Old Ways. Both Ewers and Nabakov believe that Two Leggings' search for and frequent failure to obtain power through visions was the motivation for many of his actions throughout his life. After reading this book independently, an eleventh-grade student wrote: "this story should be read by young teens. It tells how to act, and it teaches that if a person desires something, and if he works honestly for it, then he will get it. This book helps students understand pre-whiteman history."

Vizenor, Gerald (Chippewa). *Dead Voices: Natural Agonies in the New World.* Norman: University of Oklahoma Press, 1992. 144 pp.
Genre: Contemporary Novel
Themes: Remembering the Old Ways; Between Two Worlds; Cultural and Personal Loss and Survival
Grade Level: S   *NNAL* (635–648) Vizenor

From the very beginning, Vizenor admits he is playing the trickster with this novel. Through the power of imagination, story, and transformation, his modern characters survive—in the city—to realize their "human possibilities." According to the publisher's cover notes, *Dead Voices* is a cycle of tales in which "Bagese, a tribal woman transformed into a bear, has discovered a new urban world [seen] from the perspective [of cross-bloods] . . . fleas, squirrels, mantis, crows, beavers, and finally Trickster, Vizenor's central and unifying figure" (cover). *Dead Voices,* or "published stories," takes a satirical view of the European-American/Native experience with tricksters such as "exterminators" who practice chemical warfare, "hunters" who pretend to be like the animals and then move in for the kill, and fur traders. Especially for older students who are familiar with traditional trickster stories, and for adult readers who are open to the possibilities for new visions of old stories, this novel is a joy to read. Individual chapters may be read aloud to students in combination with relevant narratives and poetry. For example, sections of the chapter on "Fleas" can be used with narratives about smallpox epidemics in books such as *Fools Crow,* by James Welch.

In response to her independent reading of *Dead Voices,* an eleventh-grade student wrote that "Vizenor's people believed in Nanabozho, an all powerful trickster in the world. . . . I think if readers do not let the trickster inside themselves escape, then the book will not connect." On the basis of the lesson the *Dead Voices* storyteller learns from Bagase, "not to pretend but to see and hear the real stories behind the words, the voices of the animals in me, the definition of the words alone," this student concluded that "This book made me sit back and listen to nature." She didn't want to be "living in a world of dead voices," with one of those voices being her own.

Welch, James (Blackfeet/Gros Ventre). *The Death of Jim Loney.* New York: Penguin, 1979. 179 pp.
Genre: Contemporary Novel
Themes: Between Two Worlds; Remembering the Old Ways; Cultural and Personal Loss and Survival
Grade Level: S					*NNAL* (659–668) Welch

James Welch was born on the Blackfeet Reservation in 1940 and currently lives and writes in Missoula, Montana. Asking the question "Where do you go when no one wants you?" *The Death of Jim Loney* explores the surface problem of alcoholism, but more important, the twisted reality of the alcoholic's world and the problems of internal separation, the loss of spirituality, and the hopelessness that can happen to anyone. Although the book's characters are not classic heroes who achieve success and happiness in the end, they do grow, and students can look at what must happen before that can occur. An eleventh-grade reader identified several values he found in the novel: a respect for women, the importance of dreams, and the importance of home, landscape and nature's animals; the latter values he found evidenced in the incident where "Loney's dog dies, frozen in mud, and Loney chips away the dead dog only to bury it where it had lived all its life." Another reader described the conclusion of *The Death of Jim Loney* thus: "He usually gets drunk or close to drunk every night. Both his sister and girl friend try to save Loney and take him away from Harlem, but both are unsuccessful. Throughout all of this, he keeps seeing a black bird (an allusion to the bird in Blackfeet mythology). At the end when the police go to Mission Canyon, they find Loney and shoot him, and the last thing he ever sees is a big black bird flying away. This symbol suggests that Jim Loney, like the narrator in *Winter in the Blood*, overcomes his hopelessness by taking his place within an ancestral culture and community."

———. *Fools Crow.* New York: Viking/Penguin, 1986. 391 pp.
Genre: Historical Fiction
Themes: Remembering the Old Ways; At Home within Circles; Between Two Worlds; Cultural and Personal Loss and Survival
Grade Level: I					*NNAL* (659–668) Welch

Although Welch's poetry and earlier novels focus on contemporary themes of estrangement, search for self, and return to the Indian world, *Fools Crow*, winner of the *Los Angeles Times* Book Prize, and the Pacific Northwest Booksellers Association Book Award for 1987, portrays two years in the life of a Pikuni (Blackfeet) leader during the 1870s. The novel describes the traditional lifeways of the Pikuni people who lived below Chief Mountain in Blackfeet country and the consequent changes forced on the tribe during the time when whites migrated into Montana territory. Fools Crow (White Man's Dog) experiences conflicts with individuals within the tribe, with other bands and tribes, with Napikwans (whites), with loss of game, and with smallpox. Finally, 173 sick old men, women, and children die when "seizers" attack Heavy Runner's village, culminating in the Baker Massacre of January 1870. But the novel does not end with despair. Instead, Fools Crow remains at peace and in harmony with the earth and his people: "He felt in his heart, in the rhythm of the drum, a peculiar kind of happiness—a happiness that sleeps with sadness" (390). Students appreciate the way Welch adheres to a more traditional Blackfeet vocabulary, i.e., "wood-biter" (beaver), "ears-far-apart" (owl), and "the Backbone of the World" (Rocky Mountains). The novel encourages further interest and reading about tribal culture, values, and historical events; and students begin to ask questions of their own ancestry. When whole collections or individual Blackfeet stories, such as those by Percy Bullchild, are read or heard before reading the novel, students have a better understanding and acceptance of distinct cultural beliefs.

Fools Crow, the most widely studied Native American novel in Montana's high schools, may be paired with Ella Deloria's *Waterlily*, which features a female Dakota Sioux protagonist from the same time period as Welch's novel. After reading *Fools Crow* in a Western literature class, a German exchange student wrote that "I have always felt a terrible guilt over what the Nazis did to the Jews during World War II, but I had no idea the same kind of killing had happened with the Indians in America. I felt such a terrible sadness as I read this book."

———. *Winter in the Blood.* New York: Viking/Penguin, 1987. 176 pp.
Genre: Contemporary Novel
Themes: Between Two Worlds; Remembering the Old Ways; Cultural and Personal Loss and Survival
Grade Level: S   *NNAL* (659–668) Welch

Published globally, *Winter in the Blood* features an unnamed narrator who searches for his identity, like so many young people today, feeling distant and alienated from both the Native and non-Native worlds. However, through a conversation with his grandfather, Yellow Calf, the narrator begins to learn the importance of balance and a human being's interdependent place within the physical and spiritual universe. In Yellow Calf's world, the animals suffer and know—probably sooner than humans—when harmony within the cosmos is broken. *Winter in the Blood* demonstrates the way memories inform the present. The narrator grows when he begins to make sense of his father's and brother's deaths; he grows by regaining his personal dignity and by moving into a physical and spiritual balance with the earth. And in the end, there is his homecoming: When he saves the cow, he decides to live to free himself of the "winter in the blood" that has kept him from even his own feelings. Louis Owens, in *Other Destinies*, writes of Welch's *Winter in the Blood*, comparing it somewhat with T.S. Eliot's *The Waste Land*:

Within this drought-stricken landscape, mirroring in its sterility the inner state of the narrator, men and women seem at war with one another, communication fails repeatedly, and the present balances precariously between voids where past disappears and future cannot be imagined. The narrator's story unfolds in roughly sequential actions, the achronological tradition of Native American storytelling entering the text only as Welch allows the surrealism of dreams to interpenetrate everyday reality and exploits the familiar technique of flashback to merge past and present. (128)

———, guest ed. "Tribes." *Ploughshares*, 20.1 (Spring 1994). 210 pp. (entire issue).
Genre: Contemporary Story
Theme: Cultural and Personal Loss and Survival
Grade Level: S

As editor of this volume of *Ploughshares*, entitled "Tribes," James Welch has included works from "poets and storytellers . . . who strain *Webster's* definition of tribe," but who belong to "the tribe of good writing" (7). The volume begins with works of traditional tribal writers such as Elizabeth Woody, Simon Ortiz, Scott Momaday, Sherman Alexie, Anita Endrezze, and Diane Glancy, as well as three excerpts from Salish writer Debra Earling's novel *Perma Red*: "Bad Ways," "Winter Deeds," and "Old Ghosts." "Bad Ways" begins in "a spot in the road [on the Flathead Reservation] where the wind smells like sulfur, a dark smell, something you think you should be able to leave behind you, but it will be in your clothing and in your shoes. And there will be a darkness in the way you see things, a darkness you wish you could leave" (15). This is a dark story about Indian men who were tricked into sacrificing the woman White Crow "for the [whiteman's] promise of 'treasures.'" But the story doesn't end with White Crow dancing dead in the water: "These men, these Indians, they did back to the white man what the white man had done, not thinking of what it might do to them, not thinking what more it would take . . . (19)." Earling closes this story with the truth of the way these "Bad Ways" literally become a part of "a bad smell" in the landscape. Nevertheless, the narrator knows that recovery and survival are real; "we have to hook [the power that is leaving us], snag it like a great struggling fish and pull it back" (15–33).

Welch, James (Blackfeet/Gros Ventre), with Paul Stekler. *Killing Custer: The Battle of the Little Bighorn and the Fate of the Plains Indians*. New York: Norton, 1994. 317 pp.

Genre: Nonfiction, Personal Memoir, Historical Narrative

Themes: Lifeways and Stereotypes; Personal and Cultural Loss and Survival; Between Two Worlds

Grade Level: S   *NNAL* (659–668) Welch

This is Welch's first nonfiction work, based on the research he and director Paul Stekler conducted for their script for the American Experience documentary, "Last Stand at the Little Bighorn." Beginning with his search for answers to the questions *how?* and *why?* for his ancestors' deaths at the Baker Massacre on the Marias, Welch goes on to explore the stories and search for answers to "The Battle of the Little Bighorn."

Killing Custer represents Welch and Stekler's examinations of personal narratives, the frequently contradictory anthropological evidence, the cultural background of the Plains Indians, the economic and political situation in America at the time, and the stories behind typically empty textbook narratives.

Throughout the text, the voice and point of view shifts, providing readers with a variety of experiences and resources as they work toward discovering the answers to the questions themselves. In the storyteller's voice, through his colloquial expressions, his profound understatement, and with details that flush out the smiles, Welch resurrects a much more human and more vulnerable, and somewhat less respectable, Custer. This is a Custer who "left his column frequently to go hunting. On one such hunting trip, he was chasing a buffalo alone and shot his horse in the head when the buffalo swerved" (60). Welch also portrays the humanity and eccentricities of the Indians as well: "After much folderol, which included continuing jealousy and rivalry between Red Cloud and Spotted Tail, a spot was picked for the meeting—eight miles from Red Agency (neither chief would go to the other's agency)" (85). In the expository voice, Welch (and/or Stekler) reports the research, theories, and conclusions from anthropologists, military records, recorded interviews with participants of the Battle of the Little Bighorn, as well as with descendants living today who have the oral records of their grandfathers' experiences. First describing the battle from the Indians' point of view, telling their stories about *how* and *why*, Welch turns to describe the battle from the point of view of the military and from the individual men involved. In graphic, violent images, Welch describes the deaths and subsequent mutilations of many of the soldiers and Indians. And with Welch himself, as he looks at the battlefield, "you" are drawn to the place where this happened, to answer the questions of *how* and *why* for yourself.

Killing Custer does not resurrect the "Noble Indian." Instead, by looking at the multiple sides of this story, Welch presents to readers the complex humanity of all participants, demonstrating the terrible capabilities which may lie within us all. *Killing Custer* is one history book our young people won't be able to stuff under their desks, hoping for osmosis to work its tricks. Through the vehicle of story and the substance of myth, James Welch demythologizes Custer's ill-fated attack on a huge encampment of Plains Indians on June 25, 1876. In *Killing Custer,* Welch resurrects not only the "fleeting, a good, often exhilarating feeling" of victory, and not only the subsequent defeat which meant "death . . . of a way of life," he resurrects this truth—that the endurance of "the Indian spirit" remains "hard to break" (286).

Students can easily read this independently, but history classes should require it as evidence of the limits and possibilities in research. Critical Thinking classes should study *Killing Custer* for its demonstration of the way writers can verbally present and clarify contradictions, postulate theories, and then draw thoughtful conclusions on the basis of both available and unavailable evidence. *Killing Custer* is an excellent resource for an introduction into the culture of the Plains Indians, and much of the text represents an exploration of stereotype—the truths behind the myths and the sometimes frightening truths about those who believe the myths.

Roots and Branches

Wood, Erskine. *Days with Chief Joseph.* Vancouver, WA: Rosewind
     Press, 1970. 38 pp.
     Genre: Memoir from a Diary
     Themes: Between Two Worlds; Lifeways and Stereotypes;
     Remembering the Old Ways
     Grade Level: I, S

Lt. Charles Erskine Scott Wood, the special officer in charge of
Chief Joseph at the Colville Reservation in Northeastern Washington, was also the officer who wrote down the words of
Chief Joseph in his often quoted remark, "I will fight no more
forever." Wood continued to campaign for the right of the Nez
Perce people to return to their home in the Wallowa Valley. His
son, Erskine, wrote this diary at the age of fourteen, during his
second lengthy visit with Chief Joseph. The text includes several photographs, a preface written in 1970, in which Erskine
Wood reflects on the writing, on its accuracy, and on a few
"boyish" exaggerations; and the text closes with Wood's "recollections of Chief Joseph." The following situation demonstrates
the marked differences between the two cultures and world
views, as well as serving as an example of misunderstandings
which lead to dire consequences for many Indian people:

My father had written me to tell Joseph that if there was anything my
father could do for him he was, through me, to let my father know. I
gave this message to Joseph, and he said that he would like a good
stallion to improve the breed of his pony herd. I looked on Joseph
as . . . a noble chief driven out of his ancestral home, I revered him so,
that I thought his request for a stallion was too puny—was beneath
him. I thought he ought to ask if my father . . . could get him back a
portion of his Wallowa Valley . . . I shook my head and said, "No, that
was not what my father meant." Joseph accepted this calmly . . . but I
always regretted my utter stupidity. A fine stallion would have
upbred Joseph's herd of ponies . . . just the kind of thing in his Indian
life that he needed, and of course well within the ability of my father
to get for him. But just because I exalted him so high I deprived him
of it, and it is something I shall always regret. (38)

     The honesty in this text provides a strong contrast with
other popular literatures about Chief Joseph.

Woody, Elizabeth. (Yakama/Warm Springs/Wasco/Navajo). *Seven
     Hands, Seven Hearts.* Portland, OR: Eighth Mountain Press,
     1994. 127 pp.
     Genre: Story, Essay, Poetry
     Themes: All themes
     Grade Level: I, S

Seven Hands, Seven Hearts includes the entirety of Elizabeth Woody's highly acclaimed first book of poems, *Hand into Stone*—winner of the American Book Award—as well as new poems, stories, and essays. According to Woody's publishers, "The work is united by common themes: a rootedness in the Northwest landscape, the histories of her ancestors, and the ongoing struggle to define what it means to be a tribal member, an American, and a woman at the end of the twentieth century" (cover). Her ancestral connections are demonstrated in lines excerpted from her Introduction: "I have been learning to weave root bags. It requires a thought process I've been in need of for a long time. It claimed me, coming from women on both sides of my family who are weavers: my Navajo grandmother Annie Woody wove rugs; my Warm Springs grandmother Elizabeth Pitt wove cornhusk bags and roots bags" (15).

Joy Harjo and Simon Ortiz comment about the value of this poet's work: "In these times we are being forced to recognize the circular web that has always connected us, all of us, and to reconstruct it with the gift of our word—concurrently overturning the decay, uprooting denial—and Elizabeth Woody's work is an essential part of this transition, for she follows in the tradition of peoples who have understood the power of language, and the place of a poet/singer/storyteller at the center of the world" (Harjo). "Her gift of language, honed with compassion, wisdom, and love, offers the wonderfully affirming mythic power of her Native heritage . . ." (Ortiz). Teachers will easily find many ways to make connections for their students with this powerful book of poetry and prose.

Zitkala-Ša (Gertrude Simmons Bonnin, Yankton Sioux). *American Indian Stories.* Lincoln: University of Nebraska Press, [1900] 1985. 195 pp.
Genre: Autobiographical Essay, Short Story
Themes: Remembering the Old Ways; At Home within Circles; Change and Growth; Between Two Worlds; Cultural and Personal Loss and Survival
Grade Level: I, S   *NNAL* (169–176) Bonnin

Zitkala-Ša was born on the Yankton Reservation in 1876 to a white father and a Yankton Dakota mother, Tate I Yohin Win (Reaches for the Wind), from whom she learned the ways of her people. Three autobiographical essays originally published in 1900 in *The Atlantic Monthly* begin this collection, which also includes short stories of warriors, conflicts with the white man, and selected essay clips about "America's Indian Problem." Frequently formal, it is typical of much turn-of-the-century writing.

In the first essay, "Impressions of an Indian Childhood," Zitkala-Ša presents the late-nineteenth-century life of a young girl at home on the "Dakota" prairie, with her mother, her extended family, and her tribal community (7–45). Zitkala-Ša shares the lessons in beadwork, hospitality, generosity, and the lessons in stories from her childhood; she recognizes that the suffering Indian people have endured from contact with the white man, and she affirms the humanity and valuable old ways of her Native culture.

In the second essay, "School Days of an Indian Girl," Quaker missionaries take the eight-year-old from her reservation community to a boarding school in the East where she remains separated from her mother for three years. Her traditional values of respect for others and respect for elders conflict with her need to assert her right to remain traditionally Indian in values and behavior (47–80). The education toward assimilation that Gertrude Simmons received at distant boarding schools contributed to her mother's rejection because her mother viewed this choice as a turning away from her people. Consequently, she gave herself the name Zitkala-Ša (Red Bird) to affirm her Native identity.

In the third essay, "An Indian Teacher," the narrator returns to teach in an Indian boarding school, remaining separated from her family and community. Struggling to maintain her traditional tribal values, she works to survive and prevail in the dominant European American society (81–100).

Dexter Fisher suggests this writing "represents one of the first attempts by a Native American woman to write her own story without the aid of an editor, an interpreter, or an ethnographer" (Foreword). Although *American Indian Stories* presents a polarized view of the Indian/white conflict, Zitkala-Ša has achieved a great deal of sophistication and power in her writing by relying on her Native culture, and then uses the English language to assert the civilized and frequently "superior" humanity of her Indian people to a non-Indian audience. Mentioning neither the reservation nor the specific names of schools, the writer also communicates much more than autobiography; she communicates the very universal experience of Native American children for more than half a century. *American Indian Stories* and *Old Indian Legends* were her only formal publications, but Gertrude Simmons Bonnin continued to work as an advocate for Native American rights and for the Pan-Indian movement.

Throughout these essays and stories, Zitkala-Ša develops characters who play Iktomi (the Dakota trickster/transformer culture hero), and so students' understanding and experience with the essays can be enhanced by first reading a collection of Dakota or Sioux traditional stories. Then they can look for ways the writer and characters outsmart the trickster in Zitkala-Ša's *American Indian Stories.*

For Further Reading

Alexie, Sherman (Spokane/Coeur d'Alene). *The Business of Fancy Dancing.* Hanging Loose Press, 1992.
Genre: Poetry
Themes: Between Two Worlds; Cultural and Personal Loss and Survival
Grade Level: S
Calling his writing "Fancy Dancing," which provides an outlet for what "hurts the most," the poems in this collection feature the centrality of games (football and basketball) and ceremony to the reservation Indians.

———. *Indian Killer.* New York: Atlantic Monthly Press, 1996. 432 pp.
Genre: Contemporary Novel
Theme: Between Two Worlds; Cultural and Personal Loss and Survival
Grade Level: S

———. *Old Shirts and New Skins.* Los Angeles: University of California Press, 1993. 91 pp.
Genre: Poetry
Theme: Between Two Worlds; Cultural and Personal Loss and Survival
Grade Level: S

———. *Reservation Blues.* New York: Warner Books, 1996. 320 pp.
Genre: Contemporary Novel
Theme: Between Two Worlds; Cultural and Personal Loss and Survival
Grade Level: S

Armstrong, Jeannette (Okanagan). *Breath Tracks.* Penticton, BC: Theytus, 1991. 112 pp.
Genre: Poetry
Themes: Between Two Worlds; Cultural and Personal Loss and Survival
Grade Level: S   *NNAL* (144–148) Armstrong

————. *Slash.* Penticton, BC: Theytus, 1990. 254 pp.
Genre: Historical Novel
Themes: Between Two Worlds; Cultural and Personal Loss and Survival
Grade Level: I, S   *NNAL* (144–148) Armstrong

A teenage male protagonist experiences the major events in the Indian self-determination movement of the 1960s and 1970s across both Canada and the United States.

Benton-Banai, Edward (Anishinabe). *Generation to Generation.* St. Paul: Red School House, 1991. 21 pp.
Genre: Memoir
Themes: Remembering the Old Ways; Between Two Worlds
Grade Level: I, S

Benton-Banai's family and tribal reminiscences, which the author dedicates "To all the Grandmothers and Grandfathers who have held on so tenaciously, lovingly and with quiet, lasting hope to the meaning of Anishinabe. . . ."

————. *Mishomis Book: The Voice of the Ojibway.* St. Paul, MN: Indian Country Communications, 1991.
Genre: Memoir, Traditional Story
Themes: Remembering the Old Ways; At Home within Circles; Lifeways and Stereotypes
Grade Level: I, S

A spiritual odyssey and the teachings of the Ojibway people, contradicting the negative ways in which Native life has been presented.

Big Crow, Moses Nelson (Lakota). *Hoksila and the Red Buffalo.* Chamberlain, SD: Tipi Press, 1991. 40 pp.
Genre: Traditional Story
Themes: Remembering the Old Ways; Change and Growth
Grade Level: I, S

"One of the oldest stories" the storyteller knows, passed down from generation to generation and changing with each telling.

Bird, Gloria (Spokane). *Full Moon on the Reservation.* Greenfield Center, NY: Greenfield Review Press, 1994.
Genre: Poetry
Themes: Remembering the Old Ways; Between Two Worlds
Grade Level: S

The 1992 winner of the Native Authors First Book Award.

Brand, Johanna (Micmac). *The Life and Death of Anna Mae Aquash.* Toronto: J. Lorimer, 1978. 203 pp.
Genre: Biography
Themes: Cultural and Personal Loss and Survival; Between Two Worlds
Grade Level: S

The story of Anna Mae Aquash, a Micmac warrior from Nova Scotia and a member of the American Indian Movement, who was murdered and then had her hands severed and sent to Washington for fingerprinting.

Broker, Ignatia (Ojibway). *Night Flying Woman.* Minneapolis: Minnesota Historical Society, 1983. 135 pp.
Genre: Memoir
Themes: Remembering the Old Ways; Change and Growth; Between Two Worlds; At Home within Circles; Cultural and Personal Loss and Survival
Grade Level: I, S

Recollections from Oona, the speaker, of traditional and historical stories for her grandchildren, demonstrating the strength of Ojibway people to survive.

Brown, Emily Ivanoff (Inuit). *Tales of Ticasuk: Eskimo Legends and Stories.* Juneau: University of Alaska Press.
Genre: Traditional Story
Theme: Remembering the Old Ways
Grade Level: I, S

Traditional stories about wise old ladies, brave orphans, heroic hunters, arrogant young women, people who are clever and magical, and evil and greed.

Bruchac, Joseph. (Abenaki). *Between Earth and Sky.* New York: Harcourt, Brace, 1996. 30 pp.
Genre: Traditional Story
Themes: Remembering the Old Ways; At Home within Circles
Grade Level: P, I

A beautiful and inspiring book about some of the special places that are sacred to Native people, special places in the East, North, South, and West, as well as Above, Below, and Center.

———. *Dawn Land.* Golden, CO: Fulcrum, 1993. 317 pp.
Genre: Novel
Themes: Remembering the Old Ways; Change and Growth
Grade Level: S

Set in the Northeastern country of North America about ten thousand years ago, *Dawn Land* is a story based on the oral traditions and history of the Abenaki people that centers on the quest of Young Hunter.

————. *The First Strawberries.* New York: Dial, 1993. 30 pp.
Genre: Traditional Story
Theme: Remembering the Old Ways
Grade Level: P, I

The retelling of a Cherokee tale about the way strawberries came into the world; illustrated with watercolor paintings by Anna Vojtech.

————. *Long River.* Golden, CO: Fulcrum, 1995. 298 pp.
Genre: Novel
Themes: Remembering the Old Ways; Change and Growth
Grade Level: S

A novel about friendship, courage, trust, and adventure, with the characters who first appeared in *Dawn Land.*

————. *Native American Stories* (1991) and *Native American Animal Stories* (1993). Golden, CO: Fulcrum. 160 pp. each.
Genre: Traditional Story
Theme: Remembering the Old Ways
Grade Level: I, S

Collections of stories told by Joseph Bruchac, taken from Caduto and Bruchac's excellent educational resources, *Keepers of the Earth* and *Keepers of the Animals.*

Bruchac, Joseph (Abenaki), and Jonathan London. *Thirteen Moons on Turtle's Back: A Native American Year of Moons.* New York: Philomel, 1992. 30 pp.
Genre: Traditional Story
Theme: Remembering the Old Ways
Grade Level: P, I

A collection of storytelling poems, illustrated by Thomas Locker, which focus on Native relationships with the thirteen moons of each year.

Campbell, Maria (Métis). *Little Badger and the Fire Spirit.* Toronto: McClelland and Stewart, 1977.
Genre: Traditional Story
Themes: Remembering the Old Ways; At Home within Circles
Grade Level: P, I

The story of wisdom learned from Grey Coyote, in which Little Badger befriends the Mountain Goat, the Mountain Lion, the Grizzly Bear, the Rattlesnake, and the Fire Spirit, to bring the warmth of fire to his people.

————. *People of the Buffalo: How the Plains Indians Lived.* Vancouver: Douglas & McIntyre, 1976. 47 pp.

Genre: Culture and History

Themes: Remembering the Old Ways; At Home within Circles

Grade Level: P, I

A book showing how Plains Indians lived, a people who felt the spiritual connection between all aspects of life, and for whom "every part of life and all forms of life made up 'the whole.'" The book does much to counter the romanticized stereotypes of Plains Indians.

Charbonneau, Eileen (Cherokee). *The Ghosts of Stony Clove.* New York: Tom Doherty, 1988. 164 pp.

Genre: Historical Novel

Themes: Change and Growth; Between Two Worlds; and Remembering the Old Ways

Grade Level: I, S

A ghost story/romance and the first in Charbonneau's historical trilogy, featuring Asher Woods, the father of Joshua Woods, the protagonist of *In the Time of the Wolves.* Recommended for young adult readers.

Conley, Robert (Cherokee). *Mountain Windsong, a Novel of the Trail of Tears.* Norman: University of Oklahoma Press, 1994. 218 pp.

Genre: Historical Fiction

Themes: Between Two Worlds; Cultural and Personal Loss and Survival

Grade Level: S

A love story that brings to life the suffering and endurance of the Cherokee people.

Cook-Lynn, Elizabeth (Crow Creek Sioux). *The Power of Horses and Other Stories.* New York: Arcade, 1990. 131 pp.

Genre: Short Story

Themes: Cultural and Personal Loss and Survival; Between Two Worlds; At Home within Circles

Grade Level: I, S

Stories filled with "beauty, gentleness, charm and humor," of people living on the reservation who suffer grief when sons fight in foreign wars, when alcoholic mothers lose their children, and when the white man's injustice prevails.

————. *Then Badger Said This.* Fairfield, WA: Ye Galleon Press, 1983. 39 pp.
   Genre: Contemporary and Traditional Story, Song, Poetry
   Themes: Remembering the Old Ways; Between Two Worlds; Cultural and Personal Loss and Survival
   Grade Level: I, S

"Fictional" stories, songs, and poems, "born of a very real and usable past which remains unforgettable."

Culleton, Beatrice (Métis). *Spirit of the White Bison.* Winnipeg: Pemmican, 1985. 64 pp.
   Genre: Novel
   Theme: Personal and Cultural Loss and Survival
   Grade Level: I

A young bison growing up on the plains in the late 1800s faces peril at the hands of soldiers who are destroying the great buffalo herds as a way to control the Native tribes.

Cuthand, Beth (Cree). *Voices in the Waterfall.* Penticton, BC: Theytus, 1992. 80 pp.
   Genre: Poetry
   Themes: Remembering the Old Ways; Cultural and Personal Loss and Survival
   Grade Level: S

Dorris, Michael (Modoc). *The Broken Cord.* New York: HarperCollins, 1989. 300 pp.
   Genre: Memoir
   Themes: Between Two Worlds; Cultural and Personal Loss and Survival
   Grade Level: S

The story of Michael Dorris's adopted son, Adam, who suffered from Fetal Alcohol Syndrome.

Dudley, Joseph Iron Eye (Sioux). *Chouteau Creek.* Lincoln: University of Nebraska Press, 1992. 189 pp.
   Genre: Autobiography
   Themes: Remembering the Old Ways; Between Two Worlds; Cultural and Personal Loss and Survival
   Grade Level: S

A memoir recalling stories—including the first Wounded Knee tragedy—from Dudley's maternal Indian grandparents, who lived on the Yankton Sioux Reservation in the 1940s.

Durham, Jimmie (Cherokee). *Columbus Day: Poems, Drawings and Stories About American Indian Life and Death in the Nineteen-Seventies.* Albuquerque: West End Press, 1983. 104 pp.

Genre: Stories, Poetry

Themes: At Home within Circles; Between Two Worlds; Lifeways and Stereotypes; Cultural and Personal Loss and Survival

Grade Level: I, S

Frey, Rodney, ed. *Stories That Make the World.* Norman: University of Oklahoma Press, 1995. 264 pp.

Genre: Traditional Story

Theme: Remembering the Old Ways

Grade Level: I, S

A collection of stories compiled with the help of Tom Yellowtail (Crow), Mari Watters (Nez Perce), Basil White (Kootenai), and the Coeur d'Alene storyteller Lawrence Aripa, which uses italics, ellipses, and stage directions to show the rhythm of the Native languages.

Geronimo (Apache). *Geronimo: His Own Story.* Ed. Steven Melvil Barrett. New York: Dutton, 1970. 206 pp.

Genre: Memoir, History

Themes: Remembering the Old Ways; At Home within Circles; Change and Growth; Cultural and Personal Loss and Survival

Grade Level: I, S

The dictated story of the culture and history of Geronimo's people.

Giago, Tim (Oglala Sioux). *Notes from Indian Country.* Vol 1. State Publishing, 1984. 423 pp.

Genre: Memoir, Journalism

Theme: Cultural and Personal Loss and Survival

Grade Level: S

A collection of newspaper columns Giago has written on communications, culture, education and athletics, government, health, humor, litigation, politics, rights, religion, and the people he has observed.

Goodbird, Edward (Hidatsa). *Goodbird the Indian.* St Paul: Minnesota Historical Society Press, 1985. 78 pp.
>   **Genre:** Autobiography
>   **Themes:** Remembering the Old Ways; Between Two Worlds
>   **Grade Level:** S
>
>   The life of Goodbird, who lived from 1869 to 1938.

Grinnell, George Bird. *Blackfeet Indian Stories.* Old Saybrook, CT: Applewood, 1913. 214 pp.
>   **Genre:** Traditional Story
>   **Theme:** Remembering the Old Ways
>   **Grade Level:** I, S
>
>   Stories compiled by a respected ethnologist who lived with the Blackfeet for a time and was recognized by them as a friend.

———. *When Buffalo Ran.* Norman: University of Oklahoma Press, 1966. 114 pp.
>   **Genre:** Story, Culture
>   **Themes:** Change and Growth; Remembering the Old Ways; Lifeways and Stereotypes
>   **Grade Level:** I, S
>
>   An early account of a traditional Cheyenne boy's life, from childhood to marriage, based on Grinnell's experience of spending forty summers with the Cheyenne. Other books by Grinnell include: *By Cheyenne Campfires; Alaska 1899; Blackfoot Lodge Tales; Cheyenne Indians, Volumes 1 and 2; Pawnee Hero Stories and Folktales; Punishment of the Stingy;* and *Two Great Scouts and their Pawnee.*

Hale, Janet Campbell (Coeur d'Alene). *Bloodlines: Odyssey of a Native Daughter.* New York: Random House, 1993. 187 pp.
>   **Genre:** Autobiography, Memoir
>   **Themes:** Between Two Worlds; Cultural and Personal Loss and Survival
>   **Grade Level:** S

Harcey, Dennis W., Brian R. Croone, and Joe Medicine Crow (Crow). *White-Man-Runs-Him, Crow Scout with Custer.* Evanston, IL: Evanston Publishing, 1993. 224 pp.
>   **Genre:** History, Biography
>   **Themes:** Between Two Worlds; Cultural and Personal Loss and Survival; Remembering the Old Ways
>   **Grade Level:** S

The story of a Crow warrior who adapted to the ways of the white man in order to maintain Crow land and the survival of his people.

Heat Moon, William Least (Osage/Sioux, William L. Trogdon). *Blue Highways: A Journey into America.* Boston: Little, Brown, 1982. 426 pp.
  Genre: Memoir, Autobiography
  Themes: Between Two Worlds; Cultural and Personal Loss and Survival; Lifeways and Stereotypes
  Grade Level: S

The narrator's travels throughout the country on the nation's secondary (Blue) highways, capturing the setting and character of the people he meets.

Henson, Lance (Southern Cheyenne). *A Cheyenne Sketchbook: Selected Poems 1970–1991.* Greenfield Center, NY: Greenfield Review Press, 1992. 54 pp.
  Genre: Poetry
  Themes: Remembering the Old Ways; At Home within Circles; Between Two Worlds; Cultural and Personal Loss and Survival
  Grade Level: I, S   *NNAL* (319–324) Henson

Short imagistic poems of translated tribal songs combined with contemporary images.

Highway, Thompson (Cree). *The Rez Sisters.* Saskatoon, Saskatchewan: Fifth House, 1988. 118 pp.
  Genre: Drama
  Themes: Between Two Worlds; Cultural and Personal Loss and Survival
  Grade Level: S

A funny and powerful portrayal of seven women from a reserve who attempt to beat the odds by playing bingo—the biggest bingo in the world, with a chance to win a way out of their tortured lives—written by an award-winning playwright.

Hungry Wolf, Beverly (Blackfoot). *The Ways of My Grandmothers.* New York: Quill Press, 1982. 249 pp.
  Genre: Memoir, Traditional Story
  Themes: Lifeways and Stereotypes; Remembering the Old Ways; Cultural and Personal Loss and Survival; At Home within Circles
  Grade Level: I, S

A thorough and honest collection of stories, myths, legends, and teachings presented as told to Beverly Hungry Wolf by her grandmothers over the years, together with recipes and clothing patterns that could be used for class projects.

Johnston, Basil H. (Ojibway). *Indian School Days.* Norman: University of Oklahoma Press, 1989. 250 pp.
Genre: Memoir
Themes: Between Two Worlds; Cultural and Personal Loss and Survival
Grade Level: S   *NNAL* (353–360) Johnston

A dark story told with wit and humor about assimilation pressures that the author survived in the Spanish Indian Residential [boarding] School.

———. *Ojibway Tales.* Saint Simons Island, GA: Bison, 1993. 188 pp.
Genre: Traditional Story
Theme: Remembering the Old Ways
Grade Level: S   *NNAL* (353–360) Johnston

A collection of twenty-two stories originally collected under the title *Moose Meat and Wild Rice.*

Josephy, Alvin M., Jr., Trudy Thomas, and Jeanne Eder (Sioux). *Wounded Knee, Lest We Forget.* Billings, MT: Artcraft Printers, 1990. 55 pp.
Genre: Memoir, History, Essay
Themes: Lifeways and Stereotypes; Cultural and Personal Loss and Survival; Between Two Worlds
Grade Level: S

A powerful presentation of the "enduring nature" of the tragedy of Wounded Knee, presented through photographs, history, and memoirs from descendants of the survivors.

King, Sandra (Ojibway). *Shannon/Ojibway Dancer.* Lerner, 1993. 48 pp.
Genre: Contemporary Story
Themes: Remembering the Old Ways; At Home within Circles; Between Two Worlds
Grade Level: I

A contemporary story about young girls and the pow-wow.

King, Thomas (Cherokee). *A Coyote Columbus Story.* Toronto: Ground-wood Publishing, 1992. 30 pp.
Genre: Traditional Story
Themes: Remembering the Old Ways; At Home within Circles; Between Two Worlds
Grade Level: I

Winner of the Governor General's Award.

————. *Medicine River.* New York: Viking, 1990.
Genre: Novel
Themes: Remembering the Old Ways; Cultural and Personal Loss and Survival
Grade Level: S

A novel about the situation with mixed-bloods, especially in Canada, where only full-bloods have the right to live on the reserves, which results in drifters who are disconnected from home and culture. But through compassionate trickery, they are brought home. King wrote a screenplay for *Medicine River* for CBE-TV in 1993, and he received the PEN/Josephine Miles Award for this novel.

LaFlesche, Francis (Omaha). *The Middle Five: Indian Schoolboys of the Omaha Tribe.* Madison: University of Wisconsin Press, 1963.
Genre: Memoir
Themes: Remembering the Old Ways; Between Two Worlds; Cultural and Personal Loss and Survival
Grade Level: I, S   *NNAL* (383–390) LaFlesche

A memoir of his early childhood as a "Sacred Child" in cere-monial rituals, as well as his school years in the mid-1800s at the Presbyterian Mission, first published in 1900.

Lame Deer (John Fire, Lakota) and Richard Erdoes. *Lame Deer, Seeker of Visions.* New York: Washington Square Press, 1972. 272 pp.
Genre: As-Told-To Autobiography
Theme: Remembering the Old Ways
Grade Level: S

LaPointe, Frank. *The Sioux Today.* Orinda, CA: Macmillan, 1972. 132 pp.
Genre: Culture
Themes: Remembering the Old Ways; At Home within Circles; Between Two Worlds; Cultural and Personal Loss and Survival
Grade Level: I, S

Lowie, Robert H. *Myths and Traditions of the Crow Indians.* Lincoln: University of Nebraska Press, 1993. 308 pp.
> **Genre:** Traditional Story
> **Theme:** Remembering the Old Ways
> **Grade Level:** I, S
>
> Stories told by an anthropologist who visited the Crow people, beginning in 1907.

Marquis, Thomas B. *Memoirs of a White Crow Indian (Thomas H. Leforge).* Lincoln: University of Nebraska Press, 1974. 356 pp.
> **Genre:** As-Told-To Memoir
> **Themes:** Remembering the Old Ways; Cultural and Personal Loss and Survival; Between Two Worlds
> **Grade Level:** S
>
> A memoir, as told to Thomas B. Marquis, recounting a white man's experiences living with the Crows and scouting for the U.S. Military under Gibbon.

Mathews, John Joseph (Osage). *The Osage: Children of the Middle Waters.* Norman: University of Oklahoma Press, 1961.
> **Genre:** Memoir, History
> **Themes:** Remembering the Old Ways; Cultural and Personal Loss and Survival
> **Grade Level:** S   *NNAL* (409–416) Mathews
>
> The history of the Osage tribe, from before the arrival of the Europeans up to the present, based on oral history, and on Mathews's life with his people.

———. *Sundown.* Norman: University of Oklahoma Press, [1934] 1988. 312 pp.
> **Genre:** Contemporary Novel
> **Themes:** Between Two Worlds; Cultural and Personal Loss and Survival
> **Grade Level:** S   *NNAL* (409–416) Mathews
>
> The story of a young man who returns to the reservation after World War I and the discovery of oil on Osage land.

———. *Wah'Kon-Tah: The Osage and the White Man's Road.* Norman: University of Oklahoma Press, [1932] 1981.
> **Genre:** Historical Fiction
> **Themes:** Between Two Worlds; Cultural and Personal Loss and Survival
> **Grade Level:** S   *NNAL* (409–416) Mathews
>
> A story of the Osage people and a sympathetic Indian agent.

McGaa, Ed (Oglala Sioux). *Red Cloud: The Story of an American Indian.* Minneapolis: Dillon Press, 1971. 54 pp.

Genre: Biography, Culture

Themes: Remembering the Old Ways; Between Two Worlds; At Home within Circles; Change and Growth; Cultural and Personal Loss and Survival

Grade Level: I, S

McLaughlin, Marie (Sioux). *Myths and Legends of the Sioux.* Lincoln: University of Nebraska Press, 1990. 200 pp.

Genre: Traditional Stories

Theme: Remembering the Old Ways

Grade Level: I,S

A collection of thirty-seven traditional stories and legends—including several Inktomi (the Nakota pronunciation) stories—that represent McLaughlin's efforts to prevent the disappearance of her valued heritage.

Momaday, N. Scott (Kiowa). *The Names.* Tucson: University of Arizona Press, 1976. 170 pp.

Genre: Autobiography

Themes: Remembering the Old Ways; At Home within Circles; Between Two Worlds

Grade Level: S

The story of Momaday's roots and his boyhood grounded in landscape, using the Native spirit of storytelling.

Mourning Dove (Okanagan/Colville). *Mourning Dove: A Salishan Autobiography.* Ed. Jay Miller. Lincoln: University of Nebraska Press, 1990. 187 pp.

Genre: Autobiography

Themes: Lifeways and Stereotypes; At Home within Circles; Remembering the Old Ways; Between Two Worlds

Grade Level: S

An autobiography based on manuscripts found, organized, and edited by Jay Miller after Mourning Dove's death in 1936.

Ortiz, Simon J. (Acoma Pueblo). *The People Shall Continue.* San Francisco: Children's Book Press, 1977.

Genre: History, Culture

Themes: At Home within Circles; Between Two Worlds; Remembering the Old Ways; Change and Growth; Cultural and Personal Loss and Survival

Grade Level: I   *NNAL* (486–498) Ortiz

A story from the point of view of American Indian peoples, recounting the history of European contact on the North American continent from 1492 to the present.

Otokahekagapi (First Beginnings): Sioux Creation Story. Trans. and illus. by Thomas E. Simms. Chamberlain, SD: Tipi Press, 1987. 30 pp.
Genre: Traditional Story
Theme: Remembering the Old Ways
Grade Level: P, I, S

A Titonwan Lakota story that is as much scripture as the Bible, a story given "from God."

Owens, Amos. "Sioux/Dakota Pipe-carver." In *This Song Remembers: Self-Portraits of Native Americans in the Arts.* Ed. Jane Katz. Houghton Mifflin, 1980. pp. 64–70.
Genre: Autobiography
Themes: At Home within Circles; Remembering the Old Ways; Between Two Worlds
Grade Level: I, S

St. Pierre, Mark. *Madonna Swan: A Lakota Woman's Story.* Norman: University of Oklahoma Press, 1991. 209 pp.
Genre: As-Told-To Autobiography
Themes: Remembering the Old Ways; Cultural and Personal Loss and Survival; Between Two Worlds
Grade Level: S

Schultz, James Willard. *My Life as an Indian: The Story of a Red Woman and a White Man in the Lodges of the Blackfeet.* New York: Doubleday, Page, 1907. 204 pp.
Genre: Memoir, History
Theme: Personal and Cultural Loss and Survival
Grade Level: S

Schwartz, Warren E., and Wesley Whiteman (Black Bear) (Cheyenne). *The Last Contrary: The Story of Wesley Whiteman.* Sioux Falls, SD: Center for Western Studies, 1988.
Genre: Traditional Story, As-Told-To Autobiography
Themes: Remembering the Old Ways; Change and Growth; Between Two Worlds; At Home within Circles; Cultural and Personal Loss and Survival
Grade Level: I, S

A personal narrative of the life and beliefs of the last member of the Cheyenne Contrary (or "Clown") Society, who died in 1981.

Silko, Leslie Marmon (Laguna Pueblo). *Delicacy and Strength of Lace.* Ed. Anne Wright. St. Paul, MN: Graywolf Press, 1985. 105 pp.

Genre: Contemporary and Traditional Letters and Story

Themes: Remembering the Old Ways; At Home within Circles; Between Two Worlds; Cultural and Personal Loss and Survival

Grade Level: S   *NNAL* (575–586) Silko

Letters through which Leslie Silko and James Wright built a friendship, although they had only met twice, once at a writers' conference in Michigan in 1975, and again in January 1980 when Wright lay ill with terminal cancer.

Slipperjack, Ruby (Ojibway). *Honour the Sun.* Winnipeg, Manitoba: Pemmican, 1987. 211 pp.

Genre: Memoir

Themes: Between Two Worlds; Cultural and Personal Loss and Survival; Change and Growth

Grade Level: S

The seasonal diary of a ten-year-old child called "The Owl," who lives in a Native community in northern Ontario.

————. *Silent Words.* Saskatoon, Saskatchewan: Fifth House, 1992. 250 pp.

Genre: Young Adult Novel

Theme: Change and Growth

Grade Level: S

A funny, tragic, and moving novel for both young adult and adult readers, about a young Native boy's journey of self-discovery.

Sneve, Virginia Driving Hawk (Lakota). *High Elk's Treasure.* New York: Holiday House, 1975. 96 pp.

Genre: Story

Themes: At Home within Circles; Change and Growth; Between Two Worlds; Remembering the Old Ways

Grade Level: I

The story of Joe High Elk and his sister, who find shelter from a raging storm in a cave where his ancestor, Steps High Like an Elk, had hidden his horse from white soldiers and left behind a sacred rawhide bundle.

————. *Jimmy Yellow Hawk*. New York: Holiday House, 1972.
Genre: Story
Themes: Change and Growth; Between Two Worlds; Remembering the Old Ways
Grade Level: I

A contemporary story about a Lakota boy on a South Dakota reservation that won the 1971 Council on Interracial Books for Children Award.

————. *They Led A Nation: The Sioux Chiefs*. Sioux Falls, SD: Brevet Press, 1975. 46 pp.
Genre: History
Themes: Remembering the Old Ways; Between Two Worlds; Cultural and Personal Loss and Survival
Grade Level: I, S

————. *When Thunders Spoke*. Lincoln: University of Nebraska Press, 1993. 95 pp.
Genre: Story
Themes: Remembering the Old Ways; Change and Growth; Between Two Worlds; Cultural and Personal Loss and Survival
Grade Level: I

A contemporary story of Norman, a young Sioux, who collects rough agates to trade for candy at the trading post and makes a treacherous climb up the west side of a butte, the "place of the Thunders," because his grandfather believes something good will happen.

Standing Bear, Luther (Sioux). *My Indian Boyhood*. Lincoln: University of Nebraska Press, [1931] 1988. 190 pp.
Genre: Autobiography, History
Themes: Remembering the Old Ways; At Home within Circles; Change and Growth; Between Two Worlds
Grade Level: I, S

The home life and education of a young turn-of-the-century Sioux who learns to live the traditional life before attending Carlisle Boarding School in Pennsylvania.

————. *My People the Sioux*. Lincoln: University of Nebraska Press, 1975. 288 pp.
Genre: History
Themes: Remembering the Old Ways; Cultural and Personal Loss and Survival
Grade Level: I, S

Strete, Craig Kee. *When Grandfather Journeys into Winter.* New York: Greenwillow Press, 1977.
> **Genre:** Story
> **Themes:** Remembering the Old Ways; Change and Growth; At Home within Circles
> **Grade Level:** I
>
> A funny yet painful story about a young boy, Little Thunder, who must face the fact that Tayhua, his grandfather, is going to die.

TallMountain, Mary (Koyukon Athabascan). *Green March Moons.* Stanford, CA: New Seed Press, 1987.
> **Genre:** Young Adult Novel
> **Themes:** Change and Growth; Remembering the Old Ways; At Home within Circles; Between Two Worlds
> **Grade Level:** I, S   *NNAL* (623–627) TallMountain
>
> The story of an eleven-year-old Koyukon girl who suffers a number of tragedies—her father dies from the "whiteman's flu"; her mother dies from despair; her Uncle Vaska rapes her one night after he has been drinking—until her Aunt arranges for her to live with "old Philomena."

———. *A Quick Brush of Wings.* San Francisco: Freedom Voices, 1991. 59 pp.
> **Genre:** Poetry
> **Theme:** At Home within Circles
> **Grade Level:** I, S   *NNAL* (623–627) TallMountain
>
> Poetry, the means of survival for Mary TallMountain, who was "ripped out" of her childhood when her mother was dying of tuberculosis and moved into an Anglo school where she was mocked for her Indianness.

Vizenor, Gerald (Chippewa). *The People Named the Chippewa: Narrative Histories.* Minneapolis: University of Minnesota Press, 1984. 172 pp.
> **Genre:** History, Biography
> **Themes:** Remembering the Old Ways; Between Two Worlds; Cultural and Personal Loss and Survival
> **Grade Level:** I, S   *NNAL* (635–648) Vizenor
>
> Illustrated stories of the woodland tribal people as they meet missionaries, capitalists, government bureaucrats, and anthropologists.

————. *Summer in the Spring.* Norman: University of Oklahoma Press, 1993. 166 pp.
Genre: Poetry
Theme: Remembering the Old Ways
Grade Level: S   *NNAL* (635–648) Vizenor

Anishinabe lyric poems and stories, edited and interpreted by Vizenor.

Waheenee (Buffalo Bird Woman, Hidatsa/Mandan). *Buffalo Bird Woman's Garden.* Transcribed by Gilbert Wilson. St. Paul: Minnesota Historical Society, [1917] 1987.
Genre: Culture
Theme: Remembering the Old Ways
Grade Level: I, S

Traditional Hidatsa horticultural techniques.

————. *Waheenee: An Indian Girl's Story.* Transcribed by Gilbert Wilson. Lincoln: University of Nebraska Press, 1981. 183 pp.
Genre: As-Told-To Stories
Themes: Remembering the Old Ways; Between Two Worlds; At Home within Circles
Grade Level: P, I, S

Stories of Buffalo Bird Woman, who was born in 1839, two years after a devastating smallpox epidemic that struck the Hidatsa people.

Walker, James R. *Lakota Myth.* Ed. Elaine A. Jahner. Lincoln: University of Nebraska Press, 1983. 426 pp.
Genre: Traditional Story
Theme: Remembering the Old Ways
Grade Level: S

Stories collected by James R. Walker, a physician to the Oglala Sioux at the Pine Ridge Reservation from 1896 to 1914.

Weeks, Rupert (Shoshone). *Pachee Goyo: History and Legends from the Shoshone.* Laramie, WY: Jelm Mountain Press, 1981.
Genre: Young Adult Novel
Themes: Remembering the Old Ways; Change and Growth; At Home within Circles
Grade Level: I

The story of a young boy who learns to listen and to give up selfishness in order to grow up.

Welch, James (Blackfeet/Gros Ventre). *Indian Lawyer.* New York: Penguin, 1990. 350 pp.
Genre: Contemporary Novel
Themes: Cultural and Personal Loss and Survival; Between Two Worlds
Grade Level: S

A contemporary novel, set on the Blackfeet Reservation and in Helena, Montana, where Sylvester Yellow Calf, an Indian lawyer, has served on the state parole board.

————. *Riding the Earthboy 40.* Lewiston, ID: Confluence Press, 1971. 67 pp.
Genre: Poetry
Themes: Between Two Worlds; Remembering the Old Ways; Lifeways and Stereotypes; Cultural and Personal Loss and Survival
Grade Level: I, S

Poems representing contemporary issues and scenes from around Harlem, Montana, and Welch's family farm, forty acres leased to Earthboy.

Yellow Robe, Rosebud (Lakota). *Tonweya and the Eagles and Other Lakota Indian Tales.* New York: Dial, 1979. 118 pp.
Genre: Memoir, Traditional Story
Themes: Remembering the Old Ways; Between Two Worlds
Grade Level: P, I, S

An excellent collection of historical and legendary Lakota stories.

Yellowtail, Thomas (Crow). *Yellowtail: Crow Medicine Man and Sun Dance Chief.* Norman: University of Oklahoma Press, 1991. 241 pp.
Genre: As-Told-To Autobiography
Themes: Remembering the Old Ways; Between Two Worlds; Cultural and Personal Loss and Survival
Grade Level: S

An illustrated autobiography as told to Michael Oren Fitzgerald.

Zitkala-Ša (Gertrude Simmons Bonnin) (Yankton Sioux). *American Indian Legends.* Lincoln: University of Nebraska Press, 1985. 165 pp.

Genre: Traditional Story

Themes: Remembering the Old Ways; At Home within Circles; Change and Growth

Grade Level: I, S

Fourteen ohunkankans (traditional stories) featuring Iktomi, the trickster, which Zitkala-Ša collected when she returned to the reservation after teaching at Carlisle School.

7

Non-Native Authors and Their Stories about Native Americans

The following reviews primarily represent my own readings of several popular books by non-Native authors. However, I have relied on the insight of Beverly Slapin and Doris Seale (Santee/Cree) who have conducted critical readings of books for children in *Through Indian Eyes: The Native Experience in Books for Children.* Suggestions for books written by Native authors with similar themes and characters appear at the end of several reviews.

Banks, Lynne Reid. *The Indian in the Cupboard.* New York: Avon, 1980. 181 pp.
    Genre: Fantasy Novel
    Grade Level: I

Probably one of the most popular books for children today, this childhood novel may be characterized as fantasy, while it portrays a character with whom most children can identify. It is the story of a boy who discovers he can make plastic figures in a cupboard come alive by turning a special key. From regarding these little figures as curiosities, as extensions of himself and his own imagination, Omri learns to respect their right to a life of their own. He demonstrates this respect and choice at the end of the book when he gives his mother the key. However, the reader may expect a "return" since Omri's mother will always keep the key on a chain around her neck.

The Indian in the Cupboard represents the universal wish-fulfillment experience. Whereas so many children imagine worlds where play becomes reality, Omri's story moves one step beyond, into the magical world where plastic figures come alive, and where they require food and drink, a place to live, and meaningful and permanent relationships with others just like themselves.

While the book exhibits these positive characteristics, it also presents some serious problems for Native children as well as for those who would understand Native Americans as individuals apart from popular stereotypes.

Within the text, efforts are made to contradict stereotypes in Western films—for example, the explanation that the "designs" on tipis are unique to a tribe, so Omri can't just paint what he wants. However, inaccurate details about the Iroquois or the more general Indian experience still abound. When the narrator refers to Omri's growing ability "to see things from the Indian's point of view," it refers to the physical perspective of being small in a gigantic world, rather than "point of view" with respect to a world view and culture or with respect to relationships between people from different backgrounds. Also, reference is made to the influence of Western films: "It occurred to Omri for the first time that his idea of Indians, taken entirely from Western films, had been somehow false" (29). However, this is followed by the comment that "real Indians" didn't go home for dinner or live in houses like his. In other words, the text itself would argue this very idea. According to *The Indian in the Cupboard*, a real Indian is Little Bear, existing only in the past, valuing scalping and war, needing to be taught language, morals, and responsibility from the white boy, inspiring fear in white men, eating and moving like a predatory animal, who can't survive without the help of a white boy.

The relationship between Omri and Little Bear is a microcosm of the still acceptable—and appropriate, according to this story—paternalistic relationship between the fatherly or caregiving, morality-teaching United States government and the American Indians. Omri must teach Little Bear to be nonviolent, and to learn to be friends with white men such as Boone, the cowboy. What about the document of the Iroquois confederation which Ben Franklin relied on when writing the U.S. Constitution?

The text makes reference to the Algonquins fighting with the French and the Iroquois with the English. The following comment that "both sides had scalped like mad" implies the Indians were the perpetrators instead of both the Europeans and the Indians, although Omri discovers that scalping "wasn't at all" an Indian custom. Again, though, the text implies that ferocity is an Indian characteristic, since they are so "keen on scalping each other."

With many Indian cultures, individuals are regarded as "Chief" (or leader) when the others in the tribe honor them for their brave or generous deeds. In *The Indian in the Cupboard*, when the old chief dies, Little Bear assumes the role of Chief, demands (like a European king) that Omri bow to him, and attempts to turn Omri into a slave. And later Omri tells his friend, Patrick, that becoming Chief has "made him even more bossy and—difficult than before." This is followed by an analogy with Omri's relationship with his mother, when he was "insisting on having his own way." Again, this perpetuates the paternalistic relationship between the Indian and the white man, or the stereotype of the Indian as a "child" and the white man as his "father."

When the cowboy comes to life, he is stereotyped as standing for what is right against wrong, "fantastically brave" against the Indian. Also, the cowboy is an alcoholic, but that isn't condemned—it appears natural, another stereotype. There is another question of historical accuracy in this cowboy/ Indian conflict. If the Indian is Iroquois, he wouldn't have known a cowboy and wouldn't have had anything to fear because cowboys lived on the Great Plains more than one-hundred years after the arrival of the Europeans permanently changed the Iroquois's world.

Although the text indicates that Omri had given "Little Bear every respect as a person," teachers can encourage students to examine the concept of respect. Had Omri really given Little Bear "every respect?"

Following are several stereotypes attributed to Little Bear:

- *Alcoholic tendencies:* The Indian knows "firewater."

- *Stoic:* standing "as if nothing [Omri] did could affect him anyway" (23).

- *Savage:* He brags about how he can hunt, fight, and take many scalps. Omri doesn't want more Indians because "They'd fight," since that was the natural behavior of Indian peoples. Little Bear defines himself first in terms of violence—"[H]e's fought in wars, and scalped people, and grown stuff to eat like marrows and stuff and had a wife." The first contact between the Indian and the cowboy is violent, because Little Bear assumes the cowboy will take his land. The cowboy wants to "have the stinkin' red hide for a sleepin' bag."

- *Uncivilized:* "Omri was getting used to his Indian's ungrateful ways and was not offended." So the white boy is the understanding victim of the Indian's uncivilized behavior. Boone says, "[T]hem Injuns ain't just ornery and savage. Them's dirty . . .", although Omri clears that up by noting how dirty Boone is.

- *Vanishing Indian:* Although Omri asserts that "Little Bear isn't a toy," he does believe he is from the past, not the present.

- *Good white man who represents God to the Indian:* Omri says to Patrick, "[H]e thinks I'm some kind of spirit or something."

- *Noble savage:* Chapter 9 sounds like the ideas of George Catlin, who would put the Indians and the cowboys in a national park where they could be preserved, just like exotic animals.

From the "wild" Indian on the front cover, this book projects what many regard as racist stereotypes of Indian people. If these were limited to the point of view of the boy, we might forgive them. But the narrator's voice also exhibits such stereotypes: with "another grunt, the Indian said"; "he barked": or "The Indian was now gazing at him with something more than respect—a sort of awe [of the boy]." The Indian is "His Indian," who is afraid of the dark; ignorant of technology when whites aren't; is a "toy" turned human, and will be trained like an animal (20–21). All this on two pages. In their review of this book and its sequel, *Return of the Indian in the Cupboard,* Slapin and Seale indicate that the books have serious problems. "Although the little 'Indian' is called Iroquois, no attempt has been made, either in text or illustrations, to have him look or behave appropriately. For example, he is dressed as a Plains Indian, and is given a tipi and a horse." They go on to suggest that the battle scenes are "among the most graphic war scenes in modern children's literature. As a whole, the book is brutal, and the Indians are horrifying" (Slapin and Seale, 122).

In October 1994, a panel of three educators discussed the issue of "Censorship or a Demand for Literary Excellence." Jan LaBonty, children's literature expert at the University of Montana, Missoula, presented her research on the Iroquois culture, on Lynne Reid Banks' position as a British writer with New York publishers, and on the way the text could have easily avoided some of the above problems. Larry LaCounte (Chippewa), also from the University of Montana, commented about the effect of reading and watching films that exhibit such stereotypes: "I grew up identifying with the smart one, the good guy, the white man. And then one day I looked at myself and realized I was Indian. What does that do to a child's self-esteem?" The third panelist was Linda Pease (Crow), who read a note from her daughter who had just finished reading *The Indian in the Cupboard* in her fourth-grade class: "The book is pretty decent but some parts are not so decent . . . Now this statement is bad, 'bawling at him.' Now that is bad. I don't think Little Bear is a calf. I think he is a proud Indian and his tribe is part of him . . . and then there is this statement . . .

'grunted the miniature Indian at last.' Instead of saying that, [Banks could have written] 'said the miniature Little Bear at last.'"

When educators address the issue of stereotype and bias in texts such as *The Indian in the Cupboard,* students can learn to separate themselves from negative stereotypes, from the judgments and belief systems of others, while they establish positive images of themselves and their cultures. Two books that provide useful contradictions of—and arguments against—common stereotypes are Beverly Slapin's satirical look at stereotypes, *Basic Skills Caucasian Americans Workbook,* and Virginia Driving Hawk Sneve's contemporary story, *The Chichi Hoohoo Bogeyman.*

To her credit, Lynne Reid Banks has publicly expressed her concern with "getting things right" in the future and with trying to "avoid any mistakes." Her latest book, which will be released in 1998, is based in "firsthand" research she conducted on three Mohawk reserves in the Montreal area. It is never easy to write beyond our own biases, especially the four-hundred-year-old paternalistic American ideology that suggests that Indians will learn what to value and how to behave from non-Indian Americans, from Europeans, and that even Indian adults will learn the most important values from their "superiors." The lack of respect for the integrity of Native cultures and the lack of understanding about the history of the English devastation of eastern Native American cultures and peoples are integral to the American myth system. Consequently, neither a "sensitive" British writer, nor editors, nor "Anglo children" could ever see most books about Indians written by non-Indians as anything other than "truth" without Native peoples expressing their ideas and feelings about what is true for them. I admire Lynne Reid Banks' willingness to listen to those voices.

Benchley, Nathaniel. *Only Earth and Sky Last Forever.* New York: Harper Trophy, 1972. 189 pp.
Genre: Historical Young Adult Novel
Grade Level: I, S

Based on a traditional Lakota saying, this young adult novel tells the story of Dark Elk, an eighteen-year-old Cheyenne who had been adopted by an Oglala couple after Custer killed his people in 1868. The novel may be considered historical fiction, but the voice is definitely non-Indian directed at a non-Indian audience. Benchley has relied on the following sources regarding Crazy Horse and the Battle of the Little Big Horn:

Thomas Berger, George Bird Grinnell, Royal Hassrick, Thomas Marquis, David Miller, John Neihardt, Mari Sandoz, and John Stands in Timber (Margot Liberty and Robert M. Utley). Throughout the text, Benchley explains traditional references and ceremonial practices as though he expects his readers to be unfamiliar with the traditional Lakota culture. The story about Crazy Horse and his losing battle with the "Bluecoats" is subordinate to the central conflict—Dark Elk's effort to win the love of a Cheyenne girl, Lashuka, whose grandmother "unrealistically" demands forty horses of any young man who would marry her granddaughter. Although the narrator is a traditional Cheyenne, the non-Native voice demonstrates little respect for the spiritual aspect of ceremonies and rituals. Instead, the Vision Quest and the Sun Dance provide the means by which he might gain Lashuka's grandmother's acceptance. Set in the Dakota and Montana Plains, *Only Earth and Sky Last Forever* is a romantic young adult novel that carries the Vanishing Indian stereotype.

Resources that counter the above stereotypes include Virginia Driving Hawk Sneve's *They Led a Nation: The Sioux Chiefs,* and Charles Eastman's *Indian Heroes and Great Chieftains.* These books feature biographical essays about Crazy Horse and other Indian heroes, and *Indian Oratory* includes the last words of Crazy Horse.

Borland, Hal. *When the Legends Die.* New York: Bantam, [1963] 1984. 216 pp.
Genre: Contemporary Novel
Grade Level: S

The story begins in 1910 when a young Ute woman, her husband, who is accused of stealing and murder, and her five-year-old son flee the reservation authorities in southern Colorado. High in the mountains, she teaches her boy the old ways in song, ritual, and everyday survival, and the boy makes friends with an orphaned grizzly bear cub, taking the cub as a "brother." Sometime after both his parents are dead, Thomas Black Bull is forced into the white man's world where teachers, agents, and other Indian people remind him daily that he must forget the old ways and his Indian name, Bear's Brother, and that he must live the new way. The novel represents a polarized world where the dying old ways and the inevitable new ways remain mutually exclusive. Thomas doesn't fit into the school, where his basket weaving brings ridicule and where he must learn to farm, to "tear up the earth." A few years later, he admits to an old man that "the old way is finished . . . I have no one" (105). Following the rodeo circuit for years, "Killer" Tom Black becomes a legend from Texas to California to Montana to the East Coast. With deep and violent hatred, he punishes every horse he rides, punishes them in anger over his own loss, until the crash of one horse puts him in the hospital with more than a few broken bones. Determined to walk again, he heals and returns to his home country, where he goes to work herding sheep. There in the mountains he confronts himself, realizes that he has been trying to "kill" his past, and makes peace with himself, "a man who [at last] knew and was proud of his own inheritance, who had come to the end of his long hunt."

There is nothing bad or racist about this book. Borland never pretends to be Indian. But the definition of the old ways is limited to the spiritual and physical interaction between a Ute Indian and the earth, plants, creatures, and sky. Whereas traditional tribal peoples regard the old ways as important and still relevant because they show the way human beings should live together as relatives, *When the Legends Die* is about an individual who finds those ways only as he separates himself from the rest of the world. The character development of the lone hero, and also the title, imply the stereotype of the good but Vanishing Indian. Even at the end, Thomas Black Bull has no other human friend. It is important that literatures about Indian peoples recognize their past not as artifact but as living and useful for their community, even as they live in the world of the "white man's ways."

Students can compare one of the following Native-authored books with *When Legends Die. The People Shall Continue* by Simon Ortiz applies more to the intermediate level readers, but it does contradict the Vanishing Indian stereotype in Borland's book. On a more adult level, James Welch's novel *The Death of Jim Loney,* and D'Arcy McNickle's *Surrounded* also address the issue of living between two worlds, and the fragmentation, alienation, and tragedy mixed-bloods frequently experience.

Carter, Forrest. *The Education of Little Tree.* Albuquerque: University of New Mexico Press. 216 pp.

Genre: Novel

Grade Level: S

One of the most widely read books typically defined as Native literature, *The Education of Little Tree* was written as the autobiography of an orphan who learns the ways of the Cherokee Indians from his grandparents in Tennessee. It has sold over a million copies, was given an award as the title which the American Booksellers Association most enjoyed selling, but it has also been the subject of controversy due to the social and ethnic heritage of the author.

According to a review in the October 14, 1991 issue of *Newsweek*, *The Education of Little Tree* is not an autobiography because the author was a fraud:

> Book-publishing stories don't get much sweeter than that of *The Education of Little Tree,* by the late Forrest Carter. Presented as a folksy memoir of Carter's Cherokee upbringing, the book fairly brims with quaint mountain platitudes and affectionate ethnic stereotypes: the sage Native Americans, the thrifty Jew, the silly white folks. . . . But the story has a bitter side. According to some who knew him before he died in 1979, the author was really Asa (Ace) Carter, a former speech writer for Alabama Governor George Wallace and a notorious white-supremacist leader. . . . [George Wallace confirmed this]. . . . According to Dan T. Carter, an Emory University professor now working on a biography of Wallace, Carter formed the Original Ku Klux Klan of the Confederacy, a 100-member group responsible for the 1957 castration of a black man outside Birmingham. . . . Later, as Forrest Carter, Asa denied the previous identity, although he appears to have signed some correspondence as "Asa." (*Newsweek* 1991, 62)

Another article, in the October 14, 1991 edition of *Time,* supports *Newsweek's* claim: "old friends point out that Asa and Forrest Carter looked alike, used the same address, and were the same age." *Time* cites Dan Carter as charging that the "late Forrest Carter was not a Cherokee at all . . . but a Ku Klux Klan terrorist, right-wing radio announcer, home-grown American fascist and anti-Semite" (*Time* 1991, 33).

Henry Louis Gates Jr., professor of humanities at Harvard University, has written an article entitled "'Authenticity,' or the Lesson of Little Tree," in the *New York Times Book Review.* In this article, Gates addresses an issue that he suggests "literary critics would do well to ponder, for the belief that we can 'read' a person's racial or ethnic identity from his or her writing runs surprisingly deep" (Gates 1991, 1). Gates goes on to say that "our literary judgments, in short, remain hostage to the ideology of authenticity" (Gates 1991, 1). Making a case for the right of authors to tell stories outside their own genders, social and cultural situations, and racial backgrounds, Gates argues that *Little Tree* should not be dismissed as invalid literature because the author's background remains in question.

However, readers should be able to trust the narrators of texts, to believe that the author has done his or her homework when the story represents another's experience. But this is not true with *The Education of Little Tree.* Instead, the novel's text betrays a non-Native voice expressing a polarized world of

"Indian vs. White" and carrying such stereotypes as Noble and Conquered Savage, Childlike, and Vanishing Indian. In the fashion of New Age misappropriations of American Indian philosophies and lifeways, Little Tree communicates "perfectly" with animals and with Mother Earth. His Cherokee grandparents teach him European American culture and call it "The Way," and we wonder, where are the rest of the Cherokee? In the book, white people are universally obnoxious, ridiculing Little Tree and his family while Little Tree remains ignorant, assuming the giggles of white people on the bus represent "friendly" attitudes. In a teachers' workshop entitled "Bias and Stereotypes in Stories about Native Americans," one Native woman said, "no Indian child I know would misunderstand the laughter of white people; we learn very early to recognize ridicule." Other situations also contradict the realities of Native people that I have encountered: Little Tree is happiest when alone, living in his earthly paradise, and non-Native readers develop compassion for the young boy who never expresses anger toward those who discriminate against him.

Some Native American teachers who recognize and understand the fallacies in the book are not opposed to using it, but I suggest that the rest of us should avoid it, as enchanting as it may be. It certainly can't be regarded as Native American Literature.

Jimmie Durham's collection of poetry, *Columbus Day,* and Grant Foreman's historical accounts of *Indian Removal* will provide both contemporary and historical supplementary material that might facilitate a more critical reading of *Little Tree.*

Craven, Margaret. *I Heard the Owl Call My Name.* Garden City, NY: Doubleday, 1973. 166 pp.
Genre: Young Adult Novel
Grade Level: I, S

A young Catholic priest, with only two years to live, is sent to a Kwakiutl Indian parish on the seacoast of British Columbia. There he respects the Native people, learns their rituals and beliefs, and learns not to fear death when "the owl" calls. "And what had he learned? Surely not the truth of the Indian. There was no one truth. He had learned a little of the truth of one tribe in one village."

I Heard the Owl Call My Name honestly demonstrates the conflicts Native people face as a consequence of their encounters with the "white world": alcohol abuse, interracial marriage, the remembered importance of the Kwakwala language, the importance of education, the value of technology, the consequences of leaving their tribal community, and the shame they feel when neither the white world nor their own accepts them. This novel may be paired with "Sedna, the Woman Under the Sea," a story told by Joseph Bruchac in *Keepers of the Earth*. It is the story of a girl who makes the mistake of loving a man who will bring her harm. Also, students can compare and contrast the Kwakiutl culture with other Native or non-Native cultures.

Janet Campbell Hale's *Owl's Song,* which portrays the conflict a contemporary youth experiences when he leaves home, also includes the symbol of the owl. Native poems from Cree and Salish traditions feature the owl as the communicator of death to loved ones.

George, Jean Craighead. *Julie of the Wolves.* New York: Harper & Row, 1972. 170 pp.
   Genre: Young Adult Novel
   Grade Level: I

George's contemporary story centers on a young girl who develops a relationship with a family of wolves when she is lost and starving in the Alaskan wilderness. Referring to the Native peoples as "Eskimo" rather than Inuit, this novel presents an unrealistic and stereotypically romanticized view of Native life in Alaska. It is the story of a "white girl" with an Indian face, "a classic Eskimo beauty" (a blatant contradiction in terms—a "European" Eskimo?). She is a thirteen-year-old who leaves her husband and her evil "step-mother" to follow a dream of glamour and romance painted by her pen pal in San Francisco. Julie rejects her traditional upbringing and changes her name from Miyax to Julie; she is an individual, not a member of a community, surviving with only the help of wolves.

Teachers may use the traditional Inuit story, "Sedna, the Woman Under the Sea," in *Keepers of the Earth* by Caduto and Bruchac. Sedna falls in love with a seabird in the form of a man who lures her to his impoverished home far away. Demonstrating the value of communal survival and the foolishness of an individual's pursuit of singular happiness, students may be able to discover how this story contrasts with the predominant individualism in *Julie of the Wolves.*

Goble, Paul. *Brave Eagle's Account of the Fetterman Fight.* Lincoln: University of Nebraska Press, 1992. 47 pp.
   Genre: Historical Story, Memoir
   Grade Level: P, I, S

On December 21, 1866, Red Cloud led his people to defeat Captain Fetterman, culminating in the closure of the Bozeman Trail. According to Doane Robinson, "Red Cloud's War is the only instance in the history of the United States where the government has gone to war and afterwards negotiated a peace conceding everything demanded by the enemy and exacting nothing in return" (60). Included in Brave Eagle's narrative are commendations for the bravery of individual warriors and soldiers. Goble admits that he relied on published Indian accounts but also on white historians, "in order to give the reader a better understanding of the fight and the events which preceded it." *The Fetterman Fight* is an excellent resource for a personal and yet tribal perspective of the conflict between the Plains Indians and U.S. expansionism.

————. *Buffalo Woman.* Scarsdale, NY: Bradbury Press, 1984. 32 pp.
Genre: Traditional Story
Grade Level: P, I

Without designating a specific tribal source, Goble tells the story of a great hunter who is given a supernatural wife, but she leaves with their son because his relatives have been unkind. The hunter finds them in a herd of buffalo, and his son, Buffalo Calf, helps him. The Buffalo Nation then transforms the hunter into a "young buffalo bull." *A Legend From Crazy Horse Clan* by Moses Nelson Big Crow represents the more traditional Lakota version of this story.

Goble has spent a great deal of time with the people whose stories he uses, and his artwork is considered authentic by some. Although many traditional tribal people consider Paul Goble a respectable writer of Indian stories, others criticize him for taking the stories out of the specific cultures and "owning" them himself. By contrast, Joseph Bruchac tells stories from cultures other than his own, but he provides detailed background material about the geography, history, and culture of the tribe within which the stories originated. Teachers who use Paul Goble's books should consult collections such as Ella Deloria's *Dakota Texts* and should stress the traditional values within the stories.

————. *Death of the Iron Horse.* New York: Bradbury Press, 1987. 28 pp.
Genre: History
Grade Level: I

Death of the Iron Horse is "loosely based" on an incident in which Cheyenne warriors successfully derailed a Union Pacific train traveling from Omaha to Ft. McPherson in North Platte, Nebraska, on August 7, 1867. The story begins with the terrible "long ago" dream of Sweet Medicine, a Cheyenne Prophet, who saw hairy people coming from the East to "kill all the buffaloes, so there was nothing left to eat." When the Cheyenne saw the "Iron Horse" with the "voice of Thunder," they believed Sweet Medicine's dream had come true. To protect their people from this terrible monster, several warriors followed its trail, and in the dark they "dug down and chopped the ties in the middle, and hacked out spikes until the rails no longer joined together." After the train derailed, the Cheyenne warriors raided the boxcars, where they discovered money, household utensils, clothing, flags and musical instruments, and soldiers' uniforms and blankets; they then set the broken train on fire. Goble indicates that the "Cheyenne people have remembered [this story] with pride and amusement," ending his story with an image of Amtrak, the visual reminder of the relentless encroachment of European American technology. Nevertheless, the story proves that the Cheyenne people continued to fight to protect their territory, culture, and people, even when the odds seemed insurmountable.

Highwater, Jamake. *Anpao: An American Odyssey.* Philadelphia: Lippincott, 1977. 256 pp.
Genre: Young Adult Novel
Grade Level: I

A Newbery Honor book, *Anpao* is the mythological story about a young man who travels across America's ancient world through dangers and trials for the sake of a beautiful girl. Highwater tells a good story, the kind we like to read, the kind that follows what we expect in fantasy. Moreover, the rhythm, sound, and imagery of *Anpao* appear to represent an "Indian sensibility," as the publishers suggest: "[H]e pointed down into the moon-filled water where shimmering images of liquid-people in the drowned village at the bottom of the lake rose like smoke on a clear night" (235).

On the other hand, the bibliographic summary in the Library of Congress Cataloging in Publication Data suggests the most important reason why teachers should question the authenticity and usefulness of this book for any age group—it disregards the diversity of Indian peoples and consequently betrays their integrity as individuals: "Traditional tales from North American Indian tribes woven into one story that relates the adventures of one boy as he grows to manhood" (iv). Although many Indian people today can trace their ancestries to more than one tribal culture and history, many Native American authors are still writing from what Kenneth Lincoln calls a "sense of relatedness . . . [to] ancestral history, the remembered presence of grandmothers and grandfathers gone before" (Lincoln 1983, 8). In no way can Highwater's story be called "tribal," and in no way can it pretend to tell an "Indian" story because it betrays the very integrity of the "tribal experience." Traditional storytellers would draw on active and real memories of their ancestors' experiences, providing listeners with this shared wisdom for living in a world where present and past, vision and reality intertwine to draw the individual into a community. By contrast, Highwater's conglomeration of "woven" tales from so many very different tribes (Northern Plains patriarchal cultures, such as Crow, Blackfeet, Salish, Apache, and Southwest matriarchal cultures, among others); his varied bibliography, which reflects few "primary" sources; and his failure to call *Anpao* anything but "Indian" create not a work of art (such as the Newbery Honor suggests) but a mockery of the function of the traditional Indian storyteller and a denial of the "individual" humanity and historical experience of all descendants of tribal peoples.

Also, the publishers deny the authenticity when they regard this book as representing the "classic tradition of the storyteller." "Classic" is Greek, European, and in that sense the publishers are correct. *Anpao* is a "classic" quest, where the singular "hero" comes from some unknown origin, journeys through many trials to achieve some kind of education or self-awareness, performs sacrificial acts for the benefit of others, and finally earns the reward of nobility and the love of a beautiful woman. Unlike so much traditional literature in which Native values of generosity, respect for relatives, and the importance of community prevail, this novel portrays a very Western concept of possessions, success, individualism, and the weak position of women in society. Anpao and his brother "come as strangers" and are not accepted; the tribal people ridicule them because they are poor, and Ko-ko-mik-e-is, powerless by herself, is afraid of the Sun.

Although Highwater claims to be Blackfeet, no one on the Blackfeet Reservation in northern Montana seems to know him, and neither do the people on the Blood Reserve north of Montana. In the Summer 1984 issue of *Akwesasne Notes*, a widely distributed Native newspaper, Hank Adams (Assiniboine/Sioux) contends that Highwater is not Blackfeet but instead is Gregory J. Markopoulos, the son of Greek immigrants (Adams 1984, 10–11). A subsequent issue of *Notes* published letters from

Markopoulos and Highwater's attorneys denying the alleged connection, but as of the Early Winter 1985 issue, "NOTES still stands by Hank Adams' research linking Gregory Markopoulos to J. Marks, and thereby Jamake Highwater" (*Akwesasne Notes* 1985, 5). This issue and discussion may be important for those who are concerned about possible misappropriation of government funds intended for Native people. However, for teachers who may use the book, the possibility of Highwater not being Native may provide an explanation for the failure of Highwater's books to respect the diversity of Native peoples.

In his "Storyteller's Farewell," Highwater insinuates that he has performed the sacred storyteller role himself: "Among American Indians the teller of stories is a weaver. His designs are the threads of his personal saga as well as the history of his people" (239). Highwater has certainly "woven" a story—his own story. Teachers of non-Indian and Indian children must not mistake this for a tribal storyteller's voice, and neither should they assign the identities revealed in *Anpao* to the ancestors of any Indian children which may be sitting in their classrooms. Just as Highwater says, this is the storyteller's "personal saga," and no more. He closes his "Farewell" with a challenge to his readers: "Many of us are prepared to sail to strange places in time and in space; perhaps *Anpao* will address itself to that audience and become a personal journey for readers who wish to sail from one world to another" (246). The world of *Anpao* is a "classic" fantasy world, and no more.

Another book by Highwater, *Ceremony of Innocence*, may be compared and contrasted with Maria Campbell's autobiography, *Halfbreed*.

Hudson, Jan. *Sweetgrass*. New York: Philomel, 1989. 157 pp.
  Genre: Young Adult Novel
  Grade Level: I

Sweetgrass is a sixteen-year-old Blackfeet girl, growing up in Canada in the mid-nineteenth century, whose strongest desire is to marry her sweetheart, Eagle-Sun. However, smallpox strikes during the cold of winter, and Sweetgrass must care for her stricken family members. Although the suffering of the Blackfeet due to the "white man's illness" is clear, the numerous deaths are too quickly forgotten and de-emphasized, and there is little evidence of the tribal experience. Although Slapin and Seale admit *Sweetgrass* "lacks overt racism," they regard the portrayal of the women as "appalling" and consider much of the text contains stereotypes which are "demeaning and inaccurate" (Slapin and Seale 1992, 174).

An accurate and valuable resource for the feminine Black-feet experience is Beverly Hungry Wolf's *The Ways of My Grandmothers,* a book secondary students enjoy reading independently.

Jassem, Kate. *Chief Joseph: Leader of Destiny.* Mahwah, NJ: Troll, 1979. 47 pp.
Genre: Biography
Grade Level: I

This book covers the life of Chief Joseph (Nez Perce), his flight, and his "I will fight no more forever" speech. Doris Seale and Beverly Slapin have called the Troll series "formula non-fiction." Criticizing its "white-washing" of Indian history, they suggest that the stories reinforce stereotypical myths of the "infallibility and superiority of white American institutions" (Slapin and Seale 1992, 230). Although the story approximates Chief Joseph's flight, the dialogue is contrived, and the illustrations of Chief Joseph bear little resemblance to any available photographs. Other Troll books communicate the same romantic image of vanished Indians who lived as kings, princes, and princesses. The Troll biography of Sitting Bull closes with "Old Ways are gone," and it further suggests that Wounded Knee marked the end of Indian resistance and that the practice of the Ghost Dance disappeared after Wounded Knee—none of which is true. This Troll series can best be used as an example of stereotype and bias that ignores the serious realities of the Indian experience. When Native teachers read this book, they quickly recognize the problems indicated above, and they resent the implication of "disappearance."

Other resources about Chief Joseph include Charles Eastman's *Indian Heroes and Great Chieftains,* Erskine Wood's *Days with Chief Joseph,* and the Montana Council for Indian Education's *Chief Joseph's Own Story.*

Jeffers, Susan. *Brother Eagle, Sister Sky: A Message from Chief Seattle.* New York: Dial, 1991. 45 pp.
Genre: Oratory
Grade Level: P, I

Illustrated and written by Jeffers, the text of *Brother Eagle, Sister Sky* is based on the speech attributed to Chief Seattle, who spoke in response to an address by Governor Stevens in the

Washington Territory, sometime in 1853, after the land was designated for the town of Seattle.

In his 1991 review in *WEB (Wonderfully Exciting Books)*, Ron Hirschi objects to:

1. The stereotype presented of Indian people.

2. The simplification of and mistaken interpretation of environmental problems facing the Suquamish people.

3. The assumption that our government was coming to "buy" land from Chief Seattle and his people at the time of his famous speech.

4. The representation of Indian people as a group who can only be referred to in the past tense.

5. The choice of non-Indian people as the apparent good guys who will solve the problems illustrated in the book.

Hirschi concludes: "I do know that a lot of kids, especially Indian kids, would have been greatly uplifted if Susan Jeffers could have found it in her painting skill to paint one image of a contemporary Indian child planting that single tree. Then, she might have given us a book worth reading . . ." (Hirschi 1991, 31–34).

The front cover portrays two stereotypes: the Plains Indian as universal Indian—not at all representative of Seattle or his people, and the Environmental Indian, represented by the butterfly that easily lights on the finger of a non-Indian child. The last page reinforces the same Plains Indian stereotype, but the Vanishing Indian and the Women as Subservient stereotypes are also portrayed. Ghost-like in the background, certainly not physically part of the contemporary landscape where only non-Indians plant trees, the woman walks and carries her child while her husband follows on horseback.

Indian children who read this book must regard it as pure fantasy, or they will experience further confusion and shame at the difference between this "Perfect but Vanishing Indian" and the realities the children experience in their own homes. The consequences of non-Indian children reading this book are very serious, since Jeffers' book can only exacerbate the discrimination non-Indian children may already practice toward a group that has "apparently" fallen from such a state of grace as portrayed in *Brother Eagle, Sister Sky.*

Teachers who insist on using this book should at least read the complete text of the speech in Vanderwerth's *Indian Oratory: Famous Speeches by Noted Indian Chieftains.* The introductory comments suggest Seattle spoke in his native language, and the recorder wrote what the interpreter said. Still, some interesting comments by Chief Seattle as recorded in Vanderwerth would contradict the perfect harmony depicted in Jeffers book.

Our good father at Washington . . . will he be our father and we his children. But can that ever be? Your God is not our God! Your God loves your people and hates mine . . . we are two distinct races with separate origins and separate destinies. There is little in common between us. (Vanderwerth 1989, 119)

The text recorded in Vanderwerth concludes with the image that probably is pictured at the end of the book, but the implication is not peaceful harmony, or quiet resignation. Instead the following lines carry the possibility of threat to the white man who will also experience "the time of decay":

[W]hen the last Red Man shall have perished, and the memory of my tribe shall have become a myth among the White Men, these shores will swarm with the invisible dead of my tribe, and when your children's children think themselves alone in the field, the store, the shop, upon the highway, or in the silence of the pathless woods, they will not be alone. In all the earth there is no place dedicated to solitude . . . [the streets] will throng with the returning hosts that once filled them and still love this beautiful land. The White Man will never be alone . . . Let him be just and deal kindly with my people, for the dead are not powerless. . . . (Vanderwerth 1989, 121–122)

For literature that includes traditional tribal stories from the Northwest, teachers should refer to *The Indian Reading Series*.

Johnson, Dorothy M. *Buffalo Woman*. New York: Dodd, Mead, 1977. 247 pp.
Genre: Historical Fiction
Grade Level: I, S

A fictional account of an Oglala Sioux woman's life before, during, and after the Battle of the Little Bighorn, *Buffalo Woman* is a good account of Plains Indian life at the time of European American encroachment. Although non-Indian, Johnson was an adopted member of the Blackfeet.

Ella Deloria's *Waterlily* is a Native-authored novel that portrays a Dakota woman's experience in the middle 1800's, the time of European American contact on the Plains. Also, Zitkala-Sa's first essay in *American Indian Stories* communicates her experience as a child at the time when Yankton were moved onto the reservation. Readers can compare and contrast the different accounts.

LaFarge, Oliver. *Laughing Boy.* Boston: Houghton Mifflin, 1957. 302 pp.
   Genre: Historical Fiction
   Grade Level: S

In *Laughing Boy,* a Navajo man falls in love with a woman who has shady dealings with the white world. They fight Navajo resentment of her "white" connections and return to the "Old Ways." With respect for LaFarge and his commitment to Indian people, D'Arcy McNickle (Salish) wrote a biography called *Indian Man.*

Lesley, Craig. *River Song.* New York: Dell, 1989. 307 pp.
   Genre: Contemporary Novel
   Grade Level: S

River Song, a sequel to the novel *Winterkill,* is the culmination of a fiction fellowship granted by the National Endowment for the Arts in 1986. Lesley credits the numbers of Native people and especially the "River People [Yakima/Nez Perce], those contemporary Indians who live and fish along the Columbia River upstream from Bonneville Dam," the Oregon Historical Society, and the Yakima, Nez Perce, and the Dalles Cultural Centers. Indian students in Montana have assumed Lesley is Native American because they recognize his understanding of the cultural and personal conflicts contemporary Indians experience. *River Song* is a novel about the historical and ensuing personal conflicts that have occurred as a result of non-Indian encroachment on Yakima lands and on mining and fishing rights, but *River Song* is also about the reconciliation between father and son, between past and present, and between traditional and nontraditional Indian peoples. While Danny Kachiah tries to establish a relationship with a son from whom he has been separated for fifteen years, he searches for the meaning to a vision and meets his ancestor, Left Hand, the Nez Perce warrior. The novel closes with a salmon feast, ceremony, and giveaway. Danny wanders away from the crowd to listen to the voices that rise from the dark water of the river.

Many thousands of voices, old tongue and new, blended with the longhouse singing and echoed off the basalt hills until the valley seemed filled with their cries. They joined a deeper song borne downriver by the night wind, then fell to whispers. Stepping off the trembling platform, Danny started climbing toward the longhouse. Beneath the singing waters, Chinook glided among rocks, and campfires blazed. (305)

River Song demonstrates the distinctive nature of a particular Indian people who have depended not on the buffalo for survival, but on the salmon. The novel also reveals the importance of continuing to respect the salmon for providing life for the people. This is an excellent novel for Native young people, especially those whose ancestors and relatives have survived because of the salmon in the Columbia River.

LeSueur, Meridel. *Sparrow Hawk.* Stevens Point, WI: Holy Cow! Press, [1950] 1987. 176 pp.
Genre: Historical Fiction
Grade Level: I, S

Although LeSueur is non-Indian, she grew up in the Midwest of Wisconsin, Illinois, and Iowa, the settings for this novel. She called her work a "remembering not dismembering journey into the deepest heart of the valley of earth and man and woman." In his Foreword, Vine Deloria, Jr. praises her for risking to communicate an "Indian slant . . . with both good and bad whites and Indians." This is a growing-up story of the friendship between two teenage boys: Huck, the son of settlers who are being squeezed out by squatters, and Sparrow Hawk, from Black Hawk's tribe of Mesquakie. While the novel presents the conflicts which precipitated the final tragedy of Black Hawk's war with the U.S. military in 1832, it also carries a strong sense of the everyday Sauk culture. The as-told-to autobiography of *Black Hawk* can provide teachers with further background information.

Marriott, Alice, and Carol K. Rachlin, eds. *Plains Indian Mythology.* New York: Penguin, 1975. 175 pp.
Genre: Traditional Story, Short Story
Grade Level: I, S

This collection of thirty-one Plains Indian stories is divided into four parts: myths, stories, eighteenth- and nineteenth-century stories, and contemporary stories. In her Foreword, Marriott defines "Mythology" as "the backbone of religion; the accounts of the supernatural, superhuman beings who have become embodied in the universe: Sun, Moon, Stars, Winds, and the Earth herself." "Legendary" is defined as "explanatory stories" that provide answers to children's questions, and this includes "the accounts of men and women who actually have lived but since their lifetimes have become larger than life," while "Folklore" comprises the "lore and wisdom of the folk" (xi). A short introductory essay explaining the tribal origin and the background of the story prefaces each selection. Because Marriott is non-Indian, some individuals or culture groups might not approve of her "retelling" the stories. Although the editor makes distinctions between tribes and cultures, books such as these that don't represent direct Native voices should only be used in conjunction with more primary resources of Native stories.

McLuhan, T. C. *Touch the Earth: A Self-Portrait of Indian Existence.* New York: Promontory Press, 1971. 185 pp.
    Genre: Memoir, Oratory, Essay
    Grade Level: I, S

In this collection of short sayings (excerpts from speeches and other writings), photographs, and short background essays, "the Indians speak for themselves, of the quality of their life." *Touch the Earth* includes representations from the following nations: Lakota, Dakota, Sioux, Blackfoot, Nez Perce, Chippewa, Blackfeet, Cheyenne, Cree, Crow, and Flathead, among others. In the Introduction, the editor presents a stereotypical view of Indian peoples, saying that they "speak with courtesy and respect of the land, of animals, of the objects which made up the territory in which they lived. They saw no virtue in imposing their will over their environment. . . ." Although McLuhan may be speaking only from her understanding of the Indians she has quoted in this collection, students need to be aware that Indians did "impose their will on the land." Plains Indians burned prairies to move buffalo; the Hidatsa farmed, as did other peoples from across the continent. McLuhan's effort to rely on the voices of the peoples themselves is commendable, and so this is a valuable collection for that reason especially.

Nardo, Don. *The Indian Wars.* San Diego, CA: Lucent, 1991. 127 pp.
    Genre: History
    Grade Level: I, S

Part of the *America's War* series, and identified as "Juvenile literature," *The Indian Wars* offers an appealing format with photographs, maps, or drawings on every page, but the text would work well for secondary students. Sensitive to the influence of ethnic and social bias on historical sources, Nardo avoids adopting such bias himself: "Whites often looked upon Indians as savages who had to be reeducated to adopt civilized ways" (12), and "In their eyes, a land of Christian believers seemed ultimately more progressive and more pleasing to God than the thousands of heathen hordes that populated North America" (13). *Indian Wars* strongly attempts to contradict many stereotypes, emphasizing the strength of Indians to continue to resist encroachment, although Nardo does regard the capture of Geronimo as "The End of Apache Resistance." But Nardo stereotypes "whites," suggesting all people of that color were of the same position: "After the Indians ceased to be a threat to whites, however, some of these policies began to change" (118). While this book might portray wars between European Americans and Native Americans in more historical detail than any other American History textbook thus far, teachers should be aware of the non-Native bias of the writer, which at times tries too hard to be sympathetic to the Indian and at times avoids harsh realities.

O'Dell, Scott. *Island of the Blue Dolphins.* New York: Dell, 1960. 189 pp.
Genre: Historical Fiction
Grade Level: I, S

Scott O'Dell considers himself a writer of historical fiction, and *Island of the Blue Dolphins* may fall into that category, although Beverly Slapin strongly criticizes its use as "history" rather than fiction. It is based on the true story of an Indian woman who lived alone on San Nicolas Island off the coast of California from 1835 to 1853. For years previous to that time, her people had tolerated Russian and Aleut seal hunters who gave the island's inhabitants little return for their large catch of seals. Then one day white men came to take the entire tribe away from the isolated island. The girl jumped ship to join her brother who had remained on shore, and there she stayed for eighteen years, even after he was killed by wild dogs. *Island of the Blue Dolphins* is a Robinson Crusoe adventure and survival story. O'Dell has created a perfect hero, a rather flat character, who, in the romantic fashion of American heroes, is not only resourceful enough to survive alone but can find happiness in the effort and the experience. She befriends wild animals, makes weapons for fishing and hunting, weaves clothes, and builds a home. Even though she has lost her entire family and tribe, she is at peace. Although the book makes enjoyable reading, it provides little insight into any realistic Native personality or experience. When her brother plays "Chief," he assumes a dominant rather than a cooperative leadership position: "I am his son and since he is dead I have taken his place. I am now Chief of Ghalas-at. All my wishes must be obeyed" (51). *Island of the Blue Dolphins* also perpetuates the Vanishing Indian stereotype because the writer implies that all of these people have either disappeared or died. It is unrealistic historical fiction and should never be taught as Indian literature.

Richter, Conrad. *The Light in the Forest.* New York: Fawcett Juniper, [1953] 1995. 117 pp.
Genre: Historical Novel
Grade Level: S

For at least twenty years, Richter's young adult novel has been widely used in intermediate and secondary literature classes. Set in Ohio and Pennsylvania, the story begins as a fifteen-year-old Lenni Lenape boy, after an eleven-year separation, reluctantly returns to his white biological parents in compliance with recent treaty stipulations. Throughout the text, Richter demonstrates a sensitivity to the internal and external conflicts for both the Indians and the whites during the nineteenth century. He also depicts—with the historical accuracy of colonists such as Benjamin Franklin—the unwillingness of white children who had been adopted by Indians to return to their original families.

However, the text communicates some confusion over the historical time period of the novel, as well as over tribal beliefs and practices. For example, since the Carlisle School for Indians in Pennsylvania is mentioned, the novel must be set after 1879, and yet the relatively free existence of an Indian camp just west of the Mississippi would indicate a preremoval (1820–1830s) time period. Also, the novel implies an Indian belief in land "ownership," when they most likely practiced land "usage," not ownership. It appears violent revenge is the behavior of the entire tribe of warriors once they learn a white man has killed Little Crane. More likely, a few would have sought revenge, while the elders would have regarded Half Arrow and True Son's action toward the killer as satisfactory retribution.

Richter was a product of his time, but current recognition of the impact of stereotypical images on both Native and non-Native children warrants careful attention by teachers who would use this book. White characters realistically use the word "savage." However, with no obvious harm intended, the narrator's "objective" voice and the Introduction also use it: "As a small boy [Richter] himself had tried to run off to Indian country without the benefit of ever having lived among the savages."

Teachers who use this book should use Francis Jennings's *The Invasion of America: Indians, Colonialism, and the Cant of Conquest* as a reliable historical resource that will help address the issues of historical inaccuracy and stereotype.

Sandoz, Mari. *Cheyenne Autumn.* Lincoln: University of Nebraska Press, 1992. 281 pp.
Genre: Historical Narrative
Grade Level: S

In her Preface, Mari Sandoz strongly suggests that the United States government's Indian policy was a policy of "extermination," even during the days of Abraham Lincoln. From this point of view, she has written *Cheyenne Autumn,* a sensitive and studied portrayal of the Cheyenne's flight from the Oklahoma Indian Territory, from disease and starvation, back to the Yellowstone country (1878–1879). Across more than 1,500 miles, Chief Dull Knife led the Northern Cheyennes "through settled regions netted with telegraph, across three railroads, and straight through the United States Army." Accompanying her narrative, Sandoz provides maps, descriptions of the political situation, of historical settings and of Indian warriors, military men, and the Indian agent. She has relied on interviews with Sioux and Cheyenne people and on historical records located in Nebraska, Washington, DC, Wyoming, Colorado, Kansas, Oklahoma, and New York, and provided by the Northern Cheyenne. Still, she occasionally refers to this proud people as stereotypical children, possibly to communicate her belief in their absolute victimization. For insight into the ways the Cheyenne continued to survive and maintain their pride in spite of the pressures to destroy them, students can also read the as-told-to autobiographies of John Stands in Timber, Wooden Leg, and "Iron Teeth, a Cheyenne Old Woman" as told to Thomas B. Marquis and excerpted in *The Last Best Place.*

Speare, Elizabeth George. *The Sign of the Beaver.* New York: Dell, 1983. 135 pp.
Genre: Young Adult Novel
Grade Level: I

Twelve-year-old Matt is left to survive alone at his parents' cabin in the Maine wilderness. Following the stereotypical Indian-helps-the-white-man theme, an Indian boy and his grandfather rescue Matt from a bee attack and show him how to survive. He can choose to live with the Indians or to wait for his parents' return. Slapin and Seale criticize the "pidgin English" of the Indian speakers, the "uneven" relationship between the boys, the "white" attitudes toward women, and the missing tribal connection. *Sign of the Beaver* cannot be regarded as Indian literature. By contrast, some of the stories from Joseph Bruchac's *Turtle Meat and Other Stories* represent

Northeastern cultures and feature Native characters who are wise and witty, and who successfully outsmart those who would regard them as inferior.

Thomasma, Ken. *Soun Tetoken: Nez Perce Boy.* Jackson, WY: Grandview, 1984. 190 pp.
Genre: Historical Fiction
Grade Level: I

Mute but not deaf, six-year-old Soun Tetoken is adopted by Chief Joseph's brother just a few years before the famous 1,600-mile flight to freedom. The story centers on Soun and his adventures. To save himself and/or others, he proves his courage and bravery in the face of bears, wolves, and rushing waters. Thomasma uses documented historical dates and situations as background, but the book communicates little that is realistic to Native lifeways. This is a romanticized view of a terrible tragedy, with emphasis not on suffering but on Soun, the singular hero, who accomplishes extraordinary feats at an unusually young age. The text represents a polarized world of "Indian vs. White." Soun has no conflicts with other human beings, unless they are white; and after an internal struggle, he consents to giving his horse, Sunburst, to Chief Joseph so Joseph's grandson may ride to safety in Canada. After all, Soun's "purpose in life was to help those in need." The text switches point of view, even within paragraphs, and Chief Joseph unrealistically talks about the "importance of love." Thomasma's books may not be regarded as Indian literature, although one group of Indian teachers from Browning, Montana, commented that they had no problem using them, since they "know the difference between truth and fiction" and laugh—with their students—at the errors. Non-Indian teachers who are unfamiliar with the history and culture should avoid these books.

Ude, Wayne. *Becoming Coyote.* Amherst, MA: Lynx House Press, 1981. 165 pp.
Genre: Contemporary Novel
Grade Level: S

Ude grew up in Harlem, Montana, on the edge of the Fort Belknap Reservation (Assiniboine/Gros Ventre). A mix between traditional mythology and contemporary fiction, *Becoming Coyote* reveals the ways in which individuals can experience transformation. After breaking into a local museum and stealing saddles and bows and arrows, two Indians "hunt" one stolen buffalo into the Missouri Breaks and to the home of Charlie Coyote, an old man who personally carries the myth in his name. The main character, Snook, a tribal cop, is caught between the rational, day-to-day, explainable reality of his job and the mythical, intuitive, mystical power of his experiences surrounding a stolen buffalo. Snook, a local boy who has been hardened by his job and experiences on the reservation, is affected by this experience and develops a renewed appreciation for the spiritual power of his cultural heritage, and he grows to appreciate gifts and the importance of making offerings to the giver.

Works Cited

Adams, Hank. 1984. "The Golden Indian." *Akwesasne Notes,* Late Summer: 10–11.

Akwesasne Notes. 1985. Early Winter: 5.

Gates, Henry Louis, Jr. 1991. "'Authenticity,' or the Lesson of Little Tree." *New York Times Book Review,* Nov. 24, p. 1.

Hirschi, Ron. 1991. "Susan Jeffers' *Brother Eagle, Sister Sky.*" *WEB (Wonderfully Exciting Books),* 16.1 (Fall): 31–34.

Lincoln, Kenneth. 1983. "Sending a Voice." In *Native American Renaissance.* Berkeley: University of California Press.

"Little Tree, Big Lies?" 1991. *Time,* Oct. 14, p. 33.

"New Age Fable from an Old School Bigot?" 1991. *Newsweek,* Oct. 14, p. 62.

Slapin, Beverly, and Doris Seale. 1992. *Through Indian Eyes: The Native Experience in Books for Children.* Philadelphia: New Society Publishers.

Vanderwerth, W. C. 1989. *Indian Oratory: Famous Speeches by Noted Indian Chieftains.* Norman: University of Oklahoma Press.

Appendix A: Geographical Contexts

Native North American literatures have grown out of a wide diversity of geographical contexts, and it is important to recognize the pre-European as well as the more current cultural areas and tribal locations. Although few tribes still inhabit the same areas they did before European contact, many of the stories told today spring from those early roots. Also, many of the more contemporary literatures have been written in response to geographical movements and relocations.

"Native North America," the first of the following three maps, printed in *Keepers of the Earth,* and included with permission from Michael J. Caduto, shows most of the Native North American cultural areas and tribal locations as they appeared around 1600. The second and third maps, printed in *Native North American Writers* and included with permission from Gale Research, depict the state and federally recognized U.S. Indian Reservations and the Indian communities that exist and thrive but have not been recognized as legal entities by state or federal governments.

BERING SEA

ARCTIC OCEAN

PACIFIC OCEAN

PACIFIC NORTHWEST

WEST COAST

GULF OF MEXICO

MIDDLE AMERICA

LEGEND

—— BOUNDARIES OF CULTURAL AREAS

INNU   NATIVE NORTH AMERICAN GROUPS DISCUSSED IN
        BOOK (CAPITAL LETTERS)

Arapaho OTHER NATIVE NORTH AMERICAN GROUPS
        (INCLINED AND LOWER CASE LETTERS)

- - - - NATIONAL BOUNDARIES

········ STATE AND PROVINCIAL BOUNDARIES

CARTOGRAPHY BY STACY MILLER, UPPER MARLBORO, MD.
COPYRIGHT © 1994 MICHAEL J. CADUTO.

SCALE

0   100   200   400 STATUTE
                        MILES

Cultural areas and tribal locations of Native North Americans. This map shows tribal locations as they appeared around 1600, except for the Seminole culture in the Southeast and the Tuscaroras in the Northeast. The Seminoles formed from a group which withdrew from the Muskogee (Creek) and joined with several other groups on the Georgia/Florida border to form the Seminoles, a name which has been used since about 1775. In the eastern woodlands the Haudenosaunee (Iroquois) consist of six nations, the Cayuga, Mohawk, Oneida, Onondaga, Seneca and Tuscarora. The Tuscaroras were admitted to the Iroquois League in 1722 after many refugees from the Tuscarora Wars (1711–1713) in the Southeast fled northward. There are hundreds of other Cultures/Nations that are not included due to limited space. The generally recognized name of at least one distinct Culture is given in each area, emphasizing those with large populations, past and/or present. Traditional names are used where possible because many names in general use are not preferred by Native North Americans.

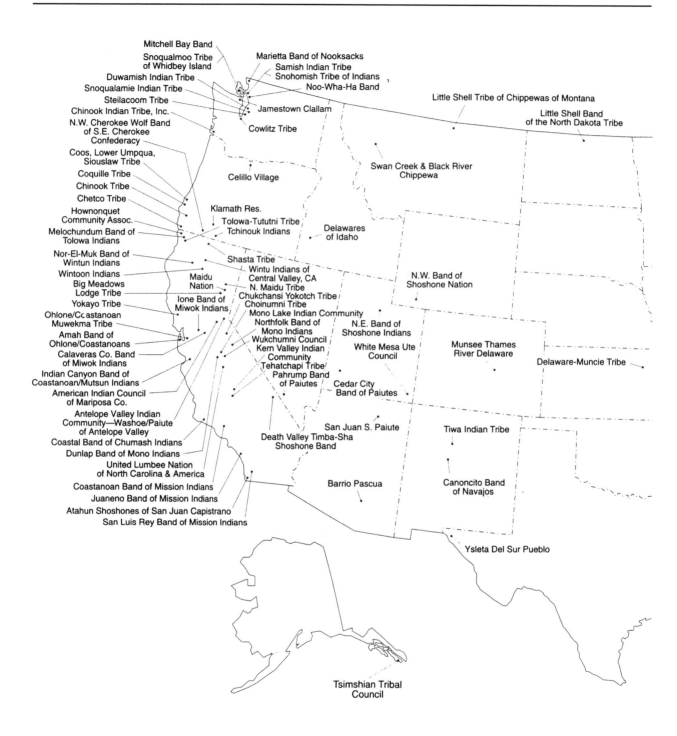

Mitchell Bay Band
Snoqualmoo Tribe
of Whidbey Island
Duwamish Indian Tribe
Snoqualamie Indian Tribe
Steilacoom Tribe
Chinook Indian Tribe, Inc.
N.W. Cherokee Wolf Band
of S.E. Cherokee
Confederacy
Coos, Lower Umpqua,
Siouslaw Tribe
Coquille Tribe
Chinook Tribe
Chetco Tribe
Hownonquet
Community Assoc.
Melochundum Band of
Tolowa Indians
Nor-El-Muk Band of
Wintun Indians
Wintoon Indians
Big Meadows
Lodge Tribe
Yokayo Tribe
Ohlone/Coastanoan
Muwekma Tribe
Amah Band of
Ohlone/Coastanoans
Calaveras Co. Band
of Miwok Indians
Indian Canyon Band of
Coastanoan/Mutsun Indians
American Indian Council
of Mariposa Co.
Antelope Valley Indian
Community—Washoe/Paiute
of Antelope Valley
Coastal Band of Chumash Indians
Dunlap Band of Mono Indians
United Lumbee Nation
of North Carolina & America
Coastanoan Band of Mission Indians
Juaneno Band of Mission Indians
Atahun Shoshones of San Juan Capistrano
San Luis Rey Band of Mission Indians

Marietta Band of Nooksacks
Samish Indian Tribe
Snohomish Tribe of Indians
Noo-Wha-Ha Band
Jamestown Clallam
Cowlitz Tribe

Celillo Village

Klamath Res.
Tolowa-Tututni Tribe
Tchinouk Indians

Delawares
of Idaho

Shasta Tribe
Wintu Indians of
Central Valley, CA
Maidu
Nation
N. Maidu Tribe
Ione Band of
Miwok Indians
Chukchansi Yokotch Tribe
Choinumni Tribe
Mono Lake Indian Community
Northfolk Band of
Mono Indians
Wukchumni Council
Kern Valley Indian
Community
Tehatchapi Tribe
Pahrump Band
of Paiutes
Cedar City
Band of Paiutes

Death Valley Timba-Sha
Shoshone Band

San Juan S. Paiute

Little Shell Tribe of Chippewas of Montana
Little Shell Band
of the North Dakota Tribe

Swan Creek & Black River
Chippewa

N.W. Band of
Shoshone Nation

N.E. Band of
Shoshone Indians
White Mesa Ute
Council

Munsee Thames
River Delaware

Delaware-Muncie Tribe

Tiwa Indian Tribe

Barrio Pascua

Canoncito Band
of Navajos

Ysleta Del Sur Pueblo

Tsimshian Tribal
Council

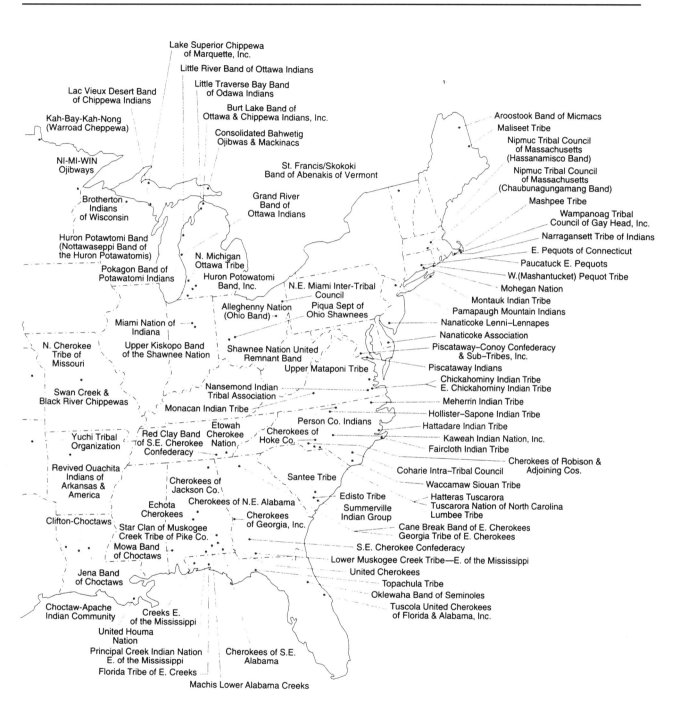

Lower Elwha   Lummi   Swinomish
Makah   Jamestown   Upper Skagit
Ozette   Klallam   Stillaguamish
Quileute   Nooksack   Sauk Suiattle
Hoh   Kootenai
Port Gamble   Tulalip   Blackfeet
Quinault   Kalispel   Rocky Boys   Turtle
Port Madison   Fort Peck   Mountain
Skokomish   Colville
Squaxin   Muckleshoot   Spokane
Island   Puyallup   Coeur
Shoalwater   d'Alene   Flathead
Chehalis   Fort Belknap
                Nisqually   Yakima   Fort Berthold
Siletz   Northern Cheyenne
                                      Nez Perce   Crow   Standing Rock
                            Umatilla
                      Warm Springs   Cheyenne River
                        Burns Paiute   Lower Brute
Fort Bidwell   Cow Creek Band   Fort   Fort Hall
                      of Umpqua   McDermitt   Wind River
                Karok   Duck Valley   Elko   Pine Ridge
                Hoopa Valley   NW Shoshone   Rosebud
                Round Valley   Summit Lake
Yerington   Pyramid Lake   Winnemucca
Carson   Reno Sparks   Te-Moak
Dresslerville   Lovelock
                Washoe   Fallon   Skull Valley
                            Yomba   Goshute
                                            Ely   Uintah & Ouray
              Numerous small   Walker River
                rancherias   Duckwater
                            Fort   Moapa   Paiute   Hopi
                        Independence   Las   Jicarilla Apache
                              Tule   Vegas   Kaibab Navajo Ute Mountain
                              River   Havasupai   Southern Ute   Picuris
Morongo   Fort   Taos   Santa Clara   Pawnee
Soboba   Palm   Santa Ynez   Mohave   San Ildefonso
Ramona   Springs   Colorado   Hualapai   Jemez San Juan   Pojoaque
Cahuilla   Cabazon   San Manuel   River   Chemehuevi   Acoma Zia   Nambe   Cheyenne
Pechanga   Augustine   Yavapai Payson   Sandia Tesuque Arapaho
Pala   Camp Verde   Zuni   Cochiti   Wichita
Pauma   Gila River   Ramah   Santo Domingo Caddo
Rincon   Santa Rosa   Navajo   Laguna San Felipe Kiowa
San Pasqual   Torres-Martinez   Alamo   Canoncito Santa Ana
Mesa Grande   Los Coyotes   Navajo
Viejas   La Jolla   Cocopah   Isleta
Jamul   Santa Ysabel   Quechin
              Sycuan   Inaha-Cosmit   Gila Bend   Fort Apache
              La Posta   Capitan Grande Papago   San Carlos   Mescalero
              Campo   Cuyapaipe   Maricopa   Tigua
                Manzanita   Papago
                                        Fort McDowell
                                        San Xavier
                                        Pascua
                                        Yaqui

                Inuit

              Athabascan

          Yupik
                            Tlingit   Kickapoo
                            Haida
                Aleut   Annette Island

              (Alaska not to scale)

Federal Indian Reservations
Federal Indian Reservations
State Indian Reservations

Appendix B: Historical Context

Few history textbooks address the issue of federal Indian policy, while most contemporary writers—from the late 1800s onward—tell stories that reflect the impact of such policies on Native lives. It is important that teachers become familiar with some of the most significant dates, policies, and consequences for tribal people. Not only have the policies resulted in Native artists' personal literary expressions—as well as deeply affecting the lives of generations of Native people—they have resulted in very personal and profoundly serious consequences, both positive and negative, for all Native children today. For a more comprehensive listing of historical and cultural events of the Native peoples of North America and Canada, teachers should consult an excellent resource for all grade levels: *Chronology of Native North American History,* edited by Duane Champagne, illustrated with black-and-white paintings and photos, and published in 1994 by Gale Research in Detroit, Michigan. In addition to federal policies, the *Chronology* includes short biographies; individual episodes of strong Indian resistance; contributions by Indians to education, literature, and the general economy; many records of smallpox epidemics in which 90 percent of whole tribes died in one winter; purposeful destruction of the buffalo; and many other stories of genocide across the continent.

In no way can *Roots and Branches* provide a complete list of U.S. government policies, acts, and programs during the past five hundred years. Neither can it begin to do justice to the devastating consequences tribal peoples have suffered and continue to suffer as a result of those policies—and as a result of countless broken treaties. However, many of the storytellers and writers listed in the current volume have born witness—and their voices testify most powerfully—to the impact of such experiences on themselves and on their ancestors. The following chronology pretends to be no more than this, a "brief" list, so that teachers might begin to understand the historical contexts of the literatures they might use.

A Brief History of Federal Indian Policy

1492—As many as 18–30 million Native Americans lived on this continent, according to current estimates by scholars.

1789–1871—Treaty Policy Period: U.S. government ostensibly treated Indian tribes—in more than 400 treaties—as sovereign foreign nations. The War Department handled these affairs from 1831 until 1859, when Indian Affairs was transferred to Department of the Interior. This policy ended with the Battle of the Little Bighorn.

1790s—As agreed to in treaties, annuity payments to tribes began for services such as education and health, money or goods, in exchange for lands treatied or for lands taken without consent.

July 22, 1790—The first Trade and Intercourse Act read that "no sale of lands shall be made by any Indians, or any nation or persons. . . ." Essentially, this meant that tribes could not sell land without federal control.

March 1, 1793—The second Trade and Intercourse Act prohibited anyone without a license from trading with the Indians and provided $20,000 for the purchase of animals and farm equipment.

1803—The "Jefferson Policy" discouraged Indian tribes from being nomadic hunters and instead encouraged and then forced them to become farmers, no matter where they lived. Congress appropriated $3,000 to civilize and educate the "heathens."

May 28, 1830—Viewing occupied Indian lands as a solution to its inability to pay soldiers who had fought in two wars against England, Congress authorized $500,000 to relocate Indian families to the Indian Territory. The Indian Removal Act determined Indian peoples—Cherokee, Choctaw, Chickasaw, Creek, Seminole, and others—would be moved west of the Mississippi to save them from European American "contamination," and to save them from "extinction." In tragic irony, 4,000 Cherokees died on that "Trail of Tears." The "Removal Era" lasted from 1830–1860.

1831—Chief Justice John Marshall's decision, regarding the *Cherokee Nation v. Georgia,* defined Indian tribes as "domestic dependent nations," subject to the U.S. Congress, not to state laws, defining the relationship between the United States government and the Indian nations as resembling that of a guardian to a ward; yet the western tribes were still handled as foreign nations until the late 1800s.

1832—A Supreme Court decision—*Worcester v. Georgia*—affirmed that Indian removal by the State of Georgia was illegal. Still, the Cherokee were forced to move west between 1835 and 1839.

1834–1836—In this period, 111 Indian schools were established by various religious organizations.

June 30, 1834—The Indian Trade and Intercourse Act insisted that all trade be conducted between tribes and the government rather than between individuals. This act defined Indian territory as "all that part of the United States west of the Mississippi . . . and not within any state to which the Indian title has not been extinguished."

1835–1850—According to Champagne, the federal government invested monies it held for tribes—monies promised to Indian nations in exchange for land—in state bonds; when the states failed to pay interest, the Indian funds earned little money.

March 3, 1847—The Trade and Intercourse Act defined the procedures for eliminating the liquor trade among the Indians.

1851–1880—Beginning with Commissioner Luke Lea's doctrine, which called for the Indians' "concentration, their domestication and their incorporation," plans developed to drastically reduce the Indians' land holdings, to make them wards of the government, and to break up the tribal structure.

July 20, 1867—The Peace Commission Act called for meetings with "hostile Indian tribes," with the intention to eliminate the "treaty process" and locate all Indians on confined areas of land. On August 13, 1868, the Nez Percé signed the last and 370th pact.

1868—The Fourteenth Amendment granted citizenship to all men but not to Indians because they were members of "foreign nations."

1870—Grant's peace policy assigned supervision of reservations to churches after Congress prohibited army officers from being Indian agents.

1871–1887—Reservation Policy Period—Land areas, created by treaties, were reserved by tribes within which they were expected to live; included in the Indian Appropriations Act was the stipulation that "no Indian Nation of Tribes within the territory of the United States shall be acknowledged or recognized as an independent nation, tribe or power with whom the United States may contract by treaty."

1883—Courts for Indian Offenses were established according to rules laid down by the Department of the Interior for the running of the reservations.

March 3, 1885—The Major Crimes Act declared that all Indian cases regarding major crimes would be tried in federal courts.

1800 to 1900s—The "Assimilation Policy," enforced through agriculture and education and Christian churches, promoted the deculturation of all Indian peoples.

Fall 1879—General R. H. Pratt established the first Indian boarding school, located off a reservation at Carlisle, Pennsylvania. Pratt's philosophy of removal of students from family and tribe and the imposition of rigid military discipline characterized Indian education for the next fifty years.

1887—The General Allotment Act (or "Dawes Act") attempted to dissolve the reservation system by forcing Indians to cease communal ways, to become individual farmers on small plots of land held "in trust" by the United States government. The reservation lands were not evenly distributed between individual tribal members or families; rather, heads of families were allotted 160 acres once they became "competent" or "civilized enough." The opportunity to become citizens would follow. The unallotted lands identified as *surplus* lands were then open to non-Indian settlement. However, this did not apply on all reservations, such as the Apache, Navajo, Papago, and Hopi.

1893—The Appropriation Act prevented rations in money or in kind from being distributed to any head of an Indian family for any children who did not attend school during the preceding year.

1887–1934—Allotment Policy Period (also known as the Assimilationist Policy Period) was finally viewed as coercive and a failure.

Consequences of the Allotment Policy for tribes were as follows:

- In 1887, Indians held title to 137 million acres.
- By 1934, 52 million acres remained.
- 25 million acres of *original* allotted land had been transferred to non-Indian people.
- Boarding school education programs were established with the purpose of separating children from their Native peoples and cultures and enforcing assimilation procedures.
- Many Indian agents governed reservations with abuse of human rights and dignity, forbidding use of Native languages and the practice of cultural traditions.
- Economic development was a disaster, funds were misappropriated, and people died of starvation and disease.
- By 1900, 250,000 Native American people remained of the estimated original 18–30 million.

July 23, 1892—The Intoxication in Indian Country Act forbid the sale and transportation of alcoholic beverages in Indian country. This was later repealed on August 15, 1953.

August 15, 1894—The Parent Consent for Education Act stressed the importance of parents or guardians granting permission for young people to attend boarding schools.

1902—The Civil Service Act was extended to the Bureau of Indian Affairs.

1910—The Sun Dance was forbidden because of the self-inflicted "torture." This proved to be a violation of the U.S. Constitution.

1924—The Indian Citizenship Act granted citizenship to those who had not become citizens through allotment.

1928—The "Miriam Report" revealed the truths of poverty and fraud, urged Congress to fulfill its treaty obligations in terms of health, education, and subsistence, and also indicted the Allotment Act for causing social genocide on the reservations.

1933—Franklin D. Roosevelt named John Collier, an Indian reformist, as Commissioner of Indian Affairs, in response to the Miriam Report.

1934–1936—Repealing the General Allotment Act, Congress replaced it with the Johnson-O'Malley Act and amendments. This act, also part of the Indian "New Deal," granted contracting authority with the states to the Secretary of the Interior for Indian education, health, social welfare, and agricultural assistance, and schools, colleges, universities, and other appropriate agencies.

1934—The Indian Reorganization Act (or "Wheeler-Howard Act") replaced treaty rights. It was written by academics who didn't like or didn't understand what was happening. The act was amended to give tribes the right to either accept or reject it. Ostensibly, it was a policy of self-determination. One hundred eighty-nine tribes agreed to its terms.

The consequences of the Indian Reorganization Act for tribes were as follows:

- gave Indian tribes the authority to form businesses and establish credit systems and rights for home rule;
- gave them the right to establish their own constitutions;
- provided clear criteria for tribal membership;
- abolished the Allotment Act of 1887;
- provided better education and economic development;
- provided the Bureau of Indian Affairs (BIA) as supervisor of funds and lands, establishing the federal government as paternal trustee;
- exempted Indians from the draft;
- represented another federal move toward assimilation;
- applied *one* policy to 250 culturally diverse tribes;
- resulted in the present system in which tribes must receive approval before passing ordinances or amending constitutions;
- gave the Secretary of the Interior power to revoke tribal constitutions, even for tribes not reorganized under the act;
- resulted in tribes under this act having fewer rights than treaty tribes;
- provided tribal monies to build federal irrigation projects.

1950s—Relocation was enacted as another attempt to mainstream Indians. The Bureau of Indian Affairs paid the expenses for an Indian family to move, helped obtain housing and jobs, and provided living expenses until the family could be self-sufficient. Over 1,000 Montana Indians moved to California. In 1965, the government was spending $15 million per year on training. By 1970, 125,000 Indians were living in urban areas, but more than one-third ultimately returned to the reservations.

The consequences of termination and relocation for Indian people were as follows:

- difficulty in adjusting to city life;
- unfamiliarity with jobs and no training;

- those who left were potential leaders, leaving behind vacuums in leadership in many communities;
- demoralization as a result of discrimination in the cities;
- severe poverty for most, while many returned to reservations;
- establishment of an employment assistance program;
- establishment of adult vocational training in 1956;
- negation of trust between the federal government and the Indian people;
- development of the general belief that termination and relocation were another form of genocide. Leonard Mountain Chief said, "The issue is still there and will never go away";
- probable beginning for the current push for tribal sovereignty;
- resulted in Indians retreating from society, becoming more defensive, and viewing the rest of the world with even more suspicion;
- termination of thirteen tribes in spite of the fact that they were too poor to have representation at hearings;
- between 1954 and 1958, 1.8 million acres of Indian-owned land passed into non-Indian hands.

1953—Public Law 280 transferred the jurisdiction over civil and criminal law from the general government to the states.

August 1, 1953—Termination Resolution—House Concurrent Resolution 108 called for withdrawal of federal services to Indians, terminating its trust responsibilities, ending tribal sovereignty, health care, and most federal obligations to Indians as specified in treaties. Ostensibly, it was intended to free Indian peoples from reservations and allow them to "get out and work, so they could take care of themselves." Not until 1958 did the law declare that the tribes would be terminated only with their consent. The Termination Act was repealed on April 28, 1988.

January 4, 1975—The Indian Self-Determination and Education Act allowed Indians to provide for some of their own services by contract with the BIA.

The consequences of Indian Self-Determination and Education Act for tribes were as follows:

- Contract schools could be governed by tribally elected school boards and operated with federal monies.
- Tribes could manage their housing programs, tribal courts, law and order agencies, career development programs, and other such entities.
- The BIA had the authority to provide technical assistance to tribes in the contract areas.
- Federal funding cutbacks affected monies for self-determination and education.

- "Great Society" programs overwhelmed Indian tribes and made it difficult to plan, set priorities, and administer them.
- Still, new hope for self-determination developed.
- In 1980, government programs decreased, and this became more of a problem for Indians since they so thoroughly depended on the federal government economically and for social services.

August 11, 1978—The American Indian Religious Freedom Act, more symbol than legal obligation, recognized Indians' "inherent right of freedom to believe, express, and exercise their traditional religions." However, it did not require an agency to change action simply because of interference with Indian custom.

August 24, 1978—The Federal Acknowledgment Program establishes parameters for recognizing an American Indian group as a tribe.

June 11, 1981—Civil Rights Commission Report chairman Arthur Flemming said that the government's policy toward American Indians has been one of "inaction and missed opportunities."

January 12, 1983—The Indian Land Consolidation Act authorized the purchase, sale, and exchange of lands by Indian tribes.

September 25, 1990—The Carl D. Perkins Vocational Education Act provided funds for "the operation and improvement of tribal controlled post-secondary vocational institutions."

November 2, 1990—The Native American Languages Act was designed to preserve, protect, and promote the practice and development of Indian languages.

In no way does the above chronology represent the entire Native historical experience. It merely recounts some of the major actions of the federal government toward Indian people in the United States.

Appendix C: Stereotypes—Sources and Definitions

The following explication of several common stereotypes can offer only a minimum background for teachers and students, since they still strongly influence young people and adults across the continent. All Native Americans must deal with these stereotypes in one way or another every day, and so an understanding of their sources is essential when reading literatures written by Native Americans as well as those written by non-Natives about Native people. When students understand the stereotypes and the ways they have been used by one group to gain power or control over another, the power of those stereotypes to negatively impact lives is diminished.

Noble Savage

The "Noble Savage" is frozen in the past, having lived in Utopia, perfectly in tune with Nature, like Adam before the Fall. According to Bernard Sheehan, the "noble" stereotype originated with Jefferson's vision of a "perfect order on earth where the noble savage was equated with the environment: impulsive, unrestrained, unburdened by social conventions, simplicity, and content in a world that demanded nothing of him" (Sheehan 1973, 89–90). The Indians' "sense of superiority," the persistent Indian belief that their "way of life [was] more attractive than the European," and the many captured whites who "refused to return to civilization," all perpetuated the idea of the Noble Savage as mythical creature (Sheehan 1973, 113). In a denial of reality, the Noble Savage lived in his pastoral garden, and his life began to be viewed in connection with the Farmer—also "in perfect synchronization with nature" (Sheehan 1973, 101). Consequently, the view of the farmer as "the very best of men," with the possibility of the Indian and farmer joining in a perfect mix, developed. The "Noble Savage" image frequently blames the bad white man for all the Indians' problems, as though the Indians are incapable of responsibly surviving themselves.

Heathen

The *Random House Dictionary of the English Language* traces "heath" to the Old English, and defines it as a "tract of open and uncultivated land; wasteland overgrown with shrubs" (*Random House* 1967, 655). The term has also been used in connection with "the area where one was born" (655). It is easy to see how the "Noble Savage" would have been regarded as a "heathen." But when interest in "civilizing" the Indian grew, demanding a change in cultural practices, the definition in America of *heathen* changed to "anti-Christian."

Savage

According to Francis Jennings, "savage" began as a French word, *sauvage,* and was associated with "wild" and "woods" (Jennings 1976, 74). From the early 1600s, European invaders regularly used the term "savage" rather than "peasant" to create—in England—favorable opinions to aggressive policies in America. However, when the colonists needed Indian peoples for trading purposes, they called them "Indians" or "native peoples," and they saved the term "savage" for occasions "when the necessity for defense [was] mentioned" (77). "To call a man a savage is to warrant his death and to leave him unknown and unmourned" (12). Indians have been depicted as loving war, when there is little evidence of much intertribal warfare before contact. According to Sheehan, "Both whites and Indians took scalps, and colonial authorities encouraged the practice by paying bounties for these trophies" (Sheehan 1973, 166). John Smith turned from calling Indians "poore innocent soules," to "perfidious and inhumane people," and to "cruell beasts with a more unnaturall brutishness then beasts" after the "Jamestown Massacre" in 1622, when 347 settlers died. (However, John Smith, ignoring his own brand of negligent brutality, was hard pressed to explain the deaths of 6,000 Jamestown settlers due to "poor management" and starvation; see Jennings [1976, 72 to 79]). "Savagery" represented the opposite of "civilization," and so later use of the word provided justification for European American efforts to educate Indian children.

Wild

The term "wild" was used to connect Indians with predatory animals, providing more justification for Europeans to control and exterminate. Shakespeare used this word to "express attributes of wildness, rudeness, bestiality and cruelty; and the words were sometimes applied to persons" (Jennings 1976, 76). Mary Gloyne Byler, in her essay "Taking Another Look," suggests that "repeated juxtaposition of person and animal serves to instill and reinforce the image of American Indians as being not only subhuman but also inhuman beings" (Byler 1992, 89).

Princess or Squaw

White male ethnographers originally defined and described Indian women according to their European cultural beliefs about the inferior roles of women. The ethnographers were no doubt influenced by early Biblical scholars and philosophers who argued that women were secondary to men since Eve had been created from Adam's rib. Some even suggested that people of color were not descendants of Adam and Eve. "Typically, the Indian woman was either glorified as a *princess,* as in the tale of Pocahontas, or denigrated as a *squaw.* Indian females were most often described as passive, submissive, and inferior. Their work was trivialized as menial and monotonous, and they were considered beasts of burden or the property of savage males"(Bowker 1993, 33–34). The word "squaw," originates from the Algonquin language feminine ending "squa" and refers to the female genitals. Native Americans very strongly disapprove of the use of this word. In detail, Bowker explains the complexity of images of Native American women, arguing that in traditional Native societies and their cosmologies, the woman was "a primary force." She closes her discussion with a quote from Ella Deloria, an early twentieth-century Sioux anthropologist:

> Outsiders seeing women keep to themselves have frequently expressed a snap judgement that [Indian women] were regarded as inferior to the noble male. The simple fact is that woman had her own place and man his; they were not the same and neither inferior nor superior. The sharing of work also was according to sex. Both had to work hard, for their life made severe demands. (Bowker 1993, 36)

Redskin

Having nothing to do with skin color, originally, the "redskin" stereotype may have two distinct sources. Europeans had applied the term to Algonquins in general and to the Delawares in particular, not because of their skin color but because they used "vermilion makeup, body paint, [made] from fat mixed with berry juice and minerals," which they would spend hours applying (*America's* 1978, 118). Indians and colonists would trade beaver skins and rabbit skins, and the term was also used by colonists who connected Indians with bloody red skins, Indian scalps that settlers would collect after conflicts with Indians.

Nomadic

Although some tribes, especially the Plains Indians, followed game across hundreds of miles, "various tribes and bands did claim sovereignty over specific areas of land, dwelling, hunting, and farming within well-established boundaries," contradicting the belief that the land lay unoccupied and free (Byler 1992, 87). The Narragansetts, an eastern woodland people, cleared twice as much land as they used each year and let half of it lie fallow; "when the ground became infertile through constant replanting, those Indians who did not fertilize their lands—some of the coastal peoples did—removed their villages to new sites." This movement was regarded as *cyclical*, not *nomadic*. "When the colonists pretended that the Indians were mere nomads, the reason was to invoke international law doctrines applicable to vacant lands; such lands were available for seizure" (Jennings 1976, 71). The "nomadic" stereotype is also connected to the "savage" stereotype because Jeffersonians believed that "such extensive acreage fostered the savage condition. The Indian was uncivilized, that is undisciplined, disordered in his manner of life, because he lived irresponsibly from the fat of the land." The Jeffersonian design for the Indians' future required that they be divested of their lands (Sheehan 1973, 169–70).

Uncivilized Savage, Existing in a Lower Level of Intellectual and Cultural Development

When Indians failed to live up to the "perfect state of Nobility," exhibiting violence in reaction to European encroachment, the "utopian idiom" grew to carry "progressivist implications and led directly to the transformation of both the land and the native culture. Indian and land became enmeshed in an elaborate ideology that established change as the basic function of nature and perfection as its end." In other words, the Indian could grow to the perfect state of "civilization" after the ultimate in human development—the European model (Sheehan 1973, 114–15). With civilization through missions, schools, and federal money, the Indian would fully assimilate and convert from the "Uncivilized Savage" to become indistinguishable from the white man (419).

Children

When the violent European American encroachment drew reactions from Indians, and when the "civilizing" programs (mentioned above) failed and Indians were dying, many reformers in government suggested programs which would treat the Indians as "children." Operating under the assumptions that they knew best, that Indians had brought about their own destruction, and that they could make the Indian act in his own best interests even though it may have been against his inclinations, these reformers used *paternalism* to manipulate the Indian. To accomplish this, reformers gave clothing, farm implements, and no money. A major promoter of the Jeffersonian "civilizing" program, Thomas L. McKenney wrote to the Senate in

1821 to explain the reasoning behind this policy: "Our Indians stand pretty much in the relation to the Government as do our *children* to us . . . equally dependent" (Sheehan 1973, 153).

Anti-education

Enforced through various Christian groups, federal government policy promoted the distant boarding school experience and the consequent kidnaping of Indian children. Once removed from their tribal environment, these groups expected that the children would forget their culture and would assimilate into the dominant European American culture. The "anti-education" stereotype today may be grounded in their ancestors' boarding school experiences. Since at least five generations of Native Americans could associate education with punishment and deprivation, Native people may still regard "education" as a negative rather than positive experience. Furthermore, Native children still experience the denegration of their cultures within contemporary public school classrooms.

Undisciplined Children

Jon Reyhner and Jeanne Eder, in "A History of Indian Education," cite a 1946 study by Pettitt which found that

> The lack of discipline [of Native children] noted by Europeans was more apparent than real. Indian communities used a number of methods to ensure the proper behavior of children, however [many Native people deemed physical punishment as inappropriate] because children needed to learn to endure pain and hardship with courage.

Since many Europeans regarded play as "sinful," having relied on physical punishment for misbehavior, they couldn't see the way Indian adults from various cultures were directing positively the behavior of their children through storytelling, shunning, and shaming (Reyhner and Eder 1992, 36).

White Man's Helper

From Indians who helped the Spanish fight against other Indians, to Squanto and Powhatan, to Pocahontas and John Smith, to the novel, *Sign of the Beaver,* and to the Indians in the film *Dances with Wolves,* Indian people are regarded as being especially good when they help white people survive and conquer. This is especially true when stories are written from the non-Indian point of view.

Vanishing Americans

Federal policy played a major role in the development of this stereotype. With the Dawes Act (1887), the stress on individual ownership of land, and the influx of non-Indian landowners on Indian reservations, policymakers believed that Indians would assimilate into the general white population, or else they would become extinct (Harger 1902, 222–25). In 1900, most non-Indians believed that the Native peoples were the "Vanishing Americans" because the population had declined from as many as 20 million across the North American continent to only 237,196 (Champagne 1994, 241). Today, many perceive the two million Indians living on reservations and in America's urban centers as a conquered people who cannot adapt to a sophisticated, technological society. Others, including federal agents, policymakers, and educators, view the whole race as "vanishing" because of the prevalence of poverty, alcoholism, and dependency on welfare, while they fail to recognize and admit these problems prevail across the entire American population. Most important, the romantic "vanishing" image serves as a deflector for honest confrontation with critical issues while it operates to cover and hide five hundred years of oppression and genocide. Furthermore, teachers and texts reinforce the "vanishing" image when they restrict their definition of Indians to terms from a precontact cultural experience.

Works Cited

America's Fascinating Indian Heritage. 1978. Pleasantville, NY: Reader's Digest.

Bowker, Ardy. 1993. *Sisters in the Blood: The Education of Women in Native America.* Bozeman: Montana State University, Center for Bilingual/Multicultural Education.

Byler, Mary Gloyne. 1992. "Taking Another Look." In *Through Indian Eyes: The Native Experience in Books for Children,* eds. Beverly Slapin and Doris Seale, 89. Philadelphia: New Society.

Champagne, Duane. 1994. *Chronology of Native North American History.* Detroit, MI: Gale Research.

Harger, C. M. 1902. "The Indian's Last Stand." *Outlook,* 70 (January): 222–25.

Jennings, Francis. 1976. *The Invasion of America—Indians, Colonialism, and the Cant of Conquest.* New York: Norton.

Random House Dictionary of the English Language, Unabridged Edition. 1967.

Reyhner, Jon, and Jeannie Eder. 1992. "A History of Indian Education." In *Teaching American Indian Students,* ed. Jon Reyhner. Norman: University of Oklahoma Press.

Sheehan, Bernard. 1973. *Seeds of Extinction—Jeffersonian Philanthropy and the American Indian.* New York: Norton.

Appendix D: Cultural and Spiritual Contexts

Philosophies from Montana Tribal Cultures

Especially when reading and hearing literatures that are centered in a particular tribal consciousness, it is important that students become familiar with the cultural and spiritual contexts. Since *Roots and Branches* began with the seven Montana tribal cultures, I asked these reservation communities to provide statements showing what is most important to their tribes. I received responses from various sources including school boards, tribal councils, tribal culture committees, and individuals who had written their own. None would presume to speak for all their people, but the philosophies as written below do represent what they, as individuals or committees, believe. Not all I received are printed in this text out of respect for their wishes that their philosophies not be included in a "book for sale." The statements included here are examples of cultural philosophies that exist in all native communities, but they are also necessary background material for the study of Montana-based literatures. I suggest teachers and students read these philosophies and study the particular tribal histories when using selections based in these cultures, always maintaining a respect for the sacred nature of cultural materials.

Assiniboine/Gros Ventre
(White Clay People), Fort Belknap

The emblem of the **Fort Belknap Reservation's seal,** as illustrated by the traditional shield, symbolizes the shield's protection of the two tribes, the Gros Ventre and Assiniboine.

The Circular shape of the shield symbolizes life itself, as perceived by the Indian belief of the constant cycle of life, each living thing dependent on each other for life. The killing of the buffalo enables the Indian to live and grow, and when his mortal remains return to the earth, it serves as food for the grasses of the prairie, which in turn feeds the buffalo, thus ensuring the constant cycle of life.

The Four Directions and the Four Seasons are symbolized in the use of the four colors: Red-Summer, Yellow-Fall, White-Winter, and Green-Spring.

Symbolizing the existence of two tribes, the Gros Ventre and Assiniboine on the reservation, who function as a whole, is the Buffalo Skull. The colors divide it, yet the skull remains as one. The Skull has a jagged line from horn to horn representing the Milk River, a major tributary of the Missouri.

Snake Butte is illustrated above the Skull. This butte is a well known landmark for Indian tribes throughout the north. The Spring, located on the north central part of the butte, is one of the few natural fresh water springs in the area.

Snake Butte is also the place to seek out visions. Many tried, but very few succeeded in acquiring sacred power at this place.

The two Arrowheads facing each other emphasize the strong traditional ties with the past.

Seven Feathers hang from the Shield. There is a feather for every two of the twelve council members representing the reservation's three districts and the center feather representing the tribal chairman.

—excerpted from the philosophy expressed in
"Seal of the Fort Belknap Reservation,"
Fort Belknap Indian Community,
Gros Ventre and Assiniboine Tribes, 1980

We recognize that the acquisition of knowledge and wisdom is a lifelong process, and we are committed to development and implementation of educational programs that will meet every individual tribal member's needs from child to elder.

—excerpted from the "Educational Philosophy
of the Assiniboine and Gros Ventre Tribes,"
Fort Belknap Reservation-Wide
Education Committee, March 1980

Fort Peck Dakota (Sioux)

The **Fort Peck Dakota Oyate** (Sioux Indian People) are spiritual beings from our mother's womb. From the time our mother acknowledges the fact of conception and on to the completion of the second year of life, this period is where her spiritual influence is critical and most important. *Ina* (mother) would choose thoughts of harmony and well-being in the quietness and confidence of her meditation, such as to instill the greater idea of life and the love of *Wakan Tanka* (the Great Mystery) into the receptive nature (soul) of the unborn child and a sense that all things are related. During her times of silence and isolation, her moments flow together with the natural orders of peace and harmony for all things good. Her words and actions reflect her conscious union with all creation. This is the *Dakota* lifeway of the expectant mother, she is as one with the universe.

When the special time in her life has come, the moment when she will be center to the miracle of life itself, she will offer prayer and give thanks. Even before Grandmothers, the Dakota women have been trained and prepared in mind, body, and spirit for this wonderment, the *Dakota* mother's holiest duty, her role in the great song of creation.

In the life of all the Dakota, there is one inevitable duty, the duty of prayer, the daily recognition of the unseen and eternal. The *Dakota* spirituality began when god began. There is no need for setting apart one day of seven as a sacred day, the *Dakota Oyate* respect each day as a life itself. The Red Road (Spiritual Journey) of the *Dakota* is a pathway that begins with each new day. The *Dakota Oyate* dress each day with the finest truth, faith, justice, of bravery/courage, fortitude, generosity and a quest for wisdom. And in memory of that daylife which has passed them by, presents of industry, parenting, honesty, and fidelity will be left for the *Dakota*.

Today, willingness and generosity are the foundation of the *Dakota*. No one person can say this is not so. The *Dakota Oyate* travel great distances to find places to share their special talents and time, as an effort to work together for the good of all life-forms.

—HECHETU, SUNG'GLESKA HEMIYE,
Poplar Creek, Fort Peck Indian Reservation

Blackfeet (The Pikuni Way)

We **Pikuni,** above all, value honor and respect for the Creator, for self, our relatives, for all that exists because we are all related. When we give honor and respect to ourselves and to all that exists, then good things happen for us. This is the sacred way to live. We believe all people are spiritual beings because the Creator made us. We are of the Creator's Spirit, and it is because of these things that we exist. We keep our spiritual status by practicing these beliefs. Children must be allowed to become involved in the ceremonial life of our people as soon as they express an interest.

We *Pikuni* affirm and demonstrate the importance of honor and respect by keeping our ceremonies, some of which are the Sweat Lodge, Give Away, Okan, Black Tail Dance, Beaver Bundle, and Thunder Pipe.

The name giving ceremony is our expression of the value and love we have for the individual child or person being honored. We give a distinct name to each person. In this way we honor each person's individual sacredness. Each person must be recognized for their differences.

We must tell the stories of our origin. The stories of *Napi* are but some of them. Many think *Napi* is just a fool and a trickster. Some *Napi* stories are meant to entertain, to make people laugh and enjoy life. But we must also remember that *Napi,* the Old Man, the Grandfather, is also a spiritual being. He is *Napi Natosi,* Sacred Elder, who was sent to earth by the Creator to help make the world.

We *Pikuni* remember that each day is good, and it is a gift from the Creator. The early summer morning time is an example. It is the time of day when the birds and the animals sing and talk to the Creator. Stormy days give us snow and rain which allow us to live.

We are given many symbols to keep us thinking of our spiritual beginning. The color red (and the reason we paint our faces with red paint) is to remind us that the blood of our ancestors is in the earth and to show the Creator we are mindful that He made us from the Mother Earth. This is the miracle of our beginning.

The responsibility of *Pikuni* adults today is to educate the children in our old ways. We must assume control of their learning. The responsibility of a Pikuni child is to listen and learn and thereby become a loving, spiritual being that is related to and respects all things. This is the only way we can live in peace and harmony. This is how we learn what it means to be a human being.

This is the *Pikuni* Way given to us by *Napi Natosi.*

—Long Standing Bear, Chief

Crow (Absorka)

The four elements the **Crows** observe are:

1. Through myth, legend, and history, the Crows believe that by displaying their loyalty, fidelity, to their clan uncles and aunts, their life will be in better harmony with their fellow tribesmen, as well as with the unpredictable elements of their immediate environment in all ways—mentally, physically or spiritually.

The two war bonnets at either side represent the thirteen original clans of the Crows, as does the rising sun, which also represents a bright future and a bright day. The Greasy Mouth Clan has the sun as its symbol. The twelve bright-orange rays represent the other twelve clans. The eleven paler-yellow rays represent the currently existing clans.

The war bonnets also represent chiefs. Among its members each clan has an outstanding chief who has distinguished himself by accomplishing all the great deeds set by Crow standards and rules to attain leadership or chieftainship.

2. The peace pipe represents just that—peace. The Crows offer peace prior to going on a journey, whether it's for a skirmish or encounter with an enemy or any other journey. They do this so they may be immune from the hazards of life and evade any misfortunate occurrence or incident. Only a chief has the right to carry the pipe.

3. The Medicine Bundle represents all the fraternities within the Tobacco Society. From myth and legend came the Tobacco Society story—that the sacred plant was a gift from the Heavens and with the practice of its rituals, members of the Society will attain spiritual harmony.

4. The sweat lodge was another gift from the Heavens which came to the people through visions of Chosen Crows. Its ceremony was to be practiced for purification. The Chosen Crows were much like prophets in teaching a way of life for their fellow tribesmen.

All of these four elements and the practices accompanying them are combined and carried out in rituals and ceremonies.

The tipi represents the home of the Crows. Each Crow believes that the home is his second parents, where he has a place to return from any journey. Crow tipis are always erected having the door facing toward the east. A Crow believes that he is entering into a new day with a bright future and leaving problems of the past with the passing darkness and coming into a bright new world again. In other words he is reborn each day.

. . . In summary, the mountains, the rivers, the wildlife, the elements of the universe, the change in cycle of seasons, the plant life—all of these were necessary for the Crows' survival in nomadic days.

The Crows believe that a supreme force somewhere designed all the elements; and the Crows observe all these blessings through their customs, traditions, their practices through nature, with the highest degree of respect. They observe these through the gifts handed down from visions of the chosen Crow Prophets.

—excerpted from the "Crow Tribal Emblem and Flag"
by Lloyd Old Coyote McGinnis, Dale K.,
and Floyd W. Sharrock. 1972. *The Crow People.*
Phoenix: Indian Tribal Series, 102–4.

Kootenai

Preserve, Protect,
Perpetuate and Enhance the
Language and Culture of the
Kootenai People

—*Kootenai* Culture Program Motto

Salish

The **Flathead Culture Committee** seeks to preserve, protect, and perpetuate the living culture and traditional way of life of our people.

We Salish cherish the gifts passed down to us from our elders, and we treasure the hope and promise embodied in our young people. The elders give us our guidance, and our hearts are grateful for their wisdom, their dreams and visions, their knowledge, their songs and words. Our elders, and our ancestors before them, received these gifts from the Creator, from Mother Earth, from the Grandfather; and it was and is their prayer that these things be carried on by the generations to come. They have always told us to never give up, to keep living our culture, to keep practicing our old ways. Their prayers are being answered in our lives, in our working to carry on our ancient ways, in passing these things on to our young people: our native language, our traditional values of respect for all of life, our knowledge of how to live upon the land, our nurturing and healing of one another as members of a tribe.

By passing on these things, we show our respect for the elders and our love for our young people; we ensure their future as Salish people. We work to mend the circle of our people, the passing of knowledge from generation to generation. It is for them, our next generation and all the generations yet to come, that we work. It is for them, and to them, that the elders wish to give the good things that we Salish have held for hundreds of generations.

—Flathead Culture Committee

Northern Cheyenne

SWEET MEDICINE, ancient prophet of the **Cheyenne** people, predicted the coming of the white man, and he predicted that many changes would then occur in the Cheyenne way of life. He foresaw the horse which would give surprising mobility to the people and that the buffalo would then disappear to be replaced by the white man's cattle. He prophesied that these events would cause the Cheyenne people to lose their old ways and to act in different and strange ways.

According to SWEET MEDICINE, when this happened, Cheyenne youth would be trying to live adult lives before they were properly prepared. All of these predictions have come to pass and today youth do face responsibilities for which they are unprepared. The Cheyenne people were told long ago by SWEET MEDICINE that these changes in the Cheyenne way would come. The time has come for us to prepare the Cheyenne youth for these changes.

In the time of the buffalo, the Cheyenne were a strong and self-sufficient people. Daily needs and constant dangers were met with pride under the leadership of wise men. The instruction by parents and relatives prepared the youth to meet the responsibilities so that when the land and the buffalo were forcibly taken from them, the Cheyenne people refused imprisonment and walked and fought from Oklahoma back to the Valley of the Rosebud in Montana. Here the Cheyenne people have lived in peace and poverty for one hundred years; however, our youth and many adults found themselves unprepared for the cultural genocide and harsh treatment in the school which was controlled by a distant government. In the past, when the school was a boarding school, it was used to separate children from their families and our culture. The school was used to repress our religion, language, and it was later used to indoctrinate our children with the values of the white man.

Always there have been some sincere educators who attempted to educate our children, not to indoctrinate them. Gradually, the quality of the school has been improved. But, we who must live with this education found it inadequate and inferior to the education of neighboring white people.

We Northern Cheyenne people know before our Creator that we are responsible for the education of our youth. Cheyenne parents, grandparents, aunts, and uncles met this educational responsibility by controlling the education for our children. As human beings, we realize and recognize our responsibility to our children, and we recognize further that time is required for dynamic community involvement in the school to be developed. Skepticism and fear of rejection based on past experiences will take considerable time to overcome.

As American citizens we understand the moral obligation (treaty with the Northern Cheyenne and Northern Arapaho, 1868) to provide us with the necessary resources to educate our children. We have, therefore, decided by vote of the People of the Northern Cheyenne Reservation to assume control with commitment born of respect for our ancestors who lived, learned and fought on this land and with a concern for their descendants who learn to live on this land and in this country.

We Northern Cheyenne believe that a good education will help provide our children with confidence, self-respect and the freedom of choice to help make them responsible adults. We believe that good education will help strengthen the self-discipline required for acceptable behavior. We believe our children should have the opportunity for a lifetime of learning and success in whatever profession they choose. We Northern Cheyenne intend to operate the Northern Cheyenne Schools by these beliefs so that when we look upon the education of our children, we will be able to say "It is good."

Goals Adopted by the Northern Cheyenne Schools, 1994

Long ago, the four chiefs and forty-four subchiefs regularly decided in council the movements and tasks for the tribe. Each morning, the subchiefs would then cry out reminders of the tasks to the awakening camp. As the designated spokesmen for education in our community, we set forth the following goals, which reflect the expectations of this Reservation.

Students should be provided a friendly and healthy educational atmosphere conducive to learning; should be encouraged to develop individual pride, confidence, self-respect, and initiative; and should be encouraged to develop responsible behavior.

—excerpted from "Philosophy of Northern Cheyenne Schools,"
Northern Cheyenne School Board Policy Handbook
(Board approved 5/11/96)

Appendix E: North Central Regional Publications

Although this list doesn't represent all publications from the seven tribes in Montana and surrounding tribal communities, it can serve nonetheless as an example of the kinds of materials that have been written and compiled in tribal communities nationwide. Teachers who wish to use literatures that more accurately represent the historical, cultural, and personal experiences of Native people may contact their local tribal college librarians, tribal education directors, and culture committee chairpersons. The complete annotated bibliography of the following resources will be available by October of 1998 through the Montana Office of Public Instruction, Helena, Montana. Wherever the title of a resource provides a clear indication of the content, the annotation is not included.

Allen, Minerva (Assiniboine). *Basal Bilingual Readers.* Illus. Hank Chopwood, Frank Cuts the Rope, and Mike Brokie. Hays, MT: Hays/LodgePole Schools, 1988. 13–15 pp. each.
Grade Level: P, I

A series of books for teaching the Assiniboine and Gros Ventre languages to first- and second-grade level students. Secondary students can also appreciate the themes, conflicts, and traditions that these stories portray.

————, ed. *Campfire Stories of the Fort Belknap Community.* Hays, MT: Hays/LodgePole Title IV Program, 1983.
Grade Level: P, I

A collection in which the voices of Fort Belknap elders can be heard as they tell the stories for their community.

——. *Spirits Rest.* Illus. Aaron Freeland. Hays, MT: Hays/LodgePole Title IV Program. 24 pp.
Grade Level: I, S

Minerva Allen's poetry, illustrated by secondary graphic art students.

——, ed. *Stories By Our Elders: The Fort Belknap People.* Illus. Frank Cuts the Rope and John D. Doney. Hays, MT: Hays/LodgePole Title IV Program, 1983. 160 pp.
Grade Level: I, S

Thirty-five illustrated stories told by Jenny Gray, Hank Chopwood, Lucille Chopwood, Wallace Chopwood, Vernie Bell, Estelle Blackbird, George Shields, Dora Helgeson, Theresa Lamebull, and Andrew Lamebull, and illustrated by Frank Cuts The Rope and John D. Doney.

Ashabranner, Brent. *Morning Star, Black-Sun.* New York: Dodd, Mead, 1982.
Grade Level: S

An examination of the issue of strip mining for coal and its impact on the reservation communities, specifically the Northern Cheyenne.

Assiniboine Memories: Legends of the Nakota People. Fort Belknap, MT: Fort Belknap Community Council, 1983. 138 pp.
Grade Level: I, S

Traditional and historical stories told by Assiniboine elders.

Bass, Althea. *Night Walker and the Buffalo.* Billings: Montana Council for Indian Education, 1972. 32 pp.
Grade Level: I

A contemporary Southern Cheyenne story.

Beaverhead, Pete (Salish). *Eagle Feathers: The Highest Honor.* St. Ignatius, MT: Flathead Culture Committee, 1978.
Grade Level: I

A story about the role of eagle feathers in the Salish culture.

——. *Legends of Scewene.* St. Ignatius, MT: Flathead Culture Committee, 1978.
Grade Level: P, I

Stories about the legendary Bigfoot.

———. *Wild Horse Roundup.* St. Ignatius, MT: Flathead Culture Committee, 1978.
Grade Level: I

Beaverhead's memories of some of the wild horse roundups on the Flathead reservation during the early years of the twentieth century before it was open to white homesteading.

Bennett, Ben. *Death, Too, for The-Heavy-Runner.* Missoula, MT: Mountain Press, 1980. 170 pp.
Grade Level: S

A historical narrative of the Blackfeet, culminating in the tragic story of the Baker Massacre in the winter of 1870.

Bilingual Readers (Cree). Box Elder, MT: Rocky Boy Transitional Bilingual Program, 1988.
Grade Level: P, I

Traditional stories that are used to teach the Cree language.

Boas, Franz. *Kutenai Tales.* Bureau of American Ethnology Bulletin 59. Washington, DC: Government Printing Office, 1918.
Grade Level: S

Traditional and historical stories in both English and the Kutenai language.

Bryan, William L. *Montana's Indians: Yesterday and Today.* Helena: Montana Magazine, 1985.
Grade Level: I, S

The geographic, economic, historical, and cultural situation of each of the seven Montana Indian Reservations: Crow, Cheyenne, Flathead, RockyBoy (Chippewa/Cree), Fort Belknap (Assiniboine/Gros Ventre), Blackfeet, Fort Peck (Assiniboine/Sioux).

Bull Shows, Harry(Crow). *Legends of Chief Bald Eagle.* As told to Hap Gilliland. Billings: Montana Council for Indian Education, 1977. 40 pp.
Grade Level: I, S

Exciting stories that are fun to read, as they demonstrate the importance of personal commitment to the welfare of the group.

Carriker, Robert C. *The Kalispel People.* Indian Tribal Series. Phoenix: University of Arizona Press, 1973.
Grade Level: I, S

An interesting history of the Kalispel people of Washington State.

Chamberlain, A. F. "The Coyote and the Owl: Tales of the Kootenay Indians." In *Memoirs of the International Congress of Anthropology,* ed. C. Staniland Wake, 282–286. Chicago: Schultz, 1894.
Grade Level: I, S

Several variations of a basic tale involving the Owl and the Coyote.

Char-Koosta. Dixon and Pablo, MT, 1956 (November)– .

The newspaper of the Salish, Pend d'Oreilles and Kootenai Tribes of the Flathead Reservation.

Charging Eagle, Tom (Dakota) and Ron Zeilinger. *Black Hills: Sacred Hills.* Chamberlain, SD: Tipi Press, 1987.
Grade Level: S

A description of the Black Hills and their value as a spiritual and physical home to the Dakota Indians.

Cheyenne Short Stories. Billings: Montana Council for Indian Education, 1977. 32 pp.
Grade Level: I, S

Some of the stories teach the importance of staying one step ahead of the enemy and surviving through wisdom rather than force. The introduction includes an explanation of the Cheyenne story-telling tradition.

Cheyenne Stories. Collected by Jennie Seminole Parker (Northern Cheyenne). Lame Deer, MT: Dull Knife College, 1993. 7 pp. (unpublished).
Grade Level: P, I

An excellent resource that includes six traditional stories with an explanation of oral traditions and their values for the teaching of children.

Chief Charlot (Salish/Flathead). "Chief Charlot's Speech of 1876." *Montana Journalism Review* 15 (1972): 20–21.
Grade Level: S

A speech against a government decision that the Bitterroot Flathead Indians were subject to state and local taxation, originally published in the *Weekly Missoulian,* April 26, 1876.

Chief Joseph (Nez Perce). *Chief Joseph's Own Story.* Billings, MT: Council for Indian Education, 1972. 31 pp.
Grade Level: I, S

The story in Chief Joseph's own words, as he traveled to Washington, DC, in 1879.

Clark, Ella. *Guardian Spirit Quest.* Illus. Alex Bull Tail. Billings: Montana Reading Publications, 1974. 35 pp.
Grade Level: P, I, S

Stories reprinted from other published sources about the guardian spirit quests of seven individuals.

Clark, Ella. *In the Beginning: Indian Legends of Creation.* Billings: Montana Council for Indian Education, 1977.
Grade Level: I, S

Creation stories that teach the consequences of irresponsible behavior and explain the differences in the races, while they demonstrate the intimate relationship between human beings and the earth and the animals.

Comes at Night, George (Blackfeet/Flathead). *Roaming Days: Warrior Stories.* Browning, MT: Blackfeet Heritage Program, 1978. 67 pp.
Grade Level: I, S

The history and culture of the Blackfeet people portrayed in ten short warrior stories that demonstrate the powerful influence of visionary and magical experiences the Blackfeet people have accepted as real.

Crow Bilingual Books and Readers. Crow Agency, MT: Bilingual Materials Development Center, 1985.
Grade Level: P, I

This Crow bilingual program includes curriculum guides, supplementary workbooks, and video materials.

1993 Crow Fair: 75th Diamond Jubilee. An illustrated "Special Supplement" from the Billings Area Newspaper Group Newspapers. 1993 (Aug. 18).

A photographic record of the annual powwow, parade, and celebration of Crow culture and community.

Crummett, Michael. *Sundance: The 50th Anniversary Crow Indian Sun Dance.* Helena, MT: Falcon Press, 1993. 92 pages.
Grade Level: I, S

An illustrated record of the 50th anniversary of the ceremony, which federal law had previously prohibited for over half a century.

Curtis, Edward. *The North American Indian. Vol. 4: The Absaroke or Crows.* New York: Johnson Reprint, 1970. 244 pp.
Grade Level: S

Originally published in 1909, this book provides a cultural review of the Crow and Hidatsa peoples.

Dempsey, Hugh A. *Big Bear: The End of Freedom.* Lincoln: University of Nebraska Press, 1984. 198 pp.
Grade Level: S

The story of the Cree's struggle for reservation land in Montana after the Riel Rebellion. Other books by Dempsey include *Crowfoot, Chief of the Blackfeet; Indian Tribes of Alberta;* and *Red Crow, Warrior Chief.*

Denny, Walter A. (Chippewa/Cree). *Bird Stories.* Box Elder, MT: Rocky Boy Transitional Bilingual Program, 1977. 36 pp.
Grade Level: P, I

Stories with names written in the Cree language using both Cree and English syllabaries, and with each story closing with a lesson.

———. *The Butterfly.* Box Elder, MT: Rocky Boy Transitional Bilingual Program, 1987.
Grade Level: P, I

This primary book teaches children to accept themselves as they are.

———. *The Eagle.* Box Elder, MT: Rocky Boy Transitional Bilingual Program, 1987.
Grade Level: P, I

The custom and significance of the eagle for the Chippewa/Cree people.

———. *How the Turtle Got Its Shell.* Box Elder, MT: Rocky Boy Transitional Bilingual Program, 1987.
Grade Level: P, I

A traditional storytelling about a wanderer who is often cold and wet, until he meets an old man who gives him "the home on his back."

———. *Stories from the Old Ones.* Ed. Harold E. Gray and Patricia Scott. Illus. William Daychild. Browning, MT: Bear Chief Educational Consultants, 1979. 79 pp.
Grade Level: I, S

A collection of twenty-three as-told-to stories, published for the first time.

Dion, Joseph P. (Cree). *My Tribe the Crees.* Calgary, Alberta: Glenbow Museum.
Grade Level: I, S

Durgeloh, Bill, et al. (Salish/Kootenai). *"Skool Loo*—Legends from Here and There." *Dovetail Magazine,* l.2 (Spring 1973): 30–40.
Grade Level: I, S

Three legends from the reservation.

Farr, William E. *The Reservation Blackfeet, 1882–1945: A Photographic History of Cultural Survival.* Seattle: University of Washington Press, 1984. 210 pp.
Grade Level: S

A photographic study of the Blackfeet from many private collectors.

Feather Earring, TurnsBack, Old Coyote, and Lela M. Puffer(Crow). *Prairie Legends.* Billings: Montana Council for Indian Education, 1978. 32 pp.
Grade Level: P, I, S

Stories reflecting the values of close observation, fortitude, commitment to a purpose, and interdependence between humans and animals.

Fitzgerald, Michael O. *Yellowtail: The Medicine Man and Sun Dance Chief Speaks of the Sacred Ways of the Crow.* Norman: University of Oklahoma Press, 1991. 234 pp.
Grade Level: S

Insights into the religious center of the Crow Indians through the eyes of Thomas Yellowtail.

Flannery, Regina. *The Gros Ventre of Montana.* Washington, DC: Catholic University Press, 1953.
Grade Level: S

Dr. Flannery obtained her stories from some of the oldest women in the tribe.

Flathead Culture Committee. *A Brief History of the Flathead Tribes.* St. Ignatius, MT: Flathead Culture Committee, 1978.
Grade Level: I, S

An introduction to the history and culture of the Flathead tribes.

Gathering. Poplar, MT: Fort Peck Community College, 1992. 43 pp.
Grade Level: S

An illustrated literary magazine, published by students at Fort Peck Community College.

Gildart, Bert. "Mary Ground: A Memory of Two Centuries." *Great Falls Tribune* (4 Mar. 1990), Great Falls, Montana.
Grade Level: I, S

Biography of Mary Ground, who died on February 8, 1990, having lived through 107 years of starvation, disease, and war.

Gilham, Dan, Sr. *Handbook of Blackfeet Tribal Law.* Browning, MT: Blackfeet Heritage Program, 1979. 73 pp.
Grade Level: S

A history of Indian law and order.

———. *Growing Up Indian.* As told to Jo Rainbolt. Billings: Montana Indian Publications, 1975. 35 pp.
Grade Level: I, S

Stories from the life of Louie Gingras, an 82-year-old Kootenai Indian.

Gingras, Louie (Kootenai). *Coyote and Kootenai.* As told to Jo Rainbolt. Billings: Montana Council for Indian Education, 1977. 35 pp.
Grade Level: P, I, S

Humorous stories about the oldtimers (animals), which teach the value of following directions, being yourself, and showing respect for wildlife, as well as communicating the importance of being satisfied with who we are, what we have, and what we can do.

Glacier Reporter (Blackfeet). Browning, MT 59417.

Official publication for the Town of Browning and the Blackfeet Reservation.

Gladstone, Jack (Blackfeet). *Noble Heart; Buckskin Poet Society; Wolves on Sea and Plain; In the Shadow of Mt. Lassen; The Buffalo Cafe.* Audio Cassettes and CDs. Kalispell, MT: Hawkstone Productions, P.O. Box 7626.
Grade Level: I, S

Original songs, based on historical events and persons and on traditional Native stories.

Gone, Fred P. (Lakota/Gros Ventre). *The Seven Visions of Bull Lodge as Told by His Daughter, Garter Snake.* Ed. George Horse Capture. Lincoln: University of Nebraska Press, 1980. 125 pp.
Grade Level: S

Healer and keeper of the Feathered Pipe, Bull Lodge was born in 1802 and died in 1886.

Good Strike, The Boy, and Joe Assiniboin (Assiniboine). *How Horses Came to the Ha'A'Ninin.* Billings, MT: Montana Council for Indian Education, 1980. 35 pp.
Grade Level: P,I, S

Three stories portraying the importance of respecting the words and advice of elders, generosity, and kindness.

Ground, Mary (Blackfeet). *Grass Woman Stories.* Ed. Janet Bailey. Browning, MT: Blackfeet Heritage Program, 1978. 59 pp.
Grade Level: I, S

Stories of the Pikuni people, including some about marriage customs and childbirth rituals, reflecting the culture from a woman's point of view, as well as some true-life stories of men, women, and children who suffer harsh and sometimes violent consequences when they neglect, betray, or show disrespect for their relatives and friends.

Harrison, Michael. "Chief Charlot's Battle with Bureaucracy." *Montana: The Magazine of Western History,* 10.4 (Autumn 1960): 27–33.
Grade Level: S

The background and story of the struggle of Charlo (Salish) to remain in the Bitterroot Valley, and General Garfield's 1872 visit to the Bitterroot Valley to negotiate with him.

Hatheway, Flora (Crow). *Chief Plenty Coups.* Billings: Montana Reading Publications, 1981. 35 pp.
Grade Level: P, I, S

The significant relationships and experiences in the life of Chief Plenty Coups (Crow) (1838–1932), from the time he was ten years old until his death.

———. *Old Man Coyote: Crow Legends of Creation.* Indian Culture Series. Billings: Montana Reading Publications, 1970. 36 pp.
Grade Level: P, I, S

Old Man Coyote is "The Wise One sometimes also called Old Coyote, as the Father of all."

———. *The Little People: Crow Legends of Creation.* Billings: Montana Council for Indian Education, 1971. 36 pp.
Grade Level: P, I, S

A collection of stories that communicate humor, gratitude for those who help and protect the people, and the importance of ceremony for the remembrance of gifts.

Hildreth, Dolly, Viola Lindblad, and Richard Albent. *The Money God: Stories of the Modern Indian.* (Taos/Navajo). Billings, MT: Council for Indian Education. 32 pp.
Grade Level: I, S

Stories demonstrating the values of the "old ways" and their continuing relevance for Indian life today while also providing a means for living "between two cultures."

History of the Flathead Reservation, 1841–1934: Study Guide. Prepared by Ron Terriault (Salish). Pablo, MT: Salish/Kootenai College.
Grade Level: I, S

A study guide for a course taught at the Salish/Kootenai College.

Holmes, Oliver M., ed. "Peregrinations of a Politician: James A. Garfield's Diary of a Trip to Montana in 1872." *Montana: The Magazine of Western History,* 6.4 (Autumn 1956): 34–45.
Grade Level: S

Holmes's version of James Garfield's diary of his trip to negotiate with Charlo in 1872.

Horse Capture, George P. (Lakota/Gros Ventre). *Pow Wow.* Cody, WY: Buffalo Bill Historical Center, 1989. 64 pp.
Grade Level: P, I, S

With color and black-and-white photographs of dress and regional participants, this book can contribute to a better understanding of the Great Plains tradition.

Howard, Helen Addison. "Indians and an Indian Agent: Chief Charlo and the Forged Document." *Journal of the West,* 5.3 (July 1966): 379–397.
Grade Level: S

The story of the removal of Charlo (Salish/Kootenai) from the Bitterroot Valley, reprinted from Howard's *Northwest Trail Blazers.*

Howard, Helen Addison. "The Men Who Saved the Buffalo." *Journal of the West,* 14.3 (July 1975): 122–129.
Grade Level: S

The story of Indian Agent Peter Ronan and Sam Walking Coyote and the establishment of the Pablo-Allard buffalo herd.

Huberman, Robert G., assisted by Karen Pale Moon Huberman. *Our Only Homeland: An Ecological Look at the Land of the Gros Ventre and Assiniboine.* Hays, MT: Hays/LodgePole Public Schools, 1980.
Grade Level: S

Hungry Wolf, Adolf. *Charlo's People: The Flathead Tribe.* Invermere, BC: Good Medicine Books, 1971.
Grade Level: S

Sketches from Flathead history and personal sketches of some Flathead leaders.

———. *Good Medicine in Glacier National Park.* Golden, BC: Good Medicine Books, 1971.
Grade Level: I, S

Inspirational photos and stories from the days of the Blackfeet People.

———, comp. *Legends from the Old People.* Invermere, BC: Good Medicine Books, 1972. 62 pp.
Grade Level: I, S

Traditional Blackfeet stories.

Hungry Wolf, Adolf, and Beverly Hungry Wolf (Blackfeet), eds. *Children of the Sun.* New York: Quill, 1987. 203 pp.
Grade Level: I, S

An illustrated collection of traditional and contemporary stories by and about Indian children who grew up during the early 1900s.

Hungry Wolf, Adolf, and Star Hungry Wolf (Blackfeet). *Children of the Circle.* Summertown, TN: Book Publishing, 1992. 160 pp.
Grade Level: P, I

Black-and-white photographs of Native children from the Plateau, Plains, and Pueblo peoples.

Indian Sentinel (Salish). St. Ignatius, MT.

A Catholic Mission publication.

In the New World. Ashland, MT: St. Labre Indian School, 1988.
Grade Level: P, I

A collection of poetry written by students of the Pretty Eagle School and the Saint Charles Mission (Crow).

Kammen, Robert, Joe Marshall, and Frederick Lefthand. *Soldiers Falling into Camp: The Battles at the Rosebud and the Little Big Horn.* Encampment, WY: Affiliated Writers of America, 1992. 229 pp.
Grade Level: I, S

An easy-to-read narrative of these two battles, which incorporates the voices of participants (Lakota and Cheyenne).

Kidder, John. "Montana Miracle: It Saved the Buffalo." *Montana: The Magazine of Western History,* 15.2 (Spring 1965): 52–67.
Grade Level: S

The story of the Pablo-Allard buffalo herd on the Flathead Reservation.

Kicking Woman, George (Blackfeet), and Molly Kicking Woman (Blackfeet). *Sikawakassi'kokaan: Black Deer Lodge Design, Blackfeet Lodge Coloring Book.* Browning, MT: Browning Bilingual Program, 1990. 20 pp.
Grade Level: P, I

Explanations in both English and Blackfeet of the design and use of the Blackfeet Lodge, using the Blackfeet elders' Black Deer Lodge design as the basis of the story.

Kipp, Neil. *Pre-Columbian History of the Red Man (Before Anglo-Saxons).* Ed. Roxanne DeMarce. Browning, MT: Blackfeet Heritage Program, 1960. 48 pp.
Grade Level: S

The author's view of the precontact Blackfeet experience, with information on how the Blackfeet communicated with other tribes, the importance of children, their religion, and different societies.

Kipp, Woody (Blackfeet). "Living in the Absence of the Sacred." *Words on Wilderness.* Newsletter of the Wildlands Studies and Information Center, Missoula: University of Montana, 1993 (Spring): 1–2.
Grade Level: S

An essay that contrasts the Native and non-Native world views, exploring such questions as "What is Sacred?" and "What on this earth is deserving of mankind's respect?" particularly in regard to wilderness issues such as the Badger–Two Medicine area and exploration for oil.

Kootenai Culture Committee. *How Martin Got His Spots.* Beaverton, OR: Educational Systems, Inc., 1978.
Grade Level: P, I

Traditional Kootenai story.

Law, Kathryn. *Salish Folk Tales.* Billings: Montana Indian Publications, 1972. 40 pp.
Grade Level: I, S

Stories showing the consequences of selfish behavior, especially when that behavior jeopardizes the life of a relative.

————. *Tales from the Bitterroot Valley and Other Salish Folk Stories.* Billings: Montana Indian Publications, 1971.
Grade Level: P, I, S

A collection of coyote stories as told by Agnes Vanderburg, Jerome Lumpry, Ignace Pierre, and Adele Adams that show the folly in setting unrealistic goals.

Lewis, Elizabeth. *Blackfeet Language Coloring Book.* Browning, MT: Blackfeet Heritage Program, 1978. 67 pp.
Grade Level: P, I

Pictures and names of animals, plant life, foods, and numbers printed in both the English and Blackfeet languages, with a Southern Piegan/Blackfeet pronunciation and spelling guide included for the teacher.

Long Standing Bear Chief (Harold Gray) (Blackfoot). *Ni-Kso-Ko-Wa: Blackfoot Spirituality, Traditions, Values, and Beliefs.* Browning, MT: Spirit Talk Press, 1992. 68 pp.
Grade Level: I, S

According to the author in his Introduction, this book represents "the values he wants his children to know, understand, and respect."

Magorian, Jim. *Keeper of Fire.* Billings, MT: Council for Indian Education, 1984. 78 pp.
Grade Level: I, S

A portrayal of both Indians and whites in a realistic coming-of-age story.

Many Guns, Tom (Blackfeet). *Pinto Horse Rider.* Browning, MT: Blackfeet Heritage Program, 1979. 67 pp.
Grade Level: I, S

The story of Many Guns's life translated from his native language, revealing the rich cultural heritage of the Blackfeet.

Martinson, David (Ojibway). *Manabozho and the Bullrushes.* Duluth,
MN: School District 709, 1975. 34 pp.
Grade Level: I, S

A story of the Ojibway trickster/transformer figure.

———. *Shemay/The Bird in the Sugarbush.* Duluth, MN: School District
709, 1975. 29 pp.
Grade Level: P

A contemporary story about a grandmother who tells a story
and a girl with a special sensitivity for the sadness of a bird.

McAlear, J.F. *The Fabulous Flathead: The Story of the Development of
Montana's Indian Reservation.* Polson, MT: Treasure State Publi-
cation Company, 1962.
Grade Level: S

Anthropological information about the tribes who now live on
the Flathead Reservation.

McDonald, W. H. *Creation Tales from the Salish.* Billings, MT: Montana
Council for Indian Education, 1973. 32 pp.
Grade Level: P, I, S

A collection of eight Coyote stories, beginning with the creation of the earth.

Medicine Crow, Joe. "The Effects of European Culture Contacts Upon
the Economic, Social, and Religious Life of the Crow Indians."
Thesis, Department of Anthropology, University of Southern
California, 1939.
Grade Level: S

Medicine Crow, Joseph (Crow). *A Handbook of Crow Indian Laws and
Treaties.* Crow Agency, MT: Daniel S. Press, 1966.
Grade Level: S

Joe Medicine Crow is the tribal historian and anthropologist.

Merriam, Alan P. "Songs and Dances of the Flathead Indians." New
York: Ethnic Folkways Library, 1953.
Grade Level: I, S

Mogor, Robert A. (Salish/Kootenai). *Flathead, Kutenai, Pend d'Oreille Flannelboard Stories.* (Mimeo). St. Ignatius, MT: Native American Cultural Awareness Program, St. Ignatius Elementary School District, 1975–76.
Grade Level: S

Traditional and historical stories of the Confederated Tribes drawn primarily from *Char-Koosta,* the Salish/Kootenai tribal newspaper.

Montana Indians: Their History and Location. Helena: Montana Office of Public Instruction, 1992.
Grade Level: I, S

One of several Indian Education Resources that are available at no cost.

Nicholsen, John. *Chii-la-pe and the White Buffalo.* Billings: Montana Council for Indian Education, 1981. 41 pp.
Grade Level: P, I

A story that teaches that rewards come to those who demonstrate respect and compassion for others.

Old Coyote, Elnora A., and Jon Reyhner, eds. *Teepees Are Folded: American Indian Poetry.* Billings: Montana Council for Indian Education, 1991. 44 pp.
Grade Level: I, S

Contemporary poetry that connects with the old ways, while it also reflects on the issues which so many young Indians experience today.

Old Coyote, Henry (Crow), and Barney Old Coyote (Crow). *Crow Stories.* Crow Agency, MT: Crow Tribal Publication, 1985.
Grade Level: P, I

Three stories, a Crow alphabet and pronunciation guide, and an appendix showing the Crow tribal structure.

Old Coyote, Mickey (Crow), and Helene Smith. *Apsaalooka: The Crow Nation Then and Now, Children of a Large Beaked Bird.* Greensburg, PA: McDonald/Sward, 1992–1993. 251 pp.
Grade Level: I, S

A comprehensive history of the Crow nation, together with the political, economic, and social situation today.

Old Coyote, Sally, and Joy Yellowtail Toineeta. *Indian Tales of the Northern Plains.* Billings, MT: Montana Council for Indian Education, 1971. 31 pp.
Grade Level: P, I

Six stories from the Blackfeet, Crow, Arapaho, and others.

———. *Indian Tales of the Northern Rockies.* Billings: Montana Indian Publications, 1971. 31 pp.
Grade Level: P, I

Several short tales from the Gros Ventre, Flathead, Crow, Shoshone, Blackfeet, and Nez Perce.

Parsons, Jackie. *The Educational Movement of the Blackfeet Indians: 1840–1979.* Browning, MT: Blackfeet Heritage Program, 1980. 45 pp.
Grade Level: S

Descriptions of mission schools, reservation day schools, government boarding schools, public and private schools on the Blackfeet Reservation.

Recollections of Fort Belknap's Past. Fort Belknap Community Council. Fort Belknap, MT: Fort Belknap Education Department, 1982. 204 pp.
Grade Level: I, S

Twenty recollections of Gros Ventre and Assiniboine tribal elders about the years 1910 through 1945.

Reese, Montana Lisle, ed. *Legends of the Mighty Sioux.* Interior, SD: Badlands National History Association, 1987. 158 pp.
Grade Level: P, I

A collection gathered by Reese and Indian workers of the South Dakota Writers' Project, representing the traditional Sioux stories, as told in their own language.

Reyhner, Jon. *Heart Butte, A Blackfeet Indian Community.* Heart Butte and Billings, MT: Council for Indian Education, 1984. 24 pp.
Grade Level: P, I

A collection of photographs published by the Heart Butte Bilingual Program, depicting student life in Heart Butte.

————, ed. *Stories of our Blackfeet Grandmothers*. Heart Butte and Billings, MT: Council for Indian Education, 1984. 23 pp.
Grade Level: I, S

Stories told by Blackfeet elders to students at the Heart Butte School during the spring of 1983, about Indian life in early Montana during the time of Indian Agency control.

Rides at the Door (Blackfeet), and Darnell Davis, comp. *Napi Stories*. Browning, MT: Blackfeet Heritage Program, 1979. 38 pp.
Grade Level: I, S

Stories of Napi, the Blackfeet trickster/transformer, through whose actions a cycle of existence began.

Riggs, Stephen R. *A Dakota-English Dictionary*. St. Paul: Minnesota Historical Society Press, 1992. 665 pp.
Grade Level: I, S

Salish Culture Committee. *Coyote and the Man Who Sits on Top* and *Coyote and the Mean Mountain*. Beaverton, OR: Educational Systems, 1978.
Grade Level: P, I

Stories illustrated for younger readers.

————. *Salish Coyote Stories*. Beaverton, OR: Educational Systems, 1979.
Grade Level: P, I

A collection of stories for the fourth-grade reading level.

Spirit Talk, 1.1 (Summer 1994). Browning, MT: Spirit Talk Press. 44 pp.
Grade Level: I, S

The first edition of a quarterly magazine published by Long Standing Bear Chief Mii-sa-mii-pai-poi-ii Nii-nohk Kyi-yo (Blackfoot), which includes book reviews, glossy color photographs, stories, articles, and poetry.

Spirit Whispers Three: St. Ignatius Anthology of Student Writing. St. Ignatius, MT: St. Ignatius High School Writing Lab. 1993. 123 pp.
Grade Level: P, I, S

A yearly publication representing the art, poetry, prose, and reading, typing, designing, editing, and organizing of St. Ignatius students in grades 7–12 on the Flathead Reservation.

Sta-Al-TSA-Nix-SIN: Ghost. Browning, MT: Blackfeet Heritage Program, 1979. 47 pp.
   Grade Level: I, S

   Stories told in the winter, and in contemporary Blackfeet life, for entertainment and for social control, reinforcing Blackfeet religious beliefs, explaining events that were forewarned, and linking the known with the unknown.

Swaney, Thomas "Bearhead" (Salish/Kootenai). "'Bearhead' Swaney Takes Strong Stand." *Montana Indian Health Board Newsletter* 1.1 (Oct. 1978): 4–6. Billings, MT.
   Grade Level: S

   A keynote address regarding the need for Indian unity for the September 1978 meeting of the Montana Indian Health Board at Billings, Montana.

Tall Bull, Henry (Cheyenne), and Tom Weist. *Cheyenne Fire Fighters.* Billings: Montana Reading Publications, 1971. 39 pp.
   Grade Level: I

   A contemporary story about Cheyenne fire fighters who battle a fire in the Bob Marshall Wilderness west of Great Falls, Montana.

———. *Cheyenne Legends of Creation.* Billings: Montana Council for Indian Education, 1972. 32 pp.
   Grade Level: P, I

   Stories beginning with Maheo, the Creator, turning mud into dust to make the "earth we walk on," and teaching about the interdependent relationship between human beings and animals, and between human beings and their environment.

———. *Cheyenne Warriors.* Billings: Montana Council for Indian Education, 1983. 32 pp.
   Grade Level: P, I

   Biographical stories of six nineteenth-century Cheyenne warriors, both men and women, and their battles as told by those who participated in these events.

———. *Grandfather and the Popping Machine.* Billings: Montana Council for Indian Education, 1970. 32 pp.
   Grade Level: P, I

   A story about old man Raven, who buys the first Ford owned by a Cheyenne and assumes that he will understand the machine since he knows how to "break horses."

————. *The Rolling Head.* Billings: Montana Council for Indian Education, 1971. 31 pp.
Grade Level: I, S

In his Introduction, Hap Gilliland explains that several plains tribes have tales about the "rolling head."

————. *The Spotted Horse.* Billings: Montana Reading Publications, 1970. 32 pp.
Grade Level: P, I

The story of a Cheyenne boy who breaks a horse, saves the herd, and learns how to hunt buffalo from his father.

————. *Ve'Ho: Cheyenne Folk Tales.* Billings: Montana Reading Publications, 1971. 32 pp.
Grade Level: P, I

Ve'Ho, the Cheyenne trickster/transformer, in stories that entertain while they teach about the importance of being very observant and cautious, and the value of using ingenuity in solving problems.

————. *The Winter Hunt.* Billings: Montana Council for Indian Education, 1971. 31 pp.
Grade Level: P, I

Three stories that teach the values of wisdom, courage, bravery, and commitment to relatives.

Tatsey, John (Blackfeet). *The Black Moccasin—Life on the Blackfeet Indian Reservation.* Ed. Paul T. DeVore. Intro. Mike Mansfield. C.W. Hill Printers, 1971.
Grade Level: S

A collection of Tatsey's weekly columns for the *Glacier Reporter* of Browning, Montana, during the late 1950s and early 1960s, including a verbatim transcription of tape recordings in which Tatsey interprets Blackfeet names, legends, and tribal ceremonies.

Teit, James A. (Salish/Pend d'Oreille). "Pend d'Oreille Tales." *Memoirs of the American Folk-Lore Society*, Vol. II, 114–18. 1917.
Grade Level: S

Six Pend d'Oreille tales told by Michel Revais.

————. "The Salishan Tribes of the Western Plateaus." *Annual Report of the Bureau of American Ethnology*, No. 45 (1927/28): 295–396.
Grade Level: I, S

Throssel, Richard. *Blue Thunder, Crow Indian Legend.* Billings: Montana Indian Publication Fund, 1976. 31 pp.
Grade Level: P, I

A story of the conflict between Little Light (Son of the Morning Star) and Blue Thunder (Crow) teaching the tragic consequences of selfish competitiveness and disregard for responsibilities between friends.

Through The Eyes of an Indian. Browning, MT.

A weekly publication serving the Blackfeet Nation.

Wagner, Curly Bear (Blackfeet). *Curly Bear's Blackfeet Stories.* Hawkstone Productions, 1996.
Grade Level: P, I, S

An audiocassette of seven Napi stories, told by a traditional storyteller who asks questions of his audience and explains the important morals or traditional values in each.

War Stories of the White Clay People. Fort Belknap, MT: Fort Belknap Education Department, Curriculum Development Project, 1982. 138 pp.
Grade Level: P, I, S

Stories told in the original local syntax that tell of the days when the White Clay People (the Gros Ventre) followed the buffalo.

Weisel, George F. *Ten Animal Myths of the Flathead Indians.* Anthropology and Sociology Papers, No. 18. Missoula: University of Montana, 1959.
Grade Level: I, S

A collection of ten animal tales of the Flathead Indians as told by Ellen Big Sam.

Weist, Katheryn. *Belle Highwalking—The Narrative of a Northern Cheyenne Woman.* Billings: Montana Council for Indian Education, 1982. 66 pp.
Grade Level: I, S

A memoir blending Cheyenne cultural ways with the ways in which historical events and government programs affected the people.

Williamson, John P. *An English-Dakota Dictionary.* St. Paul: Minnesota Historical Society Press, 1992. 264 pp.
Grade Level: I, S

Woodcock, Christine (Salish/Kootenai). *How the Chipmunk Got His Stripes on His Back.* St. Ignatius, MT: Flathead Culture Committee, 1978.
Grade Level: P, I

A traditional animal story with illustrations.

Woodcock, Clarence (Salish/Kootenai). "The Heritage of the Flathead: Worthy of Centennial Preservation." *Montana: Magazine of Western History,* 14.2 (Apr. 1964): 120–121.
Grade Level: S

An article calling for the preservation of the Flathead heritage.

———, comp. *Salish/Pend D'Oreille Coyote Stories.* Pablo, MT: Salish Flathead Culture Committee of the Confederated Salish and Kootenai Tribes, 1981. 79 pp.
Grade Level: S

A collection of stories used in a Native American studies class at the Salish/Kootenai College.

Wotanin Wowapi. Poplar, MT: Fort Peck Reservation.
Grade Level: I, S

A newspaper of the Assiniboine/Sioux people on the Fort Peck Reservation.

Appendix F: Commercial Resources

The following list is not exhaustive, but it does include some larger distributors as well as a concentration of presses and distributors within the region of Montana, neighboring Plains states, and Canada. Similar small presses and distributors exist in every state across the continent, and teachers can contact individual tribal communities or state universities for information regarding local publications.

Presses and Distributors of Native American Literatures

Akwesasne Notes
Mohawk Nation via
Rooseveltown, NY 13683
(Mohawk materials that can be used for K–12)

American Indian Curricula Development Program
c/o United Tribes Technical College
3315 University Drive
Bismarck, ND 58501
(Plains nations curricula and teacher's guides for K–12)

American Indian Studies Center
University of California–Los Angeles
405 Hilgard Avenue
Los Angeles, CA 90024

Anishinabe Reading Materials
Duluth Indian Education Advisory Committee
Independent School District #709
Lake Avenue and Second Street
Duluth, MN 55802
(Anishinabe books and teachers' guides for K–6)

Badlands Natural History Association
Highway 377 and 240
Interior, SD 57750-9710
Tel: 605-433-5489
(Dakota, Lakota, Hidatsa, Mandan, and other materials)

Blackfeet Heritage Program
Browning, MT 59417
Tel: 406-338-7411
(Blackfeet materials for K–12)

Canadian Alliance in Solidarity with Native Peoples
P.O. Box 574
Station P
Toronto, Ontario M5S 271
Canada

Canyon Records and Indian Arts
4143 North 16th Street
Phoenix, AZ 85016
Tel: 602-266-4823

Chelsea Curriculum Publications
Dept. LT94
Attn: School Division
P.O. Box 5186
Yeadon, PA 19050
Tel: 1-800-362-9786

Choctaw Heritage Press
Mississippi Band of Choctaw Indians
Route 7, Box 21
Philadelphia, MS 39350

Cross-Cultural Education Center
P.O. Box 66
Park Hill, OK 74451
(Cherokee, Creek, Chickasaw, Choctaw, and Seminole materials)

Crow Bilingual Materials Development Center
Route 1, Box 1001
Hardin, MT 59034-9707
Tel: 406-665-1304
Fax: 406-665-2784
(Crow materials for K–12)

Daybreak Star Press
P.O. Box 99100
Seattle, WA 98199
(Northwest tribal materials for K–12)

Dullknife College
P.O. Box 98
Lame Deer, MT 59043
Fax: 406-477-6219
(Northern Cheyenne materials)

Eagle Wing Press, Inc.
P.O. Box 579 MO
Naugatuck, CN 06770

Featherstone Productions, Inc.
P.O. Box 536
Agency Village, SD 57262
(Mandan, Hidatsa, Arickara, Dakota, Lakota, Ojibway, Navajo, Caddo, Kiowa, and Zuni traditional, contemporary, cultural, and historical music and stories)

Fifth House
620 Duchess Street
Saskatoon, Saskatchewan S7K 0R1
Canada
Tel: 1-800-565-9523

Flathead Culture Committee
P.O. Box 278
Pablo, MT 59855
Tel: 406-675-2700
(Salish and Kootenai materials for K–12)

Fort Belknap Education Department
Fort Belknap Community Council
P.O. Box 249
Harlem, MT 59526
(Assiniboine/Gros Ventre materials for K–12)

Fulcrum Publishing
Dept. KOE
350 Indiana Street, Suite 350
Golden, CO 80401-5093
Tel: 1-800-992-2908

Greenfield Review Press
2 Middle Grove Road, P.O. Box 308
Greenfield Center, NY 12833
Tel: 518-583-1440
Fax: 518-583-9741

Greenhaven Press, Inc.
P.O. Box 289009
San Diego, CA 92198-0009

Hays/LodgePole Public Schools
District No. 50
P.O. Box 880
Hays, MT 59527
Tel: 406-673-3120
(Assiniboine/Gros Ventre materials for K–8)

Holy Cow! Press
P.O. Box 3170
Mount Royal Station
Duluth, MN 55803
Tel: 218-724-1653

Indian Historian Press
1493 Masonic Avenue
San Francisco, CA 94117

Indian Image Productions
P.O. Box 3621
Evansville, IN 47735
(Greeting cards and calendars)

Indian Rights Association
1505 Race Street
Philadelphia, PA 19102

Minneapolis Public Schools
Planning, Development, and Evaluation Department
807 Northeast Broadway
Minneapolis, MN 55413
(Lakota, Ojibway/Chippewa, and Winnebago materials for K–12)

Minnesota Chippewa Tribe
P.O. Box 217
Cass Lake, MN 56633
(Chippewa materials for K–6)

Montana Council for Indian Education
517 Rimrock Road
Box 31215
Billings, MT 59107
Tel: 406-252-7451

Montana Office of Public Instruction
Indian Education Program
P.O. Box 202501
Helena, MT 59620
Tel: 406-444-3013

Native American Center for the Living Arts, Inc.
25 Rainbow Mall
Niagara Falls, NY 14303

Native American Cultural Awareness Program
Salish Culture Committee
P.O. Box 418
St. Ignatius, MT 59865
(Salish, Kootenai, and other materials for K–12)

Native American Materials Development Center
407 Rio Grande Boulevard, NW
Albuquerque, NM 87104
(Navajo materials)

The Native Booklist
6125-11 Street SE, #9
Calgary, Alberta T2H 2L6
Canada

North American Indian Travelling College
R.R.#3
Cornwall Island, Ontario K6H 5R7
Canada

Oyate
2702 Mathews Street
Berkeley, CA 94702
Tel: 510-848-6700
Fax: 510-848-4815

Pemmican Publications, Inc.
412 McGregor Street
Winnepeg, Manitoba R2W 4X5
Tel: 204-589-6346

Rising Wolf, Inc.
240 North Higgins Avenue, #4
Missoula, MT 59801
(Ojibway, Cree, Siksika materials for K–8)

Rocky Boy Transitional Bilingual Program
Rocky Boy Tribal High School
Box Elder, MT 59521
Tel: 406-395-4270
(Chippewa/Cree materials for K–8)

St. Labre Mission School
Ashland, MT 59003
Tel: 406-784-2347
(Northern Cheyenne materials for K–8)

Salish-Kootenai Community College
P.O. Box 117
Pablo, MT 59855
Tel: 406-675-4800
Fax: 406-675-4801

Sinte Gleska University Bookstore
Rosebud Sioux Reservation
P.O. Box 156
Mission, SD 57555
Tel: 605-856-2733
(Lakota books and musical recordings for K–12)

Spirit Talk Press
P.O. Box V
Browning, MT 59417-3022
Tel: 406-338-2882
(Blackfeet materials)

Sunset Productions Inc.
369 Montezuma
Santa Fe, NM 87501
Tel: 1-800-829-5723

Theytus Books
Box 218
Penticton, British Columbia V2A 6K3
Canada
Tel: 604-493-7181
Fax: 604-493-5302
(Coastal Salish, Metis, Okanagan and other materials for K–12)

University of Nebraska Press
P.O. Box 880480
Lincoln, Nebraska 68588-0484
Tel: 1-800-755-1105
Fax: 1-800-526-2617

University of Oklahoma Press
1005 Asp Avenue
Norman, Oklahoma 73019-0045
Tel: 1-800-627-7377
Fax: 1-800-735-0476

CD-ROM Products

Bibliography of Native North Americans. Santa Barbara, CA: ABC-Clio
(Published annually, this CD-ROM database is a source for journals, books, and film, going back 500 years. The yearly cost is $1,418.)

Internet Addresses

Book Reviews
http://www.bookwire.com/hmr/Review/htour.html

Native American Literature Online
http://web.maxwell.syr.edu/nativeweb/natlit/NAlit.html
(Books, articles, and speeches, with the possibility for downloading whole texts such as a recent essay by Michael Dorris, "Mixed Blood.")

True Stories for American Indian Youth
http://indy4.fdl.cc.mn.us/~isk/stories/stories.html
(Stories by Native Indian people—many of them students—who are on the Internet, as well as reviews and criticism of conventional publications.)

Audio and Video Distributors

The following tribal culture committees and state organizations that are connected with the National Endowment for the Humanities or the National Endowment for the Arts are examples of good resources for locally produced videos.

Big Sky Radio
247 First Avenue East
Kalispell, MT 59901
Tel: 406-758-5713
(Series of taped discussions about Northwest Native writers and their works, including D'Arcy McNickle, James Welch, Plenty Coups, Pretty-shield, and Sherman Alexie)

Educational Filmstrips and Video
1291 19th Street
Huntsville TX, 77340

GPN
University of Nebraska–Lincoln
P.O. Box 80669
Lincoln, NE 68501-0669
Tel: 1-800-228-4630

Greenfield Review Press
2 Middle Grove Road
P.O. Box 308
Greenfield Center, NY 12833
Tel: 518-583-1440

Hawkstone Productions
P.O. Box 7626
Kalispell, MT 59904

The Montana Committee for the Humanities
P.O. Box 8036
Hellgate Station
Missoula, MT 59807
Tel: 406-243-6022

Native Voice Public Television
VCB Room 224
Montana State University
Bozeman, MT 59717
Tel: 406-994-6223

Oyate
2702 Mathews Street
Berkeley, CA 94702
Tel: 510-848-6700
Fax: 510-848-4815

PBS Home Video
WMHT Public Broadcasting
P.O. Box 17
Schenectady, NY 12301
Tel: 1-800-950-9648

Author

Dorothea Susag has taught high school English in Simms, Montana, for fourteen years, receiving the Teacher-of-the-Year Award from her school district in 1990 and a Christa McAuliffe Fellowship in 1992 for her proposal to develop a curriculum using Native American literatures in Montana schools. For the past six years, she has worked with Montana public school teachers and tribal resource people from Montana's reservation communities, while she studied Native history, literatures, and cultures at the University of Montana. She has taught an elective in Montana literature, with an emphasis on Montana Native American literatures and writers, and adult education Native American literature classes. A longtime member of NCTE and the Montana affiliate, she has conducted numerous workshops for teachers, has served as a consultant to schools in regard to Native American literature resources, and has published several articles and papers.

About the Cover

The painting on the front cover was created and provided by Jack Real Bird, who belongs to the Big Lodge and Piegan clans of the Crow Indians in Montana. Real Bird graduated from Montana State University with a degree in history and art. He uses a variety of materials to create his art—rock, hide, and paint. He resides in White River, Arizona, with his wife and two sons. His artwork is intended to affirm that he is "still on this earth and still a Crow Indian."

Real Bird provides the following interpretation of his painting: The aspen tree shows the strength of the growing cycle of the earth and the power of the sun and the wind. The red on the left of the tree symbolizes summer; fall is depicted through the colors of the leaves; and the light color to the right represents winter. Winter is the time to tell stories of the tribes ("Old Man Coyote" and other stories). The coyote to the left of the tree tells humans the way his people (the coyotes) live on this land. The man on the right thinks about this and in turn tells the children, who are listening. Other symbols on the right are also traditional images. The green below the tree represents the earth. The earth takes care of all people—clothing, feeding, and nourishing. The rising sun on the left symbolizes a sacred time, the beginning of a new day. The cycle of the sun is like our lives. We can look at the image and look on our lives, or we can take it to represent just one day at a time. From observing this cycle we learn how to survive.

Index